Teach...
Inspire...
Lead...

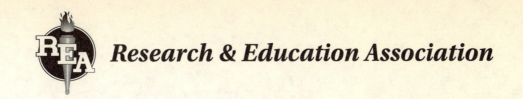
Research & Education Association

The Best Teachers' Test Preparation for the

PRAXIS II®

English to Speakers of Other Languages (0360) Test

Luis A. Rosado, Ph.D.
Professor
University of Texas at Arlington
Arlington, Texas

Visit our Educator Support Center at:
www.REA.com/teacher

For updates to the test and this book visit: www.rea.com/praxis/esol.htm

Research & Education Association
61 Ethel Road West
Piscataway, New Jersey 08854
E-mail: info@rea.com

The Best Teachers' Test Preparation for the
PRAXIS II® English to Speakers of Other Languages (0360) Test

Library of Congress Control Number 2009927260

ISBN-13: 978-0-7386-0403-9
ISBN-10: 0-7386-0403-8

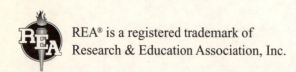

About Research & Education Association

Founded in 1959, Research & Education Association is dedicated to publishing the finest and most effective educational materials—including software, study guides, and test preps—for students in middle school, high school, college, graduate school, and beyond.

REA's Test Preparation series includes books and software for all academic levels in almost all disciplines. Research & Education Association publishes test preps for students who have not yet entered high school, as well as for high school students preparing to enter college. Students from countries around the world seeking to attend college in the United States will find the assistance they need in REA's publications. For college students seeking advanced degrees, REA publishes test preps for many major graduate school admission examinations in a wide variety of disciplines, including engineering, law, and medicine. Students at every level, in every field, with every ambition can find what they are looking for among REA's publications.

REA's practice tests are always based upon the most recently administered exams and include every type of question that you can expect on the actual exams.

REA's publications and educational materials are highly regarded and continually receive an unprecedented amount of praise from professionals, instructors, librarians, parents, and students. Our authors are as diverse as the fields represented in the books we publish. They are well-known in their respective disciplines and serve on the faculties of prestigious high schools, colleges, and universities throughout the United States and Canada.

Today, REA's wide-ranging catalog is a leading resource for teachers, students, and professionals.

We invite you to visit us at *www.rea.com* to find out how "REA is making the world smarter."

Acknowledgments

We would like to thank Larry Kling, Vice President, Editorial, for his editorial direction; Pam Weston, Vice President, Publishing, for setting the quality standards for production integrity and managing the publication to completion; Kathleen Casey, Senior Editor, for project management; Christine Saul, Senior Graphic Artist, for cover design; Rachel Di-Matteo, Graphic Artist, for test design. We also gratefully acknowledge Wendell Anderson of Northstar Writing & Editing for copyediting, Lucia Hu, M.A., for her technical expertise as a linguist; Victory Productions for development of the audio CD; S4Carlisle for typesetting; Kelli Wilkins for proofreading; and Terry Casey for indexing the manuscript.

About the Author

Dr. Luis A. Rosado is Professor of Bilingual Education and the Director of the Center for Bilingual and ESL Education in the College of Education and Health Professions at the University of Texas at Arlington. He holds degrees from the University of Puerto Rico, Boston State College, and Texas A & M University–Kingsville. He has published extensively in the areas of pedagogy and professional responsibilities, parental involvement, cross-cultural communication, Spanish linguistics and Spanish for bilingual teachers. Prior to coming to UT-Arlington, Dr. Rosado held academic appointments at Catholic University of Puerto Rico, Texas Southern University, and Texas Woman's University. Dr. Rosado has over 25 years of teaching experience at the elementary, high school, and college levels. He has taught in Puerto Rico, Massachusetts, and Texas.

Dedication

This book is dedicated to my colleague and friend Haydee Piris de Maldonado in recognition for her 60 years of service to language minority children and teacher candidates. She has been, and still is, an inspiration for me and for thousands of students in public school and in higher education.

CONTENTS

CHAPTER 4
ASSESSMENT TECHNIQUES AND CULTURAL ISSUES   **109**

CHAPTER 5
PROFESSIONAL ISSUES   **137**

PRACTICE TEST 1   **153**

PRACTICE TEST 2   **205**

INDEX   **255**

Introduction

ABOUT THIS BOOK

If you're looking to secure certification as an ESL/ESOL teacher, you'll find that nineteen states require the Praxis II English to Speakers of Other Languages (0360) test. Think of this book as your toolkit to pass the test. It will help take the mystery and anxiety out of the testing process by equipping you not only with the nuts and bolts, but also, ultimately, with the confidence to succeed alongside your peers across the United States.

We at REA have put a lot of thought into this, and the result is a book that pulls together all the critical information you need to know to pass the Praxis II English to Speakers of Other Languages (0360) test. Let us help you fill in the blanks—literally and figuratively! We will provide you with the touchstones that will allow you to do your very best come test day and beyond.

In this guide, REA offers our customarily in-depth, up-to-date, objective coverage, with test-specific modules devoted to targeted review and realistic practice exams complete with the kind of detail that makes a difference when you're coming down the homestretch in your preparation. We also include a quick-view answer key and competency-categorized progress chart to enable you to pinpoint your strengths and weaknesses.

Praxis II embraces Subject Assessment/Specialty Area Tests, of which the Praxis II English to Speakers of Other Languages (0360) is a part. The Praxis II examinations cover the subject matter that students typically study in teacher education courses such as language acquisition, school curriculum, methods of teaching, and other professional development courses. In most teacher-training programs, students take these tests after having completed their classroom training, the course work, and practicum.

The Praxis II English to Speakers of Other Languages (0360) covers the content areas of analysis of student language production, linguistic theory, teaching methods and techniques, assessment techniques and cultural issues and professional issues. This study guide will deal with each of these broader content areas and with the subareas as they relate to teaching English to speakers of other languages.

Who Takes the Test?

Most people who take the Praxis II English to Speakers of Other Languages (0360) are seeking certification in the area of ESL. You should check with your state's education agency to determine which Praxis examination(s) you are required to take; the ETS Praxis website (www.ets.org/praxis/) and registration bulletin may also help you determine the test(s) you need to take for certification. You should also consult your education program for its own test requirements. Remember that colleges and universities often require Praxis examinations for entry into programs, for graduation, and for the completion of a teacher certification program. These requirements may differ from the baseline requirements the state has for teacher certification. You will need to meet both sets of requirements.

When Should I Take the Test?

The Praxis II English to Speakers of Other Languages (0360) is a test for those who have completed or almost completed their teacher education programs. Again, each state establishes its own requirements for certification; some states specify the passing of other tests. Some states may require the test for initial certification; other states may require the test for beginning teachers during their first months on the job. Generally, each college and university establishes its own requirements for program admission and for graduation. Some colleges and universities require certain tests for graduation and/or for completion of a teacher education program. Check with your college and the state teacher certification agency for details.

When and Where Can I Take the Test?

ETS offers the Praxis II English to Speakers of Other Languages test seven times a year at a number of locations across the nation. The usual testing day is Saturday, but examinees may request an administration on an alternate day if a conflict, such as a religious obligation, exists.

How Do I Get More Information on the ETS Praxis Exams?

To receive information on upcoming administrations of any of the Praxis II Subject Assessments or any other Praxis test, consult the ETS registration bulletin or website, or contact ETS at:

ETS-*The Praxis Series™*
P.O. Box 6051
Princeton, NJ 08541-6051
Phone: (609) 771-7395
Website: www.ets.org/praxis
E-mail: praxis@ets.org

Special accommodations are available for candidates who are visually impaired, hearing impaired, physically disabled, or specific learning disabled. For questions concerning disability services, contact:

ETS Disability Services
PO Box 6054
Princeton, NJ 08541–6054
Phone: (609) 771-7780 or (866) 387-8602 (toll free for test takers in the United
        States, U.S. Territories, and Canada)
TTY only: (609) 771-7714
E-mail: stassd@ets.org
http://www.ets.org/disability

Provisions are also available for examinees whose primary language is not English. The ETS registration bulletin and website include directions for those requesting such accommodations. You can also consult ETS with regard to available test sites; reporting test scores; requesting changes in tests, centers, and dates of test; purchasing additional score reports; retaking tests; and other basic facts.

Is There a Registration Fee?

To take a Praxis examination, you must pay a registration fee, which is payable by check, money order, or with American Express, Discover, MasterCard, or Visa credit cards. In certain cases, ETS offers fee waivers. The registration bulletin and website give qualifications for receiving this benefit and describe the application process. Cash is not accepted for payment.

Can I Retake the Test?

Some states, institutions, and associations limit the number of times you can retest. Contact your state or licensing authority to confirm their retest policies.

HOW TO USE THIS BOOK

What Do I Study First?

Read over REA's subject review and suggestions for test taking. Studying the reviews thoroughly will reinforce the basic skills you will need to do well on the exam. Make sure to do the practice questions in this book so that you will be familiar with the format and procedures involved with taking the actual test.

When Should I Start Studying?

It is never too early to start studying; the earlier you begin, the more time you will have to sharpen your skills. Do not procrastinate! Cramming is not an effective way to study because it does not allow you the time needed to learn the test material.

FORMAT OF THE TEST

The Praxis II English to Speakers of Other Languages (0360) comprises 120 multiple-choice questions. Twenty of the 120 questions are part of two timed listening sections in Section I, Parts A and B. Part A is composed of ten questions designed to test your ability to recognize oral grammar and vocabulary errors, and the ten questions in Part B

Content Categories	Approximate Number of Questions	Approximate Number of Questions
Analysis of Student Languages	30	25%
Linguistic Theory	28	23%
Teaching Methods and Techniques	36	30%
Assessment Techniques and Cultural Issues	18	15%
Professional Issues	8	7%

will test your ability to recognize pronunciation errors of non-native speakers. You are given two-hours to complete the test, 30 minutes of which is spent on the 20 questions in the recorded portion of the test.

The multiple-choice questions assess a beginning teacher's knowledge of certain job-related skills and knowledge. Four choices are provided for each multiple-choice question; the options bear the letters A through D. The exam uses four types of multiple-choice questions:

1.   The Roman numeral multiple-choice question

2.   The "Which of the following" multiple-choice question

3.   The complete-the-statement multiple-choice question

4.   The multiple-choice question with qualifiers

Roman Numeral Multiple-Choice Questions

Perhaps the most difficult of the types of multiple-choice questions is the Roman numeral question because it allows for more than one correct answer. Strategy: Assess each answer before looking at the Roman numeral choices. Consider the following Roman numeral multiple-choice question:

The Praxis II English for Speakers of Other Languages includes content areas of

I.   analysis of student language production and teaching techniques
II.   linguistic theory and teaching methods
III.   literature and composition
IV.   assessment techniques and cultural professional issues

(A) I and II.
(B) II and III.
(C) I, II, and IV.
(D) I, II, III, and IV.

In reviewing the questions, you should note that you may choose two or three answers by selecting (A), (B), (C), or (D). The correct answer is (C) because it includes the three correct statements of what can be found on the Praxis II English for Speakers of Other Languages (0360) test.

"Which of the Following" Multiple-Choice Questions

In a "Which of the following" question, one of the answers is correct among the various choices. **Strategy:** Form a sentence by replacing the first part of the question with each of the answer choices in turn, and then determine which of the resulting sentences is correct. Consider the following example:

Which of the following are all American writers?

- (A)   Mark Twain, Charles Dickens, William Blake
- (B)   Mark Twain, Washington Irving, James Fenimore Cooper
- (C)   William Blake, Charles Dickens, Washington Irving
- (D)   James Fenimore Cooper, William Blake, Washington Irving

Using the suggested technique, one would read:

- (A)   Mark Twain, Charles Dickens, and William Blake are all American writers.
- (B)   Mark Twain, Washington Irving, and James Fenimore Cooper are all American writers.
- (C)   William Blake, Charles Dickens, and Washington Irving are all American writers.
- (D)   James Fenimore Cooper, William Blake, and Washington Irving are all American writers.

Read all of the options. If you know that option (A) is incorrect because Mark Twain is the only American author listed, then you know that both (C) and (D) are also incorrect because the two other writers from option (A) also appear in options (C) and (D). The correct answer is (B) since it is the only option that lists only American writers.

Not all "Which of the following" multiple-choice questions are as straightforward and simple as the previous example. Consider the following multiple-choice question that requires reading a passage such as the one below:

Read the following passage and answer the question below:

Language not only expresses an individual's ideology, it also sets parameters while it persuades and influences the discourse in the community that hears and interprets its meaning.

Therefore, the language of failure should not be present in the learning environment (i.e., the classroom) because it will have a prohibitive impact on the student's desire to learn as well as a negative influence on the student's self-esteem. The *Oxford English Dictionary* defines failure as "a fault, a shortcoming, a lack of success, a person who turns out unsuccessfully, becoming insolvent, etc." We as educators might well ask ourselves if this is the sort of doctrine that we want to permeate our classrooms. Perhaps our own university's axiom, *mens agitat molem* ("the mind can move mountains") will help us discover if, indeed, the concepts of failure are really the types of influences we wish to introduce to impressionable new students.

Is the mind capable of moving a mountain when it is already convinced it cannot? One must remain aware that individuals acquire knowledge at independent rates of speed. Certainly, no one would suggest that one infant "failed" the art of learning to walk because she acquired the skill two months after her infant counterpart. Would anyone suggest that infant number one failed walking? Of course not. What would a mentor project to either toddler were he to suggest that a slower acquisition of walking skills implied failure? Yet, we as educators feel the need to suggest that student A failed due to the slower procurement of abstract concepts than student B. It is absolutely essential to shift the learning focus from failure to success.

Which of the following statements best conveys the meaning of the passage?

(A) Learning is something that happens at different speeds and is, therefore, natural.
(B) Instructors need to be sensitive to students' individual needs.
(C) Instructors need to shift the educational focus from failure to success in learning environments.
(D) Failure is a potential hazard in the classroom and should be avoided at all costs.

The passage suggests that education today is based primarily on failure and negative reinforcement and that, in order to create a more productive and positive learning environment, the emphasis must shift to success. Therefore, the answer is (C).

Strategy: Underline key information as you read the question. For instance, as you read the previous question, you might underline or highlight the sentence: Therefore, the language of failure should not be present in the learning environment (i.e., the classroom) because it will have a prohibitive impact on the students' desire to learn as well as a negative influence on the students' self-esteem. This sentence gives you a hint of the thesis, and therefore the meaning of the passage. Highlighting will thus save you time; saving time is helpful when you must answer 120 questions in two hours.

Complete-the-Statement Multiple-Choice Questions

The complete-the-statement multiple-choice question consists of an incomplete statement for which you must select the answer choice that will complete the statement correctly. Here is an example:

The repetition of an initial consonant sound is an example of the literary device known as

- (A) metaphor.
- (B) personification.
- (C) alliteration.
- (D) denouement.

The correct answer is (C). With this type of question your strategy should be to eliminate answer choices you are certain to be wrong, thus reducing your choices.

Multiple-Choice Questions with Qualifiers

Some of the multiple-choice questions may contain qualifiers—words like *not*, *least*, and *except*. These added words make the test questions more difficult because rather than having to choose the best answer, as is usually the case, you must actually select the opposite. Strategy: Circle the qualifier. It is easy to forget to select the negative; circling the qualifier in the question stem is a flag. This will serve as a reminder as you are reading the question and especially if you must reread or check the answer at a later time. Now consider this question with a qualifier:

Which of the following is NOT an English-language proficiency test?

- (A) TESOL
- (B) TOEIC
- (C) TOEFL
- (D) LAS

You are looking for the *exception* in this question, so you would compare each answer choice to the question to find which answer is not a test that measures English-language proficiency. (B), (C) and (D) are all English-language proficiency exams: LAS is the acronym for Language Assessment Scales, a tool to evaluate reading, writing, listening, and comprehension; TOEIC is the Test of English for International Communication and the TOEFL is the Test of English as a Foreign Language. (A) is the correct answer since

TESOL is the acronym for the association of Teachers of English to Speakers of Other Languages.

New question formats will, at times, appear on the Praxis II subject assessments. If such a new format question appears on the test you are taking—don't panic! You have the tools you need to succeed. Simply follow these steps:

1. Read the directions thoroughly.

2. Read the question carefully, as you would any other question.

3. Decide what you should be trying to determine.

4. Look for the details that will help you answer correctly.

You will receive answer sheets, similar to the ones in this volume, on which you will fill in you response: (A), (B), (C), or (D). As the previous example questions have shown, there are four options for each of the multiple-choice questions; questions with more than one correct answer may use Roman numerals. Individual test items require a variety of different thinking levels, ranging from simple recall to evaluation and problem solving.

You will have two hours to complete the exam; this includes a 30-minute listening section to answer 20 of the 120 questions. This leaves you with an average of 54 seconds to spend an each question. Plenty of time!

Most of the test directions ask you to write the answer in ink. This means that you must bring your own ballpoint pen(s) and No. 2 pencil(s) for these questions; erasable pens are acceptable. The allotted time for completing the answer sheets and writing the answers to the constructed-response questions and/or the essay questions varies from test to test. Be sure to study the directions in this guide for the test that you must take and review the test directions on the day of the test.

The reviews in this book will help you sharpen the basic skills needed to approach the exams and offer you strategies for attacking the questions. By using the reviews in conjunction with the practice tests, you will better prepare yourself for the actual tests. You have learned through your coursework and your practical experience in schools most of what you need to know to answer the questions on the test. In your education classes, you gained the expertise to make important decisions about situations you will face as a teacher; in your content courses, you should have acquired the knowledge you will need to teach specific content.

The reviews in this book will help you fit the information you have acquired into its specific testable category. Reviewing your class notes and textbooks along with systematic use of this book will give you an excellent springboard for passing the Praxis test.

SCORING

The numbers of raw points awarded on the Praxis II English to Speakers of Other Languages (0360) test is based on the number of correct answers given. Most Praxis examinations vary by edition, which means that each test has several variations that contain different questions. The different questions are intended to measure the same general types of knowledge or skills. However, there is no way to guarantee that the questions on all editions of the test will have the same degree of difficulty. To avoid penalizing test takers who answer questions that are more difficult, scores are adjusted for difficulty by using a statistical process known as equating. To avoid confusion between the adjusted and unadjusted scores, ETS reports the adjusted scores on a score scale that makes them clearly different from the unadjusted scores. Unadjusted scores, or "raw scores," are simply the number of questions answered correctly. Adjusted scores, which are equated to the scale ETS uses for reporting the scores, are called "scaled scores." For each edition of a Praxis test, a "raw-to-scale conversion table" is used to translate raw to scaled scores.

The easier the questions are on a test edition, the more questions must be answered correctly to earn a given scaled score. The college or university in which you are enrolled may set passing scores for the completion of your teacher education program and for graduation. Be sure to check the requirements in the catalogues or bulletins. You will also want to talk with your advisor. The passing scores for the Praxis II tests vary from state to state. To find out which of the Praxis II tests your state requires and what your state's set passing score is, contact your state's education department directly.

Score Reporting

When Will I Receive My Examinee Score Report and in What Form Will It Be?

ETS mails test-score reports six weeks after the test date. There is an exception for computer-based tests and for the Praxis I examinations. Score reports will list your current score and the highest score you have earned on each test you have taken over the last 10 years. Along with your score report, ETS will provide you with a booklet that offers details on your scores. For each test date, you may request that ETS send a copy of your scores to as many as three score recipients, provided that each institution or agency is eligible to receive the scores.

STUDYING FOR THE TEST

It is critical to your success that you study effectively. The following are a few tips to help get you going:

- Choose a time and place for studying that works best for you. Some people set aside a certain number of hours every morning to study; others may choose to study at night before retiring. Only you know what is most effective for you.

- Use your time wisely and be consistent. Work out a study routine and stick to it; don't let your personal schedule interfere. Remember, seven weeks of studying is a modest investment to put you on your chosen path.

- Don't cram the night before the test. You may have heard many amazing tales about effective cramming, but don't kid yourself: most of them are false, and the rest are about exceptional people who, by definition, aren't like most of us.

- When you take the practice tests, try to make your testing conditions as much like the actual test as possible. Turn off your television, radio, and telephone. Sit down at a quiet table free from distraction.

- As you complete the practice test, score your test and thoroughly review the explanations to the questions you answered incorrectly.

- Take notes on material you will want to go over again or research further.

- Keep track of your scores. By doing so, you will be able to gauge your progress and discover your strengths and weaknesses. You should carefully study the material relevant to your areas of difficulty. This will build your test-taking skills and your confidence!

STUDY SCHEDULE

The following study course schedule allows for thorough preparation to pass the Praxis II English to Speakers of Other Languages (0360) test. This is a suggested seven-week course of study. However, you can condense this schedule if you are in a time crunch or expand it if you have more time. You may decide to use your weekends for study and preparation and go about your other business during the week. You may even want to record information and listen to it on your MP3 player or CD as you travel in your car. However you decide to study, be sure to adhere to the structured schedule you devise.

THE DAY OF THE TEST

Before the Test

- Dress comfortably in layers. You do not want to be distracted by being too hot or too cold while you are taking the test.

- Check your registration ticket to verify your arrival time.

- Plan to arrive at the test center early. This will allow you to collect your thoughts and relax before the test; your early arrival will also spare you the anguish that comes with being late.

- Make sure to bring your admission ticket with you and two forms of identification, one of which must contain a recent photograph, your name, and your signature (e.g., a driver's license). You will not gain entry to the test center without proper identification.

- Bring several sharpened No. 2 pencils with erasers for the multiple-choice section; pens if you are taking another test that might have essay or constructed-response questions. You will not want to waste time searching for a replacement pencil or pen if you break a pencil point or

Week	Activity
1	After reading the first chapter to understand the format and content of this exam, take the first practice test. Our score chart will indicate your strengths and weaknesses. Make sure you simulate real exam conditions when you take the test. Afterward, score it and review the explanations for questions you answered incorrectly.
2	Review the explanations for the questions you missed, and review the appropriate chapter sections. Useful study techniques include highlighting key terms and information, taking notes as you review each section, and putting new terms and information on note cards to help retain the information.

Week	Activity
3 and 4	Reread all your note cards, refresh your understanding of the exam's subareas and related skills, review your college textbooks, and read over notes you took in your college classes. This is also the time to consider any other supplementary materials suggested by your counselor or your state education agency.
5	Begin to condense your notes and findings. A structured list of important facts and concepts, based on your note cards, college textbook, course notes, and this book's review chapters will help you thoroughly review for the test. Review the answers and explanations for any questions you missed on the practice test.
6	Have someone quiz you using the note cards you created. Take the second practice test, adhering to the time limits and simulated test-day conditions.
7	Review your areas of weakness using all your study materials. This is a good time to retake the practice tests, if time allows.

run out of ink when you are trying to complete your test. The proctor will not provide pencils or pens at the test center.

- Wear a watch to the test center so you can apportion your testing time wisely. You may not, however, wear one that makes noise or that will otherwise disturb the other test takers.

- Leave all dictionaries, textbooks, notebooks, calculators, briefcases, and packages at home. You may not take these items into the test center.

- Do not eat or drink too much before the test. The proctor will not allow you to make up time you miss if you have to take a bathroom break. You will not be allowed to take materials with you, and you must secure permission before leaving the room.

During the Test

- Pace yourself. ETS administers the Praxis II English to Speakers of Other Languages (0360) in one two-hour sitting with no breaks.

- Follow all of the rules and instructions that the test proctor gives you. Proctors will enforce these procedures to maintain test security. If you do not abide by the regulations, the proctor may dismiss you from the test and notify ETS to cancel your score.

- Listen closely as the test instructor provides the directions for completing the test. Follow the directions carefully.

- Be sure to mark only one answer per multiple-choice question, erase all unwanted answers and marks completely, and fill in the answers darkly and neatly. There is no penalty for guessing at an answer, do not leave any answer ovals blank. Remember: a blank oval is just scored as wrong, but a guessed answer has a chance of being right!

Take the test! Do your best! Afterward, make notes about the multiple-choice questions you remember. You may not share this information with others, but you may find that the information proves useful on other exams that you take.

Relax! Wait for that passing score to arrive.

CHAPTER 2

Linguistic Theory

This chapter introduces the concepts of phonology, morphology, lexicon, syntax, semantics, and pragmatics, and their importance in language teaching and learning. It also presents an overview of theories of first- and second-language acquisition and the interdependence between a learner's native language (L1) and the new language the learner is learning (L2).

COMPONENTS OF LANGUAGE

Language is a system composed of the following subsystems: phonology, morphology, syntax, lexicon, discourse, and pragmatics. An analysis of these components follows:

Phonology

Phonology is the study of the sound system of the language. The sound system of a language is composed of a finite number of phonemes, the basic units of sounds. English has 44 phonemes (sounds) and only 26 graphemes (letters) to represent them. Some of the English phonemes are represented by multiple graphemes, which suggests that the grapheme phoneme correspondence of English is not consistent. This lack of correspondence between graphemes and phonemes makes English phonology a challenging task for English-language learners (ELLs) as well as for teachers. For example, in English, the consonant sound /Š/, as in the initial sound of the word, *shower*, can be represented by as many as six different graphemes: *sh, c, t, ch, s,* and *ss.* The vowel sound /e/, as in the word, *feet,* can be represented by three different graphemes: *e, ee,* and *ea.* Table 2.1 presents evidence of the grapheme–phoneme correspondence of these particular sounds.

Table 2.1 Examples of Grapheme–Phoneme Discrepancy in English

Phoneme	Grapheme	Examples of Words
/Š/	*sh, c, t, ch, s, ss*	*shell, delicious, nation, **chef**, sugar, mission*
/e/	*e, ee, ea*	*behold, beet, meat*

Decoding and pronouncing ***consonant diagraphs*** can also create challenges for ELLs. Consonant diagraphs occur when two consonants or two vowels represent a single phoneme. Some examples of consonant and vowel diagraphs—identified in bold—are presented here:

Consonant Diagraphs   **Vowel Diagraphs**
What, **wh**en, **ph**oto, tou**gh**   B**ee**f, b**ea**t, b**oo**k, f**oo**l

In addition to the challenges of consonant diagraphs, English also has words with graphemes that are not pronounced at all. For example, the word *through* has an initial diagraph and two final graphemes that are not pronounced. That is, the word contains seven graphemes (letters) to represent only three phonemes, *thru* or [θru]. Most ELLs will attempt to pronounce all the letters of the word, resulting in nonstandard and often unintelligible pronunciation.

To represent phonetic transcriptions of English words, we will use the symbols of the American Phonetic Alphabet (APA). Individual sounds will be represented within slashes / / and word transcriptions will be done using brackets [ ]. For example, the word through used above was represented as [θru].

Unlike English, a language like Spanish has a consistent grapheme–phoneme correspondence. Spanish has 26 graphemes to represent 27 sounds. With the notable exception of the grapheme *h*, every letter in Spanish is pronounced. This consistency can lead to negative transfer when Spanish-speaking ELLs attempt to pronounce every single letter in diagraphs and English words like *island, palm, calm,* or *although.*

Allophones

Allophone is used to describe the process whereby a phoneme that occurs in complementary distribution results in two different but similar phonemes. Because they occur in complementary distribution—when one occurs, the other will not—these sounds are predictable. Let us examine the oral–nasal vowel dichotomy in the following sentence:

Sam the **cat sat** and ate the **ham**.

Notice the vowel sounds in the words *Sam*, *cat*, *sat*, and *ham*. What is the difference among these vowel sounds? In all four words, the vowel represents the same phoneme /æ/; however, in two of these words, the phonemes are nasalized. Pronounce them again to see if you can notice the difference between the vowel sounds in the words *Sam* and *ham*, as opposed to the sounds of the vowels in the words *cat* and *sat*.

In the words *Sam* and *ham*, the vowels precede a nasal sound /m/; thus, through a process called **assimilation**, the vowel sound becomes nasalized. In phonetic transcription, a tilde [~] is used to identify nasal sounds /æ/. In any other conditions, the vowel is pronounced as an oral sound. Based on these principles, the allophones of the vowel sounds can be easily predicted through a basic rule: When a vowel sound precedes a nasal sound, the vowel becomes nasalized. In any other conditions, the vowel sounds remain an oral sound.

Let us now examine an allophone involving consonants. In this case, we will analyze the **aspirated-unaspirated** dichotomy of the three English stop consonants /p/, /t/, and /k/. The **aspiration,** or puff of air, of these phonemes occurs in initial position in a word or a syllable. For example, the initial phoneme in the word *pork* produces a puff of air. To represent this feature, the phoneme is transcribed with a small superscripted symbol, /p^h/. In other positions, the sound of the graphemes *p, t,* and *k* is unaspirated, and it is represented in the traditional fashion, /p/.

Let us examine the way in which we pronounce the grapheme *p* in the words *park* and *spark*. To make the explanation more concrete, place a sheet of paper in front of your mouth while producing the /p/ sounds in these two words. In the production of the first one, *park*, you will notice a puff of air moving the paper indicating aspiration; whereas in the second word, *spark*, the puff of air is not there or it is not as strong as the first one. Thus the rule for aspirated and unaspirated stop sounds is also predictable. In this case, when the phoneme /s/ precedes the phoneme /p/, the sound is unaspirated. Additional information about grapheme correspondence and articulators used to produce English sounds is presented later in this chapter.

The /k/ sound can be represented by the graphemes *c, ch,* and *k* in words like *court,* *chrome,* and *kangaroo*. The rules apply to these situations too.

Morphology

Morphology is the study of the structure of words and word formation. Words are made of units of meaning called **morphemes**. Common English words can have a minimum of one morpheme and as many as four or five. For example, the word *car* has a single morpheme, a **free morpheme**: car. It is called a free morpheme because it has meaning by itself. Whereas the word *careful* is made up of two morphemes, the basic word or root word *care* and the adjective morpheme *–ful*. The first part of the word, *care,* is a free morpheme, and the second component, *–ful,* is a **bound morpheme**. A free morpheme can occur in isolation because it represents a word. As previously indicated, whereas the word *care* is a free morpheme and can occur in isolation, the morpheme *–ful* cannot because it is a bound morpheme. Bound morphemes are attached to words, root words, or another morpheme. For example, the word *predetermined* contains three morphemes: a root word (*determine*), a prefix (*pre–*), and suffix (*–ed*). The morphemes *pre* and *ed* are bound morphemes because they cannot convey meaning in isolation. They have meaning only when attached to a root or free morpheme like the word *determine*.

Affixes describes both prefixes and suffixes. **Prefixes** are morphemes placed before the root word, and **suffixes** are those morphemes placed after the root word. A large number of English affixes come from classical languages like Latin and Greek, and these are common to a number of Indo-European languages, including English, Spanish, French, and German. The use of these prefixes and roots creates **cognates**, words that are spelled and pronounced similarly in two or multiple languages. See the examples of affixes and root words used in English and Spanish and the cognates that these create.

Table 2.2 Root Words in English and Spanish

Roots	Meaning	English Words	Spanish Words
bio	life	symbiosis	simbiosis
fobia (phobia)	fear of	xenophobia	xenophobia
fono (phono)	sound	phonetics	fonética
foto (photo)	light	photography	fotografía
geo	land, earth	geology	geología

Table 2.3 Affixes in English and Spanish

Suffixes	Meaning	English	Spanish
–ism	action or progress	heroism	heroísmo
–logy	study of	biology	biología
–acy	quality/state of	democracy	democracia
–tion, –ción	state of	celebration	celebración
–ous, –oso	full of/with	mysterious	misterioso

Morphemes are further classified into two large categories: derivational and inflectional.

Derivational Morphemes

The concept of **derivational morphemes** describes the units of meaning that can be attached to a word or root word. These morphemes often can change the syntactic classification of the word. Most of these morphemes have been borrowed from foreign languages—mostly from Greek and Latin—and can be used as prefixes and suffixes. For example, the word *subconsciously* contains four morphemes: a root word, *consci* or *conscience*, and three derivational morphemes, *sub–*, *–ous*, and *–ly*. The first is the prefix morpheme (*sub–*); the second is an adjective morpheme (*–ous*); and the third (*–ly*) represents an adverb. By transforming the word *subconscious* to the word *subconsciously*, we just changed the syntactic classification from an adjective to an adverb.

Inflectional Morphemes

Inflectional morphemes, or **inflectional endings**, are a second type of morpheme. These morphemes do not change the syntactic classification of the word attached, and they typically follow derivational morphemes in words. They are also called inflectional endings because they occur at the end of the word.

As previously indicated, inflectional morphemes do not change the syntactic classification as most derivational morphemes can. For example, the word *greater* is composed of the adjective *great* and the comparative *–er*. Adding the inflectional ending and changing the word from *great* to *greater* did not affect the syntactic classification of the word; both words are adjectives.

Table 2.4 Inflectional Morphemes in English

Morpheme	Example
progressive (ing)	She is **working**.
third person singular (s)	She **works** at the zoo.
possessive ('s)	**Mary's** favorite animal is the cougar.
the plural (s, es)	She cleans ten **cages** and two **sheds** daily.
regular past tense (ed)	Yesterday, she **designed** a new exhibit area.
past participle (en)	Mary has **worked** at the zoo for two years.
the comparative (er)	She is **better** than most workers at the zoo.
the superlative (est)	Mary is the **best** zookeeper in the city.

Syntax

Syntax describes the organization or sequence of words in a sentence. English has specific syntactic rules to account for word order, sequence of morphemes, and grammatical and logical relations of words within sentences (Fromkin, Rodman, & Hyams, 2003). English contains a specific number of basic *phrase structure rules* to account for sentence formation in the language. Some of these rules are presented later in this chapter.

Traditionally, an English sentence is divided into two main components: *noun phrase* (NP) and *verb phrase* (VP). The basic noun phrase in English can be a subject or an object. It can have multiple variations that follow specific syntactic rules. A noun phrase can be formed through multiple combinations of these components. Here are some possible combinations.

noun	Mark, she, it
article + noun	the boy, the dog, a house
article + adjective + noun	the nice boy, the brown dog, the ugly car
Adjective + noun	wonderful people, smart folks, tall babies

Verb phrases, on the other hand, can contain a verb by itself, or they can have a verb followed by any other constituent like a noun phrase or a prepositional phrase, among others. Let us examine some of the constituent rules for the formation of the verb phrases.

verb	ran, cries, sobbed
verb + noun phrase	called the dog
verb + prepositional phrase	hide inside the closet
Preposition + noun phrase	in the house

Phrase Structure Rules

The noun phrase and the verb phrase presented earlier can be used to create multiple sentences.

Classification of Verbs

To understand the rules for sentence formation, it is important to examine the classification of English verbs and how they are used in sentences. English verbs can be clas-

Table 2.5 Syntactic Rules

Rules	Examples
Sentence = noun phrase + verb phrase.	**The young man lives in a cozy cabin**.
Noun phrase (NP) = noun	The young **man** lives in a cozy cabin.
NP = article + noun	**The** young **man** lives in a cozy cabin.
NP = adjective phrase (AP) AP = adjective + noun	The **young man** lives in a cozy cabin.
Verb phrase (VP) = verb	The young man **lives** in a cozy cabin.
VP = verb + noun phrase (NP)	The young man **lives** in a cozy **cabin.**
VP = verb + prepositional phrase (PP) PP = preposition + NP	The young man lives **in a** cozy **cabin.**
VP = verb + AP	The young man lives in a **cozy cabin.**
AP = adjective + NP	

sified in multiple ways; however, we will discuss two major categories here: transitive and intransitive.

Transitive verbs are those verbs that can take objects, whether these are direct or indirect objects. Let us analyze how the direct and indirect objects are used in the following sentences:

> Jennifer and Martin called the **waiter** (direct object).
> The waiter gave **them** (indirect object) the **bill** (direct object).

To identify the direct object, use the verb of the sentence to ask the following question: Jennifer and Martin *called* what or whom? The logical answer to the question is the direct object, **waiter**. To identify the indirect object we can use a similar question: The waiter *gave* the bill to whom? Here we use the indirect object to answer the question, **them**.

Traditionally, people link transitive verbs with action verbs and verbs of motion; however, this is not totally correct. Verbs of motion are generally intransitive. An analysis of intransitive verbs and verbs of motion follows.

Intransitive verbs cannot take objects; instead, they serve as *linking verbs*. They link the subject with a *predicate adjective*, a *predicate nominative*, or a *complement* in general. A predicate adjective describes the subject, and a predicate nominative reinstates the subject. Let us examine two examples:

Hugo Chávez is a colorful leader.
He is the president of Venezuela.

In the first example, the subject is described as "a colorful leader." Thus the structure is noun phrase (NP) + intransitive verb (IV) + predicate adjective (PA). In the second example, the subject is being reinstated, or identified, as "the president of Venezuela." The structure for the second sentence is NP + IV + predicate nominative (PN).

All forms of the verb *to be—am, is, are, was, were, been*—and verbs like *seems* and *becomes* are also linking verbs. Linking verbs as well as all intransitive verbs require a subject complement to complete the meaning of the sentence. Some linking verbs can convey motion, which can be confused with the term *action verbs*. A lot of verbs of motion are intransitive; however, there are others that can be either transitive or intransitive, depending how they are used. For example, the verb *smell* conveys some kind of motion; it can be used as either a transitive or an intransitive verb. Let us examine the following two sentences:

Transitive: I smell my **mother's cooking** (direct object).
Intransitive: Mother's cooking smells **good** (predicate adjective).

In the first sentence, we can ask, "what do I smell?" The answer points to the direct object: mother's cooking. In the second sentence, the adjective *good* describes mother's cooking. Following are some examples of linking verbs and specifically verbs of motion:

appears, become, grow, remain, seen, get, grow, look, sound, smell, feel, taste, continue, runs

In summary, linking verbs, verbs of motion, and all forms of the verb *to be* are intransitive verbs that cannot take objects. Let us examine how the rules for intransitive and transitive verbs apply to the formation of common sentence structures in English.

ENGLISH SENTENCE STRUCTURES

English has basic sentence patterns known as kernel sentences. Some examples of kernel sentences follow.

subject + intransitive verb	Mark cried.
subject + intransitive verb + adverb	Eugenia runs fast.
subject + transitive verb + direct object	Obama won the presidential election.
subject + transitive verb + direct object + object complement	Jack found the treasure very quickly.
subject + intransitive verb + predicate adjective	The tour was wonderful.
subject + intransitive verb + predicate nominative	The Boston Celtics are the new world champions.

Lexicon

Lexicon refers to the vocabulary of the language. This component of the language is also the most versatile and changeable component. Words can change meaning based on context and historical period. For example, today the word *cool* can have different meanings based on how it's spoken. This word can refer to temperature (The room is cool.); to imply good (The party was cool.); or to describe someone (The teacher is cool.). Because lexicon is used to describe our culture and lifestyle, new words are required to represent changes in people's lives and accomplishments.

In addition to vocabulary use in daily life, we have a large number of vocabulary words used in the content areas of mathematics, science, and social studies that ELLs need to master to function effectively in school and in society in general. A large number of words in the content areas are common to multiple Indo-European languages. These words are known as cognates, Table 2.6 on the next page, illustrates cognates found in four major languages.

Knowledge of cognates can increase the vocabulary of ELLs and can support language and knowledge transfer from L1 to L2.

Table 2.6 English, German, Spanish, and French Cognates

English	German	Spanish	French
anatomy	anatopmie	anatomía	anatomie
magnificent	-------	magnífico	magnifique
excellent	exzellent	excelente	excellent
pharmacy	pharmazie	farmacia	la pharmacie
April	April	Abril	Avril
biology	biologie	biología	biologie
elegant	elegant	elegante	élégant
nation	nation	nación	nation

Semantics

Semantics is the component of the language that conveys the meaning system. Language represents the meaning system based on the culture and context of the conversation. It uses literal (denotation) or implied (connotation) meaning to achieve this goal.

Denotation refers to the literal meaning of words and ideas. For example, a sign that reads "Dog Bites" seems obvious because all dogs have such capability (literal meaning). However, communication pragmatics will guide people to go beyond literal meaning and understand the intended meaning of the statement: *the dog is aggressive and might attack* (Rosado, 2007).

Connotation refers to the implied meaning of words and ideas. Idiomatic expressions frequently use implied meaning as a communication tool; thus speakers need to be familiar with the cultural framework embedded in the communication to understand the intended message. ELLs might have problems getting the meaning intended in statements such as "George is always *passing the buck*." They might know the two meanings of the word *buck*—male deer or a dollar—and still be unable to understand the implied meaning, that is, passing the responsibility to someone else.

Idiomatic Expressions

Idioms are expressions that traditionally use connotative meaning to communicate information. English uses multiple idiomatic expressions in daily conversation. These expressions use culturally bound information, which makes them particularly difficult for

ELLs. The use of idioms presents a challenge for learners who are new to the language and culture. ELLs often take these expressions in literally, creating miscommunication and embarrassing situations for them. Let us examine the following examples. Imagine the implications of taking these expressions literally.

Keep your nose clean. (behave properly)

Joe kicked the bucket early this year. (died)

He is passing the buck. (giving responsibilities to someone else)

Stop beating about the bush. (go straight to the point)

It is raining cats and dogs. (raining a lot)

Keep an eye on the baby. (check on the baby)

Not all idioms are as colorful as the ones just listed. Some we use daily without paying attention to how they are constructed and how difficult they might be for students new to the language.

The Amelia Bedelia series written by Peggy Parish (Harper Collins) represents a good example of how idioms can create communication problems. In this series, the main character, Amelia Bedelia, interprets everything literally, and this lack of understanding creates multiple problems. Teachers of ESL can use this humorous series to introduce ELLs

Table 2.7 Selected English Idioms and Their Meanings

Idioms	Meaning	Example
as far as	to this extent	As far as I know, idioms are cool.
broke up	to separate	Marcos broke up with Judy.
by the way	incidentally	By the way, Judy has a new boyfriend.
find out	discover	Marcos just found out about it.
better off	in a better situation	She is better off without him.
as long as	on the condition that	Marcos will be fine, as long as he does not see them together.

to American idioms. They should also be guided to recognize and analyze idioms used in class, in songs, and in television. For a detailed analysis of American idioms, see *Idiom Connection* available at www.idiomconnection.com.

Discourse

Discourse describes the ability of speakers to combine sounds into words, words into sentences and larger units cohesively to achieve oral or written communication. Oral and written discourse uses a variety of strategies and cohesive devices to deliver the message and achieve the intended goal. However, the strategies and cohesive devices used in L1 to communicate might be different from the ones required in English. Whereas English narrative follows a linear discourse, languages like Arabic, Russian, and the Romance languages in general follow a more curvilinear approach (Kaplan, 1966). That is, English speakers generally present the thesis of the argument and provide supporting details with minimal deviation from the main idea. In the curvilinear, or associational, style, people present the thesis and the supporting details, but they embellish the content in such a way that it can lead them away from the main topic, without being penalized for it. However, when ELLs use the curvilinear approach to communicate in English, they get penalized when they are assessed using the linear approach required in formal English. Teaching the linear progression required in English is paramount for the success of ELLs in their attempt to master oral and written communication.

Pragmatics

Pragmatics describes the role of context in the production and interpretation of communication. Pragmatics describes the hidden rules of communication shared by native speakers of the language. It includes the use of euphemism (the use of less offensive words), paraphrasing, and the use of direct and indirect communication. For example, instead of telling someone to be quiet, a person might choose to make a comment about the noise level in the room. The speaker can also say, "I have problems concentrating when people are talking aloud." Others might choose a direct but sensitive approach by saying, "Could you lower you tone of voice, please?" Another speaker might choose a more direct and assertive approach by asking the person directly to be quiet. Often these options and rules are not evident to ELLs. Additionally, they might not have yet mastered the vocabulary and the linguistic sophistication to choose the appropriate format to sound polite or to get the point across.

ARTICULATORY PHONETICS

To become an affective ESL teacher, you will need to understand the physical properties of sounds and the way sounds are produced in English. These areas of linguistics are called *acoustic phonetics* and *articulatory phonetics*. Knowledge and awareness of your vocal tract and the position of your articulators in the production of sounds are paramount to develop an understanding of articulatory phonetics.

Exploring Your Vocal Tract

Developing an awareness of the vocal tract can improve teachers' ability to produce and explain how English sounds are produced. The best way to accomplish this goal is to explore your vocal tract using one of the most important articulators, the tongue. Follow the steps here to discover the articulators used to produce English language sounds:

Lips together: Put both lips together and conceptualize English sounds that we can produce in this manner. These types of sounds are called *bilabial* sounds, as in the initial sound in the words *mother*, *past*, and *boy*.

Lower lips touching upper teeth: Guide you lower lips and upper teeth to come together, as in the initial sound of the word, *view*. If the upper teeth are touching the lover lip, we produce *labiodental* sounds, as in the initial phone of the words *vine* and *fine.*

Tongue between the teeth: Move the tip of you tongue between the upper and lower teeth and allow the tongue to stick out a little bit. Sounds that are produced in this way are called *interdental* sounds. English has two interdental sounds: /θ/ as in the initial voiceless phoneme of the word *thanks*, and the voiced counterpart /ð/, as in the word *them*.

Alveolar ridge: Move your tongue from the lower part of the upper teeth all the way up until the gum begins. Feel the connection between the teeth and the bony part of the gum. This part of your gum is called the alveolar ridge, and the sounds produced in this environment are called *alveolar sounds*. The initial sound of the words *tip*, *do*, *no*, *some*, *zoo*, and *low* represents alveolar sounds.

Hard palate: From the alveolar ridge continue moving your tongue toward the back to feel the hard palate. Notice the concave shape of you hard palate. Sounds produced in this environment are called *palatal sounds*. The graphemes in bold in the following words represent palatal sounds: *shower*, *chart*, *Cajun*, and *seizure.*

Velum (soft palate): From the hard palate continue moving all the way toward the back until you can feel the softer part of the palate, the velum. Sounds produced in the soft palate are called *velar sounds*. The initial phoneme of the words *gate*, *car*, *when*, and *water*, and the final sound in the word *sing* are velar sounds.

Uvula: Now get a mirror and open you mouth wide, just like when your doctor is going to check your throat, and notice the fleshy pendulum-like shape hanging from your soft palate. That is the uvula. Sounds produced behind the uvula and before the glottis (vocal folds) are called *glottal sounds*. The initial sound of the word *home* represents a glottal sound.

Nose: With your thumb and index fingers, pinch your nose and produce the following sounds: /m/, /n/, and /ŋ/. Notice the vibration going through your nose. Sounds produced in this manner are called *nasal sounds*. The initial, medial, and final sounds of the word *morning* are nasal sounds.

Now that you are more familiar with articulators and your vocal tract, let us explore the *types of sounds* that these articulators produce.

MAJOR PHONETIC FEATURES OF THE LANGUAGE

English sounds are identified as *pulmonic sounds*. They are produced when air from the lungs goes through the vocal tract and the nose. Sounds can be pushed through the oral cavity to produce oral sounds or through the nose to make nasal sounds. When the sounds go through these two channels, they produce one of two kinds of sounds, voiced or voiceless. Additional information about these broad phonetic features follows.

Oral and Nasal Sounds

Most sounds in English are identified as *oral sounds*. Oral sounds are produced when the velum (soft palate) is raised stopping access through the nose and forcing the air to go through the mouth. Nasal sounds are produced when the velum is lowered, allowing the air to escape through the nasal cavity. Only three sounds in English are classified as nasal: /ŋ/, /m/, and /n/; the rest of the sounds are classified as oral. See the following examples of nasal sounds in the words *sing*, *come*, *new*. The feature oral/nasal also occurs with vowel sounds. Notice that the vowel sound in the word *new* is also identified as a nasal sound.

Through the rule of assimilation, the nasal sound of the phoneme /n/ transfers toward the vowel, creating a nasalized sound for the vowel.

Voiced and Voiceless Sounds

Voiced sounds are created when the airstream from the lungs moves through the trachea (windpipe) and through the openings between the vocal folds (glottis). When the air goes through the vocal folds, the glottis vibrates, creating voiced sounds. *Voiceless sounds* are created in a similar fashion; the only difference is that the air goes through the cavity above the vocal folds. Because the glottis does not obstruct the sound, it does not vibrate, creating voiceless sounds. Because the vocal folds are not engaged, voiceless sounds are generally softer to the ear.

> When people try to have a private conversation, they artificially disengage the vocal folds and produce voiceless sounds (Fromkin, Rodman, & Hyams, 2003). If they try to increase the tone of voice, the vocal folds become engaged, and they are no longer whispering.

Place and Manner of Articulation

English sounds are further categorized based on the articulators involved in the production of phonemes and the manner in which the sounds are produced. An analysis of these two components follows.

Place of Articulation

As previously mentioned, the place of articulation of English sounds is classified under five areas: bilabials, labiodental, alveolars, velars, and palatals. Table 2.8 on the next page, describes each category and introduces their phonetic representations with the corresponding examples.

Manner of Articulation

The manner of articulation is another category used to describe the consonant sounds of the language. Five categories will be analyzed: *stops*, *fricatives*, *affricates*, *liquids*, and *glides*.

Table 2.8 Place of Articulation of English Sounds

Type of Sound	Place of Articulation	Examples
Bilabials	Both lips together	/p/ plan /b/ boy /m/ mother
Labiodental	Upper teeth touching the lower lips	/f/ five /v/ view
Interdental	Tip of the tongue (apex) between the upper and lower teeth	/θ/ think /ð/ them
Alveolars	Tip of the tongue touching beginning of the gum right behind the teeth (alveolar ridge)	/t/ Tim /d/ dark /n/ no /s/ some /z/ zoo
Velars	Raising the back of the tongue to touch the soft palate (velum)	/k/ cake /g/ gate /ŋ/ sing
Palatals	Front part of the tongue raised touching the hard palate	/Š/ shower, sugar, caution /Ž/ pleasure, seizure /č/ church / ǰ / judge

Stop sounds: The stop sounds are produced when the air going through the vocal tract stops or dies out. English has six stop sounds, presenting three types of sounds: bilabial, alveolar, and palatal. Table 2.9 presents the three voiceless sounds in English and their three voiced counterparts.

Table 2.9 English Stop Sounds

Type of Sound	Voiceless	Example	Voiced	Example
Bilabial	/p/	paper	/b/	baby
Alveolar	/t/	Tom	/d/	donkey
Palatal	/k/	cake	/g/	gate

Note: The stop sounds /p/, /t/, and /k/ have aspirated phonetic variations identified by a superscript *h*: /p^h/, /t^h/, and /k^{Hz}/.

Fricative sounds: Fricative sounds are produced when the air from the lungs is partially obstructed creating friction or a hissing sound. English has eight fricative sounds representing four types of sounds: labiodental, interdental, alveolar, and palatal. Table 2.10 presents four voiceless fricative sounds and their voiced counterparts.

Table 2.10 Fricative Sounds

Type of Sound	Voiceless	Example	Voiced	Example
Labiodental	/f/	first	/v/	view
Interdental	/θ/	think	/ð/	them
Alveolar	/s/	some	/z/	zoo, has, runs, cars
Palatal	/Š/	shower, sugar, citation	/Ž/	pleasure, leisure
Traditionally, the grapheme *s* represents a voiceless sound. However, when the grapheme follows a voiced sound (vocal folds vibrate), as in the word *has* or *calls*, through the process of sound assimilation the grapheme *s* is transformed into the voiced counterpart, /z/.				

Affricate sounds: Affricative sounds are produced when the air from the lungs is stopped in the vocal tract and slowly released. In simple terms, an affricate sound is a combination of stop and fricative sounds. English has two affricate sounds representing one type of sounds, *palatal*. Table 2.11 presents the voiceless sound and the voiced counterpart.

Table 2.11 Affricate Sounds

Type of Sound	Voiceless	Example	Voiced	Example
Palatal	/Č/	church	/ǰ/	judge

Liquid sounds: Liquid sounds are produced when the airstream finds some degree of obstruction inside the vocal cavity that does not bring to a close the sound nor creates friction; instead, the flow of air passes through the sides of the vocal cavity. English has two sounds identified as liquid and voiced sounds: the /l/ (lateral) and the /r/ (retroflex). The /l/ is identified as a *lateral sound*. The sound is produced with the tip of the tongue (apex) touching the alveolar ridge (apico-alveolar). The /r/ is identified as a *retroflex sound*. The retroflex is produced when the tip of the tongue forms an arch that touches the alveolar ridge producing a movement toward the back (apico-alveolar).

Table 2.12 Liquid Sounds

Type of Sound	Voiced	Example
Lateral	/l/	local
Retroflex	/r/	rerun

Glides: Just as the name suggests, glide sounds are produced when the airstream passes through the vocal tract with little or no obstruction (gliding). The sounds occur before or after a vowel, gliding toward or away from the vowel sounds. These sounds are also known as *semivowels* because they resemble vowel sounds. However, contrary to the vowels, glides are not always voiced sounds and do not form the crest of a syllable (stress vowel of the syllable). Four sounds fall under this category:

- The /j/, represented by the grapheme *y*, is a voiced palatal sound produced when the edges of the tongue are raised and touch the hard palate.

- The /w/ is a voiced labiovelar (lips and velum) sound produced by rounding the lips and at the same time raising the tongue toward the velum (soft palate).

- The /hw/ is a voiceless labiovelar sound produced by rounding the lips and at the same time raising the tongue toward the velum.

- The /h/ is a voiceless glottal sound produced when the air passes through uninterrupted through the opened glottis (vocal folds).

Table 2.13 Glide Sounds

Type of Sound	Voiceless	Example	Voiced	Example
Palatal			/**j**/ (y)	you
Labiovelar	/**hw**/	when	/**w**/	water
Glottal	/**h**/	home		

THE ENGLISH VOWEL SYSTEM

English has twelve vowel sounds represented by five graphemes and three additional sounds identified as *diphthongs*: /ɔj/ as in *boy*, *koi* (type of fish); /aw/ as in *cow*, *about*; and /aj/ as in *I*, *die*. The number of vowel sounds together with the small number of graphemes that represent them can create problems for ELLs. Speakers of languages with a different grapheme–phoneme correspondence than English has found this discrepancy difficult to understand, and they struggle to decipher and interpret the multiple graphic representations of the twelve phonemes in English.

Description of the Vowel System

The vowel sounds of English are illustrated using three main descriptors: the relative position of the tongue in the vocal cavity (high, mid, low), the shape of the lips (rounded or unrounded), and the part of the tongue activated to produce the sound (front, central, back).

Tongue height: This component describes how high or low the tongue is inside the vocal cavity. Another way of looking at this descriptor is to observe the openness of the mouth when the vowel sounds are produced. Vowel sounds are identified as being **high**, **mid**, or **low**. For example, the sound where the tongue is at the highest point in the mouth is the **/i/** as in the word *bee*. Pronounce this sound and notice how high your tongue is in the vocal cavity. Now, pronounce the vowel sound in the word *cat*. Notice the relative position of the tongue when you produce this vowel sound. If you did it correctly, the position of the tongue should be very low in the mouth.

Part of the tongue: Three parts of the tongue are activated to produce language sounds: **front**, **central**, and **back**. If you produce the two sounds /i/ and /æ/, you will notice that two different portions of the tongue are raised for their production. That is, in the production of /i/, the tip of the tongue should be raised, whereas in the production of /æ/, the tip of the tongue should remain lower in the mouth while the back is raised.

The position of the lips: The position of the lips can be unrounded or rounded. Now, produce the two sounds again and notice the position of the lips. Are the lips rounded or unrounded? When you produce /i/, your lips should be unrounded. How about when you produce the sound /æ/? Are your lips rounded or unrounded? The position of the lips in the production of this sound should also be unrounded. Now, let us practice the sound of the /o/ as in the word *old*. Are the lips rounded or unrounded when you produce the initial vowel sound? The /o/ is a typical rounded vowel.

Table 2.14 English Vowel System

Tongue Height	Front [Lips Unrounded]	Central	Back [Lips Rounded]
High ▲	beet / i / bit / I /		fool /u/ full /ʊ/
Mid	bait / e / bet / ɛ/	cut /ʌ /(stressed) sofa /ə/(unstressed)	grow / o / saw / ɔ /
Low ▼	bat /æ/		bar / a /

SUPRA SEGMENTAL ELEMENTS OF ENGLISH

Up to this point, we have emphasized how phonemes can convey meaning in oral communication. However, a large number of languages in the world can also convey meaning through phonological components beyond the phoneme. These languages use *pitch* at the syllable, word, or sentence levels to convey meaning. The use of these features beyond the phoneme level is known as *suprasegmental features* of the language. Three suprasegmental components will be analyzed in this section: tone, intonation, and word stress.

Tone

Tone describes a language feature where speakers use different levels of pitch at the *syllable level* to change the meaning of words. Speakers of a tonal language like Thai, Chinese, or Vietnamese can pronounce a word using different tones—low, mid, high, falling tones, and rising tones—to communicate as many as five different meanings using the same word (Fromkin, Rodman, & Hyams, 2003). Many languages in the world are tonal languages; these include Chinese, Thai, Burmese, Vietnamese, Lao, and many African and Native American languages. Because English is not a tonal language, ELLs who are speakers of tonal languages face a particular challenge to master English pronunciation.

Intonation

Intonation pattern describes how pitch at the sentence and word levels can convey meaning or alter the emphasis of the communication. In intonation languages like English, the *pitch contour* plays an important role in pronunciation. However, the pitch is important mostly at the word, phrase, and sentence levels. This distinction, for example, can create the difference between a question and a reply or what part of a sentence is highlighted. Let us analyze how the intonation pattern of English is able to change meaning in the following utterances.

(Note: Capital letters in bold are used to indicate the primary stress.)

How **ARE** you?—the question

How are **YOU?**—the reply

In the first sentence the verb, **ARE**, is emphasized to signify a question, whereas in the second utterance, the noun, **YOU,** is emphasized as a reply to the question. In this case, the intonation pattern was able to change the meaning in identical sentences.

Intonation patterns can also be used to emphasize key words and ideas in utterances. Traditionally, there are key words in the subject (noun phrase) and predicate (verb phrase). These are used to identify key components of the communication. For example, let us examine the following two sentences to see how the pitch contour can change the emphasis and the purpose of the communication.

John McCain was the **REPUBLICAN** candidate for the presidency.

John McCain is the Republican candidate for the **PRESIDENCY**.

SARAH PALIN'S SON is **A SOLDIER** in a combat brigade in the U.S. Army.

SARAH PALIN'S SON is a soldier in a **COMBAT BRIGADE** in the U.S. Army.

In the first sentence, the key element is to emphasize that John McCain is **REPUBLICAN**, not Democrat. Notice the lack of stress in the subject—John McCain—because the speaker did not want to emphasize his name, only the fact that he was the **REPUBLICAN** candidate. In the second sentence, the key element is to emphasize that he is a candidate for the **PRESIDENCY**, not for any other elective office. In the third example, two elements are emphasized, one in the noun phrase—**SARAH PALIN'S SON**—and one in the verb phrase—**A SOLDIER**. No emphasis is given to the fact that he is a soldier in the U.S. Army. In the last sentence, another component is emphasized; he is in a **COMBAT BRIGADE**. Notice that in all these sentences, most of the words emphasized are content words. Moreover, when we communicate these sentences, the stressed words are pronounced with a higher pitch, louder and longer, to make the listeners aware of the intent of the communication. That is, speakers use the intonation pattern of the language to guide listeners to pay attention to specific ideas and to disregard others.

Word Stress

In addition to the intonation pattern at the sentence or phrase level, English uses *word stress* to change the meaning and often the syntactic classification of a small number of words: homographs. *Homographs* are words with identical spelling but with an alternate pronunciation. For example, when we change the stress in the word *SUBject* (noun) to *subJECT* (verb), it results in the creation of a different word. This linguistic feature is called *phonetic stress*. Notice that when we change the stress, the syntactic classification of the word also changes from a noun to a verb. See additional examples of homographs that follow the same pattern.

Table 2.15 Phonetic Stress

Nouns	Verbs
ADDress	ad**DRESS**
At**tribute**	at**TRI**bute
CONcert	con**CERT**
CONduct	con**DUCT**
CONtract	con**TRACT**
CONvert	con**VERT**
DIgest	di**GEST**
INsert	in**SERT**
OBject	ob**JECT**
PERmit	per**MIT**
PROduce	pro**DUCE**
PROgress	pro**GRESS**
PROject	pro**JECT**
PROtest	pro**TEST**
Record	Re**CORD**
Rebel	re**BEL**
Renegade	rene**GADE**
SUSpect	sus**PECT**
TRANSfer	trans**FER**
SUBject	Sub**JECT**

In addition to phonemic stress, English uses at least three levels of stress to pronounce words: primary, secondary, and unstressed. These kinds of stress do not necessarily change the meaning of the word; instead, they serve as a guide for pronunciation. Teachers of ELLs have to become aware of these patterns so they can support students in their attempt to master English pronunciation. To accomplish this task, teachers have to guide ELLs to identify at least the primary and secondary stress in words. For example, study the primary and secondary word stress in the following words.

(Note: Capital letters in boldface are used to represent primary stress, and italics are used to represent secondary stress.)

Two-syllable words: **COM***pass,* **PRO***file,* **TA***ble*

Three-syllable words: *com***PO***site, Im***por***tant,* **PHO***to*graph

Four-syllable words: **ME**lan*cho*lic, **E**du*ca*ted, *mis*un**DER**stand

Notice that in the two-syllable words, the stress falls on the next to last syllable in all three examples. Also in the rest of the examples, the stress falls at the beginning of the word or in the middle. We could say that English words have the tendency to place the stress at the beginning or the middle syllables of the word. However, this observation is not specific enough to guide an effective preparation or to teach the stress pattern of English words. There are a few general rules to teach the stress pattern of English; these are presented later in this section.

Teaching the Stress Pattern of English

In normal oral communication, English speakers stress key words in the sentence, whereas the others words are quickly spoken. That is, in English, we stress content words and quickly glide over function words. ***Content words*** refer to words with high semantic value: nouns, verbs, adjectives, and adverbs. ***Function words*** refer to words that are required to comply with grammatical conventions: articles, prepositions, auxiliaries, conjunctions, and pronouns. It is common in English sentences to stress content words, as opposed to function words, because content words can communicate more information than function words can.

Romance languages—French, Italian, and Spanish—follow intonation patterns that are different than those in English. Romance languages use a similar intensity of word stress for each word in the sentence. For that reason, when English speakers hear communication in these languages, they might perceive a string of monotonous word patterns with no specific high or low points and without word boundaries. On the other hand, when speakers of these languages fail to provide the appropriate sentence stress and rhythm required in English, the sentences might not sound like English, and the communication might lose the intended meaning.

Like native English speakers, ELLs might need to learn word stress as they learn new vocabulary words. However, there are a few rules to identify the position of stress in English words with more than one syllable. In compound words, the first word is generally stressed:

BUTTERflies, **BIRD**house, **BOOK**store.

The same rule applies to compound nouns such as **COMPUTER** programmer, **FRENCH** fries, **NAIL** polish. When using two- or three-word phrases, the preposition gets the stress:

Two-word phrases: shut **UP**, turn **OFF**, pick **UP**

Three-word phrases: pick me **UP**, turn me **ON**, turn it **DOWN**

PHONETIC ALPHABET

The two most common phonetic alphabets used to describe languages are the International Phonetic Alphabet (IPA) and the American Phonetic Alphabet (APA). IPA is used to describe languages throughout the world, and APA is used exclusively to describe English sounds. With the exception of a few phonemes, both systems use similar symbols. Table 2.16 presents the symbols used in the APA to describe consonants, and Table 2.17 on the next page, presents those symbols that differ in the two systems.

Table 2.16 Summary of Consonant Sounds of English

Type of Sound	Bilabial	Labiodental	Interdental	Alveolar	Palatal	Velar	Retroflex	Glottal
Stop	/p/ (vl) /pʰ/(vl) /b/ (vd)			/t/(vl) /tʰ/ (vl) /d/ (vd)		/k/ (vl) /Kʰ/(vl) /g/ (vd)		
Nasal	/m/(vd)			/n/ (vd)		/ŋ/(vd)		
Fricative		/f/ (vl) /v/ (vd)	/θ/ (vl) /ð/ (vd)	/s/ (vl) /z/ (vd)	/š/ (vl) /ž/ (vd)			
Affricate					/č/ (vl) /ǰ/ vd)			
Glide					/j/ (vd)	/hw/(vl) /w/(vd)		/h/(vl)
Liquids				/l/ (vd)			/r/ (vd)	
Phonetic symbols taken from UCLA Division of Psychology and Language Sciences, retrieved on August 11, 2008, from www.phon.ucl.ac.uk/home/wells/phoneticsymbols.htm.							

Table 2.17 Symbols for the American English Phonetic Alphabet

Symbol in the American Phonetic Alphabet (APA)	Equivalent symbol in International Phonetic Alphabet (IPA)
/č/ church	/tʃ/
/ǰ/ judge	/dʒ/
/š/ shower	/ʃ/
/ž/ pleasure	/ʒ/

Difficult English Sound for ELLs from Multiple Language Groups

The inconsistency between grapheme and phoneme in English can create challenges to speakers from multiple language groups. Problems with the sounds represented by *ch* and *sh* are examples of this faulty correspondence. Study the examples provided here:

ch pronounced as /š/: **ch**ef, **ch**evron, ma**ch**ine, **Ch**evrolet

s*s*, *ti*, *s*, *ci* pronounced as /š/: mi**ss**ion, cau**ti**on, **s**ugar, deli**ci**ous

ch pronounced as /k/: **Ch**rist, **ch**rome, **ch**emistry

The issue is not whether ELLs can produce the /č/ or /š/ phonemes; rather, the issue is to identify when the grapheme–phoneme is consistent and when it is not. One of the main reasons for this grapheme–phoneme inconsistency is the use of loan words from various languages—French and Native American groups, mostly. Traditionally, when English sounds are not present in the L2, students have the tendency to substitute them for the similar sounds in their native language. Table 2.18 presents sounds not present in various language groups with the resulting phoneme substitution (Chamot, De Mado & Hollie, n.d.; Kress, 1993).

Table 2.18 Challenging English Sounds for Various Language Groups

Sounds	Examples	No Equivalent Sounds (Substituted Sounds Are in Parentheses)
/b/	Book, bit, beet, baby, ball	Cantonese and Hmong (substitute /p/), Korean (substitute /p/)
/w/	Work, want, war, water	Vietnamese and Hmong (substitute /u/)
/f/	First, forward, **ph**one	Filipino and Korean (substitute /p/)
/š/	shell, delicious, nation, chef, sugar, mission	Spanish (substitute for /s/ or /č/, Cantonese (substitute /s/), Japanese /s/
/θ/	thank, think, math, bath	Spanish and Mandarin (substitution /s/, /t/), Cantonese, Vietnamese, Hmong (substitute /t^h or /f/), Korean (substitute /t/).
/ð/	them, these, rather, either	Vietnamese, Hmong and Korean (/d/), Cantonese (/t/ or /f/)
/ ǰ /	**j**ust, gauge, **j**udge	Hmong and Korean (/ č /)
/ ž /	Measure, pleasure	Spanish (/z/ or / ǰ /), Vietnamese and Cantonese (/s/)
/z/	zoo, ha**s**, wa**s**, cars	Spanish and Cantonese (/s/)
/v/	**V**ery, **v**iew, **v**owel	Spanish, Filipino, and Korean (/b/) Cantonese (/f/), Mandarin (/w/ or /f/)
L clusters	**Cl**ass, **Spl**ash, **pl**ane, **cl**ever	Chinese, Korean, Vietnamese, Japanese, and Italian
R clusters	**Cr**y, **pr**ize, **br**ibe	Chinese, Korean, Vietnamese, and Japanese
Initial S clusters	**Spr**ing, **sc**ale, **sm**all	Spanish
Final Clusters	E**nd**, calle**d**, fir**st**	Greek, Italian, Spanish

Communicative Competence

Communicative competence describes the ability of second-language learners to apply the rules and use language appropriately. In the 1960s, Dell Hynes coined the term to describe the second-language acquisition process and to expand Noam Chomsky's concepts of *competence* used to describe first-language acquisition. Canale and Swain (1980) later redefined communicative competence based on the following components:

- Sociolinguistic: the ability to switch from register based on context and purpose of communication

- Grammatical: the application of grammar rules for the language, that is, phonology, morphology, syntax, semantics, and pragmatics

- Discourse: the ability to achieve cohesion and coherence in communication

- Strategic: the use of techniques of communication to achieve the communicative purpose and to avoid breakdowns in communication

These components of communicative competence have to be taught explicitly to ELLs. With effective instruction, ELLs can develop the communicative competence needed to function effectively in school and in society.

BICS and CALP

Jim Cummins (1981) defined the concept of communicative competence based on two distinct components: **basic interpersonal communication skills** (BICS) and **cognitive academic language proficiency** (CALP).

Basic interpersonal communication skills describes the type of proficiency that ELLs need to communicate in face-to-face and highly contextualized situations and in daily activities. Based on the superficial nature of this proficiency, children are able to master it after to two to four years of exposure to the language.

Cognitive academic language proficiency describes a higher level of linguistic development required to understand instruction in decontextualized situations. It covers the type of language needed to understand and use higher-order thinking skills and instruction typical of the content areas. ELLs must master CALP to be able to compete in mainstream class-rooms. Students who are exited from the ESL or bilingual program before achieving this level of linguistic development generally cannot compete academically with their native English-speaking peers.

THEORIES OF SECOND-LANGUAGE ACQUISITION

Healthy young children acquire a first language in natural settings with minimum conscious effort. Following this universal achievement, researchers in second-language acquisition studied first-language acquisition to identify ways in which this process can be replicated to teach a second language. Their views are presented based on the same three dominant theories of first-language acquisition: *behaviorist*, *innatist*, and *interactionist*.

Behaviorist Views

Behaviorists see second-language learning as a process of habit formation through the use of stimulus, response, and reinforcement. Following these principles, the behaviorist developed the *audiolingual method*. The method uses imitation, repetition, and reinforcement to teach a second language. Behaviorists promote the use of memorization of dialogues and pattern drills as a foundation to teach the grammar of the language. Errors are corrected immediately to avoid the formation of bad linguistic habits, and reinforcement is used to maintain the correct structures. This method influenced the teaching of second and foreign language during the 1950s and 1960s, but its influence virtually ended in the late 1970s.

Innatist Views

Innatists believe that children are born with the capability to learn languages. This *innate mechanism* is equipped with a grammar template that allows children to construct the grammar of their native language through the process of hypothesis testing. According to Chomsky, children develop the rules of their language with minimal support from parents. The role of adults in this theory is restricted to building the lexicon of the language and teaching rules to develop sociolinguistic competence.

Following Chomsky's views of language, innatists developed the *creative construction theory*. Proponents of this theory suggest that second-language learners follow similar strategies and make the same kinds of errors as native speakers do in the process of language mastery. Following these principles, Stephen Krashen (1985) developed one of the most comprehensive theories of second-language acquisition. This theory is composed of the following five hypotheses:

- **Acquisition versus learning**: Acquisition and learning represent two different processes. Acquisition takes place through meaningful and natural language interaction with speakers of the language, with no conscious efforts to comply with grammar conventions. It is meaning driven and characterized by language discovery in a low-anxiety environment. Furthermore, acquisition is informal and resembles the way in which children acquire their native language. In opposition, learning describes the formal and highly restrictive cognitive activities typically found in teacher-centered classroom instruction. **Implications**: Implementing strategies that resemble the L1 acquisition process can promote second-language acquisition. Teachers need to use inductive teaching and promote language development through fun and interactive activities that lead to self-discovery.

- **Comprehensible input**: Children must understand the content of the communication in the target language to acquire the language. However, for real acquisition to take place, the input must be a little bit above the current linguistic level of the learner. In summary, language is acquired by understanding input that contains linguistic structures that are beyond the current level of linguistic competence. **Implications**: Implement meaningful activities in contextualized situations to ensure that ELLs understand the content of the communication. Implement ESL methods that attempt to re-create the way that children acquire a first language, that is, the natural method and total physical response.

- **The monitor hypothesis**: Learners exposed to formal language instruction develop an internal mechanism able to assess language and make corrections. However, to use this language editor, the learner must have explicit knowledge of the rules and time to apply them. **Implications**: The monitor hypothesis has limited implications for the development of the speaking ability in L2. However, teachers can guide students to internalize the rules to a point where these rules become automatic and can be easily applied subconsciously. Conscious knowledge of the rules can be beneficial to polish the language and to monitor writing samples.

- **Affective filter hypothesis**: Students perform better when they feel motivated and relaxed. When they are relaxed, the affective filter is lowered, allowing linguistic input in the language acquisition device (LAD). **Implications**: Create a low-anxiety environment in which students feel secure. Students should not be forced to communicate before they are ready. Allow students to remain silent, but provide them with comprehensible input to develop the language needed to begin oral communication.

- **Natural order hypothesis**: ELLs acquire English structures in a predictable sequence with small variations depending on the influence of L1. This sequence is guided by the communicative value of the structures and the frequency of required usage. For example, forms of the verb *to be* are used more frequently and convey more information than the third-person singular; thus, they are acquired earlier. **Implications**: Avoid the teaching of English following a grammatical sequence. Instead, develop rich linguistic activities where students are able to use a variety of structures. The communicative acts and the needs of the learners will determine the acquisition sequence of the language structures.

Interactionists' Views

Interactionists conceptualize the existence of the LAD but believe that the role of parents and caregivers in the innatist theory is too narrow. Interactionists believe that caregivers play a vital role in adjusting language to facilitate language acquisition. Parents and caregivers become sympathetic listeners and provide needed language support through *conversational scaffolding*. Parents scaffold conversation by repeating and modeling the words that the child produces, checking for understanding by prompting questions at the end of the child's statements and by making the child feel confident in his or her ability to communicate. The interactionist theory is currently the prevailing theory used to explain the process of first-language acquisition.

Krashen's comprehensible input is a key concept in the interactionist view of second-language acquisition. Interactionists emphasize the way that native speakers deliver comprehensible input and the way they negotiate meaning with ELLs. **Implications**: Teachers should be encouraged to use nonverbal communication, drawing and modified speech (foreign talk) to deliver comprehensible input. They should also develop strategies where ELLs interact with native speakers and are guided to negotiate meaning in real-life situations.

Interdependence of L1 and L2

A strong cognitive and academic development in the first language has a positive effect in the acquisition of the second language. Academic skills and content knowledge, literacy development, and metacognitive strategies transfer to L2 (Ovando, Combs, & Collier, 2006). Jim Cummins (1991) called this interdependence the common underlying proficiency.

Multiple situations and conditions can affect the acquisition of a second language. Some of the elements and concepts are discussed in this section.

Interlanguage

An *interlanguage* describes a transitional construction students develop in the process of mastering a second language. It is usually caused by language interference or by the complexity of the structure of the language. Interlanguages are developmental in nature and generally disappear once mastery in L2 is achieved. If the nonstandard structures persist, then we say that the structures have been *fossilized*. The development of an interlanguage is not generally a group effort; instead, interlanguages are unique to individual second-language learners.

The Threshold Hypothesis

Jim Cummins believes that language learners should arrive at a given academic and literacy level in L1 in order to transfer elements from L1 to L2. This age-appropriate threshold is generally reached after four or five years of effective L1 instruction. This theory explains why ELLs taught only in L2 may experience academic difficulties in school. ELLs who received services through a late-exit program may have cognitive advantage over monolingual students (Baker & Jones, 1998).

Language Interference

Language interference is errors caused by the interference of L1 over the structures of the new language. For example, because Spanish does not have the voiced alveolar sound /z/, Spanish speakers substitute the sound with its equivalent in Spanish, /s/. This substitution can result in the creation of nonstandard homonyms when speakers replace the /z/ for /s/, creating confusion with words like *zoo*, which can be pronounced as *sue*.

Cross-Linguistic Language Transfer

Positive transfer occurs when structures of L1 help in the acquisition of structures of a second language. For example, most concepts related to writing in Indo-European languages, such as Spanish, French, and German, transfer to English. Children do not have to learn to read again; instead, they need to learn the vocabulary and the syntactic and semantic features of the language to obtain meaning.

Code Switching

Code switching describes the alternating use of two languages in communication. This linguistic behavior is typical of bilingual people, and it is done for a variety of reasons. People switch languages because the word or expression is not available or does not convey the same message in the language of communication; they do not know the word in the language of communication; or they want to convey the idea that they are bilingual.

There are two identified forms of switching: intrasentential and intersentential code switching. In the intrasentential (within the sentence) code switching, speakers combine words of two languages within the same sentence. **Example**: I went to the party with my best *cuates* (friends). In the intersentential (across sentences) format, speakers produce one sentence in a given language and a second in a different language. **Example**: At the party we danced all night long. *Nosotros bailamos hasta salsa y reggaetón* (We even danced salsa and reggaeton.).

Code switching is a normal feature among bilingual speakers; however, teachers need to be sure that learners can separate the two languages so they can function effectively in both linguistic environments.

Stages of Second-Language Development

The stages of second-language acquisition are similar to first-language acquisition. Five stages have been identified. A description of these stages follows.

Preproduction or Silent Stage

- Communicates with gestures and actions

- Lacks receptive vocabulary and shows problems comprehending messages

- Might prefer to remain silent (silent phase)

- Might experience frustration and anxiety

- Relies heavily on nonverbal communication; can lead to miscommunication

Early Speech Production

- Increases comprehension

- Communicates using yes or no, and one-word statements

- Expands receptive vocabulary

- Understands language in contextualized situations

Speech Emergence

- Communicates in phrases using words with high semantic context: verbs, adjectives, nouns, and adverbs

- Continues gaining receptive vocabulary

- Communicates more effectively in contextualized situations, face-to-face interactions

- Understands more than is able to communicate

Intermediate Fluency

- Communicates using simple sentences

- Over generalizes because of intralingual and interlingual interference

- Becomes more acculturated and feels more comfortable in school

Advanced Stage

- Develops the academic language and might be ready to be mainstreamed

Elements that Affect Language Acquisition

Personality Factors

Extroversion describes individuals who are outspoken and have well-developed social skills. Extroverted people seek contacts and negotiate meaning with native speakers of the language. Extroversion can be linked to the interpersonal intelligence described by Howard Gardner. This type of personality definitely contributes to second-language acquisition.

Tolerance for ambiguity is the ability to avoid frustration in instructional situations characterized by lack of organization and guidance. To cope with this situation, individuals generally create their own structure to complete the task. Individuals who can cope with ambiguity are generally good language learners and do better academically.

Positive Self-Esteem

Self-esteem is defined as the value that people assign to themselves. Having *positive self-esteem* correlates to language learning and academic success in school. Students with positive self-esteem are risk takers, which also correlates to language learning.

Impulsiveness versus Reflection

Impulsive students are those who attempt to address issues or answer questions without having a clear view of the issue in question. *Reflective students*, on the other hand, step back and analyze the issues or questions before attempting to address them. Impulsive students might develop the language faster than reflective students might, but reflective children will develop a more polished form of the language.

High Anxiety

Environments characterized by high stress can impair learning and second-language learning. However, some levels of anxiety (facilitating anxiety) can guide students to take responsibility for the learning process and become effective language learners.

Instrumental and Integrative Motivation

The type of motivation that learners may have can affect the rate and quality of second-language acquisition. Two types of motivation are commonly discussed in the area of second-language acquisition: instrumental and integrative.

ELLs with an *instrumental motivation* want to learn the language for specific purposes, to travel, to gain admission to college, to take a proficiency test. ELLs with an *integrative motivation* want to learn the language to understand the people and culture and to function effectively in society. The type of motivation can affect the rate and the quality of second-language development achieved. For example, ELLs with instrumental motivation might lose interest once their specific reasons for learning the language are met. On the other hand, students with integrative motivation will be prone to learn the social aspect of language faster than the academic part of it.

Previous Schooling or the Absence of Schooling

Students with strong academic backgrounds are able to transfer academic and language skills to the new language. However, those students who have experienced interrupted schooling or have never attended schools represent a unique challenge to public schools. Generally, these students cannot be placed in the regular classroom before they receive attention to meet their linguistic and academic gaps. Traditionally, these students are served in newcomer centers or through a pullout programs to provide basic skills instruction and training to facilitate their adjustment to school and life in their new country.

Socioeconomic Background

Traditionally, students from low socioeconomic backgrounds do not receive the verbal, literacy, and social stimulus to do well in school. Most of these students are served through specialized programs sponsored with funds from Title I of the No Child Left Behind legislation.

Age and Second-Language Acquisition

The critical period hypothesis suggests that children might have an advantage over adults in the development of pronunciation. Children are also more willing to take risks than adults are; thus they might develop the language faster. However, the ideal time for second-language learning is not necessarily the early age of development, birth to 6 years old. Instead, the acquisition of a second language is best achieved after the child develops a strong foundation in the first language. Children generally arrive at this plateau in their first language around ages 8 to 12 (third to sixth grade). Once children arrive at this threshold, and with appropriate instruction, they can easily transfer skills and content to the second language. Moreover, these students will have sufficient time in school to strengthen knowledge in L2 and to meet the academic gap that traditionally exists between ELLs and native English speakers (Hadaway, Vardell, & Young, 2009).

Adults, on the other hand, generally develop a language ego that might affect their willingness to seek contacts with native speakers to practice the language. However, in general, adults have advantages over children in the mastery of more abstract components of the language and overall language proficiency.

Home and Community Environment

Children who live in ethnic enclaves where L1 is extensively used might not get the language support needed in L2. Most of the time the L2 is not needed to function in this environment; thus, the motivation to learn the language decreases.

Time and Expected Time of Residence in the Country

Students who plan to remain in the country for an extensive period will make an effort to learn the language. However, transitory or migrant students might not be motivated to learn the language because they know that eventually they will return home.

CONCLUSIONS

In this chapter, we introduced the concepts of phonology, morphology, lexicon, syntax, semantics, and pragmatics, and their importance in language teaching and learning. We emphasized the description of English sounds and the articulators involved in their production, including the place and manner of articulation.

We also presented an overview of theories of first- and second-language acquisition. Finally, we introduced elements that affect second-language acquisition, such as previous schooling, age of exposure to the language, cross-linguistic transfer, and language interference. These principles were presented to provide a foundation for identifying best methods and strategies to meet the needs of English-language learners.

REFERENCES

Baker, C., and S. P. Jones. 1998. *Encyclopedia of bilingualism and bilingual education.* Philadelphia: Multilingual Matters.

Canale, M., and M. Swain. 1980. Theoretical bases of communicative approaches to second language teaching and testing. *Applied Linguistics* 1:1-47.

Chamot, A., J. De Mado, and S. Hollie. (n.d.). *Longman Keystone B: Teacher's edition.* White Plains, NY: Pearson Education, Inc.

Cummins, J. 1991. Interdependence of first- and second-language proficiency in bilingual children. In *Language processing in bilingual children*, ed. E. Bialystok, 70–89. Cambridge: Cambridge University Press.

_____, J. 1981. The role of primary language development in promoting educational success of minority students. In *Schooling and language minority students: A theoretical framework*, ed. California State Department of Education 3–49. Los Angeles: Evaluation, Dissemination and Assessment Center, California State University.

Fromkin, V., R. Rodman, and N. Hyams. 2003. *An Introduction to language*, 7th ed. Boston: Thompson Heinle.

Hadaway, N. L., S. M. Vardell, and T. A. Young. 2009. *English language learners.* New York: Pearson.

Kaplan, R. B. 1966. Cultural thought patterns in intercultural education. *Language Learning* 16: 1–20.

Krashen, S. 1985. *The Input Hypothesis: Issues and Implications.* Beverly Hills, CA: Laredo Publishing Company.

Kress, J. E. 1993. *The ESL Teacher's book of lists.* West Nyack, NY: The Center for Applied Research in Education.

Ovando, C. J., V. P. Collier, and C. B. Combs. 2006. *Bilingual & ESL classrooms: Teaching in multicultural context.* 4th ed. Boston: McGraw-Hill.

Rosado, L. 2007. *The best teachers' test preparation for the TExES generalist EC–4* (101). Piscataway, NJ: Research and Education Association.

Teaching Methods and Techniques

This chapter presents a description of the learning theories that have been used to develop methods to teach ESL. It presents an overview of the proficiency levels used to describe the development of English, the language the student is learning (L2) and the methods and strategies used to teach the receptive and productive English skills. The chapter also addresses factors that influence the development of a second language and discusses how teachers can use this information to promote second-language acquisition. The chapter also summarizes information about the integration of language and content, and content-based language programs. Lastly, it presents information about programs (cooperative learning, critical pedagogy, and accelerated learning) that have been successful in bridging the gap between native English speakers and English-language learners (ELLs).

APPROACHES, METHODS, AND STRATEGIES

Various approaches, methods, and strategies have been used to develop programs of study to address the linguistic and cognitive needs of ELLs. The term *approach* describes the learning theories, theoretical and philosophical foundations, and the principles used for the development of methods and strategies. A *method* is the actual implementation of the learning theories in a program of study. A *strategy* refers to specific techniques and activities to implement the method. For example, the audiolingual method is based on behaviorism and the principles of the structural school of linguistics. One of the

Figure 3.1 The Connection among Approach, Methods, and Strategies

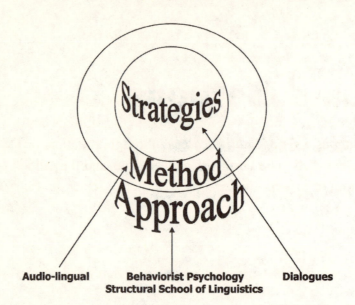

main principles of these two schools (structural–behaviorism) is that learning is a set of habits that can be isolated and taught through conditioning. That is, specific language components can be isolated and taught through repetition drills and positive reinforcement. Using these and other principles, linguists developed the audiolingual method. This method uses strategies like memorization of dialogues and repetition drills to teach languages. Figure 3.1 presents a visual representation of the connection among approaches (behaviorist–structural), the method (audiolingual), and strategies used to implement the method.

Learning Theories: Schools of Psychology and Linguistics

Psycholinguistics represents the merging of the school of psychology with the school of linguistics. This merging initiated what has been refered to as the *scientific approach* for the teaching of languages. In psycholinguistics, psychologists deal with language teaching and learning, and linguists study the multiple components of language and language acquisition. As a result of the fusion of these two distinct theoretical components, new models to explain language acquisition and language learning emerged. An analysis of the theoretical framework for the development of English-as-a-second-language (ESL) methods is presented in this section.

Behaviorist–Structural School

The behaviorist–structural school emerged in the late 1950s as result of the work of psychologists Ivan Pavlov, John B. Watson, and B.F. Skinner, and the linguists Ferdinand de Saussure, Leonard Bloomfield, Robert Lado, and Charles Fries. The behaviorist school of psychology emphasizes the use of observable behavior as a foundation to study and assess learning processes. The behaviorists believed that measurable behaviors could be described and used as a foundation to determine if learning is taking place. They conceptualized learning as a *set of habits acquired* through imitation, drills, and reinforcement. Children were believed to be born with a clean slate, and they added language to the slate through imitation of parents and caregivers.

On the linguistic side, the structuralists saw language primarily from the oral point of view and emphasized mostly the overt components of language: phonology and morphology. As the result of these views, language acquisition was perceived as a habit-forming process through operant conditioning learned inductively through imitation and memorization. Research done in second-language acquisition developed two key theories explaining second-language acquisition: contrastive analysis and error analysis.

From behaviorists and through the influence of the school of structural linguistics, the following key language and learning principles emerged.

- Frequent and intensive practice will lead to mastery.

- Conditioning through stimulus and response can be used to promote learning.

- Language is best learned indirectly and inductively.

- Pattern drills should be taught without explanations (subconscious learning).

- Practice should precede any explanation.

Behaviorism was the leading school of psychology in the United States from the 1940s to the 1970s. During the same period, structural linguistics was the dominant school in the United States. One key ESL method was developed following behaviorist–structural principles: the audiolingual method. This method will be discussed later in this chapter.

The Contrastive Analysis Theory

One key linguistic theory linked to the work of the behaviorist–structural group is the theory of ***contrastive analysis (CA)***. This theory was developed in the 1940s and was used extensively in the audiolingual method. Charles Fries and Robert Lado popularized the theory and applied the principles to the teaching of ESL in the United States. An analysis of this theory follows.

Proponents of CA suggest that through an analysis of the student's native language (L1) and L2, it is possible to predict problems that ELLs will encounter in the acquisition of the target language (L2). Let us study an example from Spanish and English. An analysis of the two languages revealed the following features:

- Spanish does not have words that begin with *s* clusters, such as *sp–*, *sk–*, *sm–*, *spr–*, *st–*, *sn–*, and *sl–*.

- These clusters occur only in medial positions in Spanish, and they are always preceded by the vowel *e*.

- English has multiple words that begin with these clusters: *speak*, *school*, *smoke*, *spring*, *state*, *snow*, *slate*, and others.

Taking these findings as a foundation, CA can predict that Spanish-speaking ELLs will not only have problems with these clusters but also they will add an *e* in front of these English consonant clusters, producing nonstandard pronunciation such as *espeak* [EspIk], *eschool* [Eskul], *esmoke* [Esmok], *espring* [Espri], *esnow* [Esno], and *eslate* [Eslet]. The CA theory revolutionized the teaching of ESL in the 1960s; however, the theory had one main flaw: It could not predict or identify every single error made by ELLs. The CA theory is still used today; however, a second theory was developed to compensate for its shortcoming, error analysis.

Error Analysis Theory

The error analysis (EA) theory was developed in the 1970s to compensate for the flaws of the contrastive analysis theory. In EA, linguists examine not only the issue of language interference but also the inconsistent and developmental language features of the target language, including errors typical of native speakers. When the complexity of the target language and the contrastive features of both languages are taken into account, it produces a more accurate picture of the performance of ELLs. As a result of this analysis, the performance of ELLs is used as a foundation for lesson planning.

Cognitive-Generative-Transformational

The cognitive-generative-transformational school emerged in the 1960s as a result of the work mainly of the psychologist Jean Piaget and the linguists Eric Lenneberg and Noam Chomsky. Cognitive psychology studies human behavior, processes used for problem solving, the use of memory as a learning tool, and the language-acquisition process. This school of psychology has its foundations in the work of Jean Piaget and his theory of the stages of cognitive development typical of children and young adults.

Cognitive generativists conceptualized the acquisition of languages as a mental process using innate mechanisms. Chomsky labeled this mechanism the language acquisition device (LAD). He believed that once this mechanism is activated, children acquire a set of universal grammar rules that allow for language acquisition. Following the same principles, the generative-transformational (GT) school proposed that language is composed of a finite set of universal rules that children acquire and apply to create language. They believe that the main components of language are semantics and syntax. Once children internalize the set of rules (syntax), they can generate their own sentences to communicate (semantics) and eventually master the language. Other linguistics concepts linked to the work of the cognitive-generative-transformational school are the critical period hypothesis and the theory of the lateralization of the brain. An analysis of these theories follows.

The Critical Period Hypothesis and the Lateralization of the Brain

Proponents of the *critical period hypothesis* posit the idea that there is an ideal time for language acquisition (Chomsky, 1975; Lenneberg, 1967). This theory is based on another concept, the *lateralization of the brain*. The lateralization of the brain describes the alignment of brain functions and the articulators used in the production of language. That is, neurons transmit nerve impulses to specific articulators to produce the sounds and other language functions of the mother tongue. It has been suggested that the process begins at birth upon contact with the language, and it reaches its peak around puberty, when the brain functions become settled or assigned. Once the lateralization of the brain occurs, second-language acquisition becomes more difficult.

It has been conceptualized that the brains of young children are more elastic and flexible than the brains of adults are; thus, young ELLs may have certain advantages over adults. However, convergent research shows that this advantage might be restricted at the phonological level only. For this reason, people who learn the language after puberty might develop a foreign accent, whereas children generally develop native-like pronunciation.

Humanistic Psychology (1950s-present)

Humanistic psychology has also impacted the development of ESL methods. This school of psychology emerged as a reaction to behaviorism and its lack of understanding of emotions and their impact on learning. Humanistic psychology is concerned with the human components of the learning process. These human components are best represented in the work of Abraham Maslow's theory of the hierarchy of human needs and Carl Rogers's ideas on the development of positive self-concept and the student-centered approach for teaching. Maslow believed that learners have basic physical and emotional needs, and meeting these needs can enhance and facilitate learning. These basic human needs include safety, love, affection, belonging, and positive self-esteem. He believed that once these needs are met, people are able to reach the top of their development, or self-actualization. Carl Rogers's student-centered approach and Maslow's hierarchy of needs are considered the cornerstone for the development of methods and strategies for teaching and learning. Thus teachers ought to strive to develop the classroom conditions where students can become physically and emotionally ready to learn.

Three main approaches have been used to develop modern ESL methods: behaviorist–structural, cognitive–transformational, and the principles of humanistic psychology. An analysis of methods developed before the development of the concept of psycholinguistics is presented, followed by the methods linked to these approaches.

METHODS FOR TEACHING ESL

The Direct Method (Natural Method)

Target population: Beginner, intermediate, or advanced ELLs

The **Direct Method** originated in the nineteenth century as a reaction against the grammar translation method, a method originally developed to translate classic literature from the Greek to the Latin. The Direct Method is based on the way in which children acquire a first language. The method tries to replicate the first-language acquisition process; however, it is traditionally delivered through *teacher-centered* practices, as opposed to the ***child centeredness*** typical of the first-language acquisition process.

The use of the native language is prohibited in this method; children are exposed to the language using the target language only. One of the main principles of this method is that second-language learners acquire vocabulary in a manner similar to children acquiring the first language, through direct association of words and phrases with objects and ideas (word concepts). Following the principles of first-language acquisition, grammar rules are not taught explicitly; instead, the rules of the language are internalized through the use of language.

Characteristics

Language learning should start with **here-and-now situations.** Communication is conducted in the target language. The teacher uses classroom objects and activities that the child will need to function in the new language and culture. This component is usually delivered through the use of pictures representing situations typically encountered in the new language and culture.

Vocabulary development is a key component of the method, and it is taught through paraphrasing and through nonverbal communication using visuals and concrete objects typical of the target culture. The lessons are essentially developed around pictures representing scenes from the target culture.

Listening comprehension and **oral communication** is heavily emphasized and presented in a graded progression. Correct punctuation and pronunciation are emphasized. Communication activities are geared toward questions and answers between teachers and students in a small-group format.

Grammar rules are learned subconsciously through indirect teaching (inductive method). If grammar is explicitly taught (deductive method), the target language is always used. The expectation is that through the use of the target language, learners will internalize the rules.

Principles of the **Direct Method** are still being used today to teach foreign languages. The **Berlitz method** is one of the most successful variations of the Direct Method. It has been used to teach foreign languages for more than 100 years in schools established worldwide. The Berlitz method emphasizes vocabulary development and conversation as a key program component (Berlitz Method, n.d.). This and other more modern adapta-

The Grammar Translation Method was originally developed to translate literature from the Greek to Latin. Eventually, in the nineteenth century, it was adapted to teach foreign languages. The method uses the students' native language to teach and analyze grammar and to introduce vocabulary. Because of the method's limited scope and ability to support all four components of the language—listening, speaking, reading, and writing—it was excluded from further analysis in this chapter.

tions of the direct method are currently being used to teach ESL in American schools. Some of these methods will be discussed in this chapter.

The Audiolingual Method (Adaptation of the Direct Method and the Army Method)

Target population: Beginner, intermediate, or advanced ELLs.

The **Audiolingual Method** was developed under the structural–behaviorist umbrella. It borrowed heavily from the principles of the Direct Method and the research conducted under the structural–behaviorist approaches. Using research in second-language acquisition, the audiolingual method initiated the scientific approach to language teaching and learning. Contrary to the Direct Method, the Audiolingual Method does not rely heavily on vocabulary development; instead, teachers use drills and practice as a way to teach the grammar of the language.

Proponents of this method believe that language is primarily oral; thus phonology and morphology are the primary focus for instruction. They also believe that language instruction should be carefully sequenced; consequently, the skills of listening and speaking precede the formal components of the language, reading and writing.

Characteristics

The Audio-lingual Method follows the law of Exercise and Intensity to teach language. Practitioners believe that frequent and intensive practice and drill will lead to learning. Piaget's concept of operant conditioning—learning through stimulus and response—promotes language acquisition. Through the use of language exercises, students will learn the grammar of the language subconsciously.

The use of the native language should be avoided during instruction. In this way, learners will have to use the new language and acquire it faster.

Practice should precede grammar explanation. Pattern drills, dialogues, grammar transformation, and applications are traditionally used to teach language, and these

---

The Army Method was developed during the 1940s as a way to expedite second-language acquisition to communicate with speakers from multiple language groups involved in the war effort (World War II). The method uses principles of the direct method and a small-group format to promote language development. It uses a native speaker of the target language (or a record containing the speech of native speakers) and a linguist in a team-teaching format to model oral production and teach the grammar of the language.

---

should always be presented without explanations. If grammar explanations are needed, these should be brief and through the use of the target language.

MODERN ADAPTATIONS OF THE DIRECT METHOD

The Total Physical Response (TPR) (Adapted from Asher)

Target Population: The method is for beginner ELLs, who might be going through the silent phase of second-language acquisition.

The **Total Physical Response** (TPR) method is a modern adaptation of the direct method. It attempts to re-create the process of first-language acquisition and the types of interactions that characterize it. The method uses Stephen Krashen's theory of the comprehensible input, the speech emergence theory, and the silent period hypothesis as a foundation for the development of the method. (See Chapter 2.) According to these three principles, students should always understand the communication presented (input hypothesis), and they should never be forced to speak (silent period hypothesis); they will speak when they are ready to do so (speech emergence theory). Another characteristic of this method is that language is best introduced through multiple sensory systems, including kinesics (movement). That is, language should be presented not only visually and orally but also through kinesics. Through the use of commands that require a physical response, students are guided to link the command to specific physical responses; thus, the language input is presented and received through multiple sensory routes.

Characteristics

The method uses commands and nonverbal communication to provide the comprehensible input. The learner is not required to respond orally; instead, the expectation is that the learner understands the command and executes it. Commands are used to promote listening comprehension, which traditionally precedes speaking skills.

Initially, the teacher produces the commands and guides the learners to follow them. If they do not understand it, the teacher models it or uses nonverbal communication to get the point across. Later, children can trade roles and produce the commands for other children and the teacher to follow. Commands can be as simple as *Stand up and walk* or as sophisticated as *Come to the board, erase your name, and replace it with the name of the person sitting next to you.*

The Natural Approach (Adapted from Krashen and Terrell)

Target population: Appropriate for beginner ELLs who might be going through the silent phase of second-language acquisition but can also be used to address the needs of intermediate and advanced learners.

The Natural Approach is a research-based adaptation of the direct method. This method is also based on Stephen Krashen's theories of second-language acquisition (Krashen, 1985). Vocabulary development is the key component for language development. Thus, the method relies heavily on the teaching and practice of vocabulary. Because the most important goal of the method is communication, it places little emphasis on the accuracy of language usage. Because direct corrections can inhibit communication, students are in communication activities. If corrections are needed, they are done through modeling.

Characteristics

Class period is devoted to communication; explanations and practice of grammar should be done outside the classroom (modules and homework).

Error correction is not emphasized; corrections inhibit communication and affect the students' motivation and self-image.

Learners are not forced to speak (silent phase); when the learner is ready to talk, he or she may use L1 or L2. In this case, techniques from the total physical response method are used to address the needs of learners at the silent stage of second-language development.

Listening comprehension is promoted through the use of TPR techniques.

Real objects, pictures, paraphrasing (foreign talk), and nonverbal communication are used to promote comprehensible input.

HUMANISTIC PSYCHOLOGY: CLIENT CENTERED

Community Language Learning (Adapted from Curran)

Target population: It can be used with beginners, but it is more appropriate for ntermediate and advanced learners. This method requires the appropriate planning so that the teacher can spend quality time with a small number of students (6 to 12) at a time, while the rest of the class is engaged in other learning activities. Unless the teacher organizes the classroom to offer small-group instruction, this method might be impractical for large classes typical of public schools in the United States.

Community Language Learning is the method that best represents the principles of humanistic psychology, including the student-centered approach. A *communicative-based* method takes into account the physical, cognitive, and emotional needs of the students. In this method, teachers serve as facilitators of learning; they do not teach but rather facilitate the acquisition of learning. The creation of a relaxed, nonthreatening, and cooperative environment constitutes the main principle in this ESL method.

Characteristics

The method delivers instruction using a small-group format engaged in communication. Students are organized in a group of 6 to 12 learners, forming a circle. The main strategy of the method is to guide students to have a conversation with group members. The teacher provides the necessary support to guide students to communicate. A tape recorder is placed on the table to record the verbal interaction among group members.

One of the key features of this method is the connection and trust that the teacher/counselor provides to the learners. The teacher lets the students know that his or her main function is to support them in the effort to communicate and learn the language. For beginner students, the teacher is available to serve as translator. The client (student) tells the counselor (teacher) the information that he or she wants to share with the group, and the teacher tells the students how to say it the target language. More advanced students begin addressing the group without direct support from the teacher. Language support is available only at the request of the speaker or other members of the group.

At the more advanced stages, students feel more confident with the language and are ready to accept direct corrections. At this stage, teachers provide input to enrich and polish the language. Once the conversation is finished, the linguistic data gathered through the tape recorder are used to teach grammar concepts and for more advanced students to promote self-correction.

The Silent Way (Adapted from Gattegno)

Target population: It can be used with beginners, but it is more appropriate for intermediate and advanced learners because they can produce more speech samples. The use of color-coded charts to guide pronunciation can be modified to meet the needs of ELLs at different stages of development.

The **Silent Way** shares components of cognitive and humanistic psychology. It is a *communicative-based* method whose main goal is to promote in students the principles of independence, autonomy, and responsibility. Students are encouraged to take responsibility for their own learning. However, they can get language support from their peers. Students are encouraged to correct themselves or to get support from peers. The role of the teacher is not necessarily to correct students but to guide them in the acquisition of language.

Characteristics

In this method, the teacher is silent most of the time while the students are actively speaking. Colored wooden rods are used to create situations where students can use language and learn vocabulary and concepts. Color-coded wall charts are used to teach phonology and to guide pronunciation in general. For example, the color blue and green can be used to guide students to distinguish between the sound of the /s/ and /z/. That is, teachers can use blue to signal the /s/ and green to highlight the /z/. Using this system, students can grow more confident in their ability to produce English sounds.

Suggestopedia (Adapted from Lozanov)

Target population: This method uses a bilingual approach; thus, it can be used with beginner, intermediate, and advanced language learners. However, because this method requires the creation of a specific environment (soft light and comfortable seating) away from disruptions, it might be impractical for use in public schools.

Suggestopedia is another method that relies heavily on the principles of humanistic psychology and the power of engaging students in the learning process. To relax and guide the learner to a state of concentration, the method uses soft lights, comfortable seating, and Baroque music. This state of relaxation can help learners in awakening the subconscious. The method also uses dramatic readings to guide students to a subconscious state to support language acquisition.

Characteristics

The class is always accompanied with Baroque music in the background. New material is then presented in context through lengthy dialogues representing typical situations in the target culture. Instruction is presented through two stages identified as Concert 1 and Concert 2.

In Concert 1, the teacher reads the dialogue using dramatic features (active concert). To ensure comprehension of the content, students are provided with a copy of the dialogue written in the native language and the target language. While the teacher reads the dialogue, students follow the reading using the bilingual text.

In Concert 2, students are motivated to relax and listen to the reading with their eyes closed (passive concert). Dialogues have continuity and present colorful characters with vivid names to enhance understanding and to make it interesting. Role playing is done to promote language practice.

After the concert, an eight-hour follow-up is conducted. In this activation stage, role playing is done to promote language practice. The content of the dialogue is also used to introduce additional language concepts and to review concepts learned.

For more information about this method or to contact Dr. Lozanov visit his website at http://lozanov.hit.bg/.

Baroque music is a lively and melodious type of composition developed in the seventeenth century in Europe. The term *Baroque* was originally used to describe highly decorated and exuberant European artwork, and eventually the term was extended to describe music. It uses simplistic melody and harmony with sensitive and relaxing poetry. Some of the best-known composers of this music were Antonio Vivaldi and Johann Sebastian Bach. To learn more and to listen to Baroque music, go the webpage of Michael Sartorius at www.baroque-music.org/index.html.

Notional-Functional Approach (Adapted from Finocchiaro and Brumfit)

Target population: Can be used with beginner, intermediate, or advanced ELLs and with either children or adults.

The *notional-functional syllabus* is a precursor of the *communicative-based* approaches developed in Europe in the 1970s. It was designed to teach the language structures and vocabulary needed for a variety of situations and speech acts. The term *notions* describes particular situations or context in which people interact and communicate. Some of the notions typically covered are shopping, health issues, travel, personal identification, and social conventions. *Functions* cover the different reasons or purpose for communication. Some of the functions commonly identified are greetings, asking for clarification, expressing an opinion, lodging a complaint, asking for advice, and apologizing. For example, conducting business in a bank is a notion that requires multiple language functions, such as asking for an account balance, requesting an explanation of expenses, or complaining about a bank charge. The key advantage of this method is that it identifies specific real-life context and provides language support and information to communicate in these situations.

Characteristics

The class content is typically introduced through dialogues covering multiple notions and functions. Students practice the dialogue with classmates and practice the appropriate vocabulary to address each of the functions (Finocchiaro & Brumfit, 1983).

To activate the knowledge, students may create their own dialogues, which are also used for practice. To activate the concepts learned, students are asked to supply the appropriate words or phrase in a variety of written dialogues.

Students may continue to expand on the concepts, seeking situations to practice the notions and functions in real-life situations. After practicing the specific functions in real life, students are asked to discuss their experiences as a way to refine their performance in future situations.

DIFFERENTIATING INSTRUCTION AND SECOND-LANGUAGE PROFICIENCY

Differentiated instruction attempts to promote equity among learners. The concept of equity implies that children learn differently, have different needs and interests, and exhibit potential differently. To meet the needs of the learners, teachers have to modify classroom activities so all students, despite their ability, can learn effectively (Tomlinson, 2001). Thus teachers ought to analyze learners' particular situations and provide instruction and opportunities to meet their education needs. For ELLs, differentiated instruction takes into account their cultural, linguistic, and experiential background to design programs to meet their particular needs and expectations. For example, a child that comes from a war-torn country, with interrupted instruction, requires a different language program than a student who is literate in L1 and comes to the new country performing at grade level. Both students will be required to meet the same curriculum requirements, but the route to get there and their instructional modification are different.

A variety of instructional components has been identified to support learners in the content areas and language (Quiocho & Ulanoff, 2009; Tomlinson, 2001a). First, it is important to notice that the goal of differentiated instruction for ELLs is to teach the same content and level of complexity required from native English speakers. However, the way to reach the instructional targets can be modified. Typically, the teacher scaffolds instruction to make it cognitively accessible to ELLs. Following are some of the suggested modifications:

- Use materials written at different levels of readability, and match the materials to the level of the learners.

- Provide and discuss content vocabulary so that children have an idea of the key terms and concepts linked to the new information presented in lessons.

- Allow flexible grouping to facilitate working and supporting students. That is, provide instruction using a variety of instructional formats, including learning centers, small-group format, individualized instruction, and the buddy system to provide content and linguistic support to peers.

- Use ongoing assessment to check for understanding, and provide individualized support as needed.

- Use audio recorded versions of narratives in the content areas to support struggling readers. If recorded versions are not available, teachers can ask advanced readers to read the passages for other children. In both instances, students can listen to the narrative while following the written page. In this way, the effort required to decode written text can be devoted to comprehension.

- Allow students to use a bilingual glossary with pictures and explanations of key concepts. If the glossaries are not available, seek the support of bilingual teachers to develop it. To prepare for this kind of support, ESL teachers have to read the content before introducing it and identify words or concepts that might create reading or conceptual problems for ELLs. For advanced students, teachers can give the vocabulary words as an extension of the lesson and/or in preparation for future lessons.

- Supplement instruction with the use of concrete objects, hands-on instruction, nonverbal communication, and contextualized instruction to enhance comprehension. When content is cognitive accessible, students not only will learn it but also will acquire language components indirectly.

- Use literature and activities that reflect the experiential background of different cultural groups, especially those ethnic, linguistic, and racial groups represented in the classroom.

- Develop a routine so that ELLs know how to get support when the teacher is not readily available to help them. For example, when the teacher is not available, ELLs could have the option of consulting with more advanced students or consulting reference materials, including electronic media.

When checking for understanding with ELLs, teachers have to avoid rhetorical questions, such as, *Do you understand? Do you have questions?* These questions should never be asked because teachers will not get reliable answers, if they ever get one. Most of the time, learners new to the English language will answer in the affirmative or remain silent, giving the impression that they understood the lesson. Questioning the instructor could also be inappropriate in some cultural groups, and it is rarely done. Thus, teachers have to look for more reliable ways to determine if students understand the communication and the content presented. One way to determine if they understand the concepts is through performance-based assessment, where students perform a task to demonstrate understanding.

- Identify cognates (similar words in two languages) used in the content areas, and guide students to identify them in reading. Develop a word wall with common cognates for each of the content areas.

The concept of differentiated instruction can be expanded to the assessment component of the teaching process. Assessing students in a language that they do not understand can invalidate assessment data. To minimize the effect of language on content-area testing, students can be provided with specific linguistic accommodations. Testing accommodations for ELLs are presented in Chapter 4.

LANGUAGE PROFICIENCY AND EDUCATIONAL IMPLICATIONS

The delivery of developmentally appropriate instruction for ELLs constitutes another challenge for differentiated instruction. Teachers have to identify current levels of language development and, based on these, provide appropriate language instruction. The American Council for the Teaching of Foreign Languages (ACTFL) has identified four levels of language proficiency (novice, intermediate, advanced, and superior) to describe the development of L2 in the areas of listening, speaking, reading, and writing. These levels resemble the four levels identified by Krashen for second-language learners: preproduction, early productive, intermediate, and advanced proficiency. (See Chapter 2) Teachers need to have a clear understanding of these stages and use these as a foundation for planning instruction and assessing language development and academic progress. A summary of key features for each stage, together with instructional implications, is presented next.

Stage 1: Novice (Preproduction and Early Production Stages)

- Communicates minimally with memorized materials

- Responds briefly to questions with words and phrases that have been memorized: colors, numbers, foods, days of the week, names of family members (function at the vocabulary level)

- Experience difficulties in producing sentence-type utterances and encounters difficulties in being understood by native speakers

- Produces discrete and isolated words and phrases but might not be able to put them together in a coherent fashion; examples: *That's cool! Yes, ma'am.* (common in southern United States)

Educational implications: Use strategies from the total physical response (TPR) and the natural method to deliver comprehensible input. Provide opportunities for active listening, and use visual and concrete objects to contextualize instruction. Introduce hands-on activities and group activities where students can support each other. Avoid direct corrections because they can inhibit communication. Develop and introduce functional vocabulary needed to be successful in daily life. Initially, avoid the use of contractions. Use the long forms together with the contracted version. Identify and introduce idioms in contextualized situations to ensure comprehension. If students do not understand their meaning, define them and provide examples. Avoid continuous direct corrections in communication activities. Provide corrective feedback indirectly through modeling. Modeling is the preferred strategy for students in early childhood. For students in upper elementary and beyond, correct errors through explicit grammar instructions at the end of the communication activity. Listen and identify most common errors made by the students in the group and then develop a lesson to address those.

Stage 2: Intermediate (Higher Level than the Early Production Stage)

At this stage, students

- Are able to create language by combining or recombining learned elements

- Are able to ask and answer questions as well as initiate and minimally sustain conversations about familiar topics: home, school, friends, personal history, and family members

- Can be understood by sympathetic learners/listeners—people who will make an effort to understand them—even though they are likely to have problems with grammatical accuracy and strong interference from L1

- Produce discrete sentences and strings of sentences in isolation; examples: *That's radical. That's awesome. May I help you?*

Educational implications: Continue providing contextualized instruction, and avoid direct correction in communication activities. If communication is unintelligible (cannot be understood), ask for clarification or to repeat the statement. Provide corrective feedback indirectly by modeling using foreign talk (exaggeration). For students in upper elementary and beyond, you can also develop explicit lessons to address common errors among them.

Begin instruction by asking questions that require a one-word answer, yes/no questions, and either/or questions until students are ready to produce responses that require more language input. Provide opportunities for self-correction by highlighting errors. That is, identify the source of the problem and guide the learner to self-correction.

Stage 3: Advanced (Higher than Intermediate Fluency)

At this stage, students

- Have moved from sentence-level utterances to paragraph-length connected discourse

- Can narrate and describe present, past, and future activities

- Can talk about a variety of concrete topics: personal background, family, travel, interests, and events they have experienced or read about

- Are able to express facts, report accidents, and make comparisons but may have difficulties supporting an opinion with examples or arguing against an opposing viewpoint

- Produce paragraph discourse with some level of language and conceptual interference from the first language and culture

Educational implications: Guide students to develop and self-correct oral and written narratives. Instead of using a red pen to correct all the errors, use a highlighter to identify areas that might need further refinement, and ask them to make the appropriate changes. Discuss technical vocabulary from the content areas before reading for content. Introduce the concept of cognates and guide students to recognize them in content area text. If cognates are used in direct instruction, make students aware of the similarities with words in their native language. In pronunciation, identify sounds that can cause language interference, and begin polishing pronunciation. Provide practice with word stress and the intonation pattern of the language. Guide students to notice how stress can change the meaning of words (word stress).

Stage 4: Superior Level (Advanced Fluency)

At this stage, students

- Are able to participate effectively in most formal and informal conversations on topics connected to practical, social, professional, and abstract concerns

- Can support their opinion and hypothesize about abstract topics, offering detailed narration and description with native-like discourse strategies

- Are able to function effectively with most native speakers

- Produce extended discourse with minimal language interference

Educational implications: Continue expanding academic vocabulary development and polishing pronunciation. Fluency at this level can be deceptive; thus, check for comprehension continuously. Teach reading strategies for different purposes. That is, guide students to read for the main idea only or scan for specific words or details.

ACTIVITIES TO PROMOTE ORAL COMMUNICATION

Pronunciation and oral development in general is best learned in meaningful and real-life situations. When students see the need to communicate, they will make an extra effort to produce intelligible utterances. For young children, pronunciation is best presented through modeling.

However, for students in middle school and high school, modeling alone might not be sufficient. They might need specific explanations about pronunciation problems and how to correct them. This explanation will require information about the articulators used in the production of sounds, word and sentence stress, and nonstandard pronunciation caused by language interference. Teachers do not have be linguists to teach pronunciation, but they should have a working knowledge of English sounds and how they are produced. (See Chapter 2.)

In classroom situations, teachers can organize activities to resemble real-life situations to promote communication among students. Some of the activities are listed here.

Dramatic Play

Dramatic play using prompts is an ideal activity to develop communication that resembles real-life situations. Students are given a situation and a specific role to play, and they improvise communication to play individual parts. For example, one child can play the role of a parent, another the role of a student in trouble, and someone else can play the role of a teacher.

Language Play

Language play involves the use of language in rhyme, alliteration (repeated consonant sounds in initial position), songs, and repeated patterns to amuse children. Tongue twisters are commonly used to practice pronunciation and language patterns. Through these activities, children acquire language knowledge in a relaxed and fun environment. Teachers also use nursery rhymes, poems, and stories that contain rhyme to introduce these language features.

Show and Tell

In *show and tell activities*, children bring artifacts and personal items to class. They show the object and describe its features to the class. In addition to the obvious benefit of oral communication, this kind of activity can be used to promote home and cultural pride.

Hand Puppets Show

Hand puppets, finger puppets, and string puppets can be used to promote confidence among children. They communicate orally using the puppet as a cover for any errors made in communication. The use of puppets is an enjoyable and motivating activity for young learners.

Pair Interview

Another interesting strategy to promote oral communication is the *pair interview*. In this strategy, children are paired to learn information from each other and to make a report to the larger group. This strategy is ideal for the first days of class when students want to get to know each other. This strategy can also be used to learn how much a student knows about a particular topic. For example, a child can interview a peer to get explanations about the cycle of water. As part of the interview process, students can share information and clarify the content.

Presentations to Address Different Audiences

Children can develop short presentations for a given audience and then modify the ideas to present the same information to address a different kind of audience. For example, children can be led to prepare an oral presentation to persuade parents to donate money to purchase more computers for the school. Once the presentation is delivered, the second activity is to modify the presentation to address members of the school board or a business executive.

Teaching Vocabulary and Vocabulary Transfer

Students, who are literate in L1 at a level proportionate with their grade placement, bring strong word recognition skills to L2. For speakers of Indo-European languages, this transferability is supported by the historical and linguistic connection among these languages and the Greek and the Latin. Establishing a connection between these two languages has impacted modern languages and can help in the development of English vocabulary. There are multiple roots and affixes from the Greek and Latin common to most Indo-European languages, such as Spanish and English. Most of these roots and affixes are used in academic areas, such as the sciences, law, and mathematics. This connection has resulted in the development of multiple cognates, or words similar in two languages. The cognitive academic language proficiency (CALP) that students need to be successful in the regular classroom can be delivered through this comparison. A few examples of the connection between English and Spanish follow.

Greek Prefixes	English	Spanish
anti–	antifreeze	anticongelante
amphi–	amphibious	anfibio
auto–	autobiography	autobiografía
bio–	biography	biografía
demo–	democracy	democracia

Latin Prefixes	English	Spanish
ante–	antecedent	antecedente
bi–	bicycle	bicicleta
extra–	extraordinary	extraordinario
infra–	infrared	infrarojo
inter–	international	internacional

Suffixes	English	Spanish
–ist	artist	artista
–or	actor	actor
–logy	biology	biología
–al	abdominal	abdominal
–tion, –ción	demonstration	demonstración

Teaching Listening

Native English speakers develop listening skills inductively with little or no instruction. They begin making sense of the oral sounds of the language through meaningful interaction with native speakers. Native speakers use commands, repetitions, and the use of concrete objects and context to ensure comprehension. Based on this description, listening comprehension can be perceived as a natural process that does not require explicit instruction. However, when working with ELLs, teacher do not use the same strategies to make oral messages comprehensible; instead, they make linguistic demands beyond the linguistic reach of the child. Thus we cannot assume that ELLs will master listening comprehension the way native speakers do, without appropriate modifications and instruction.

When teaching listening comprehension to ELLs, it is important to guide them to listen for different purposes. Sometimes they can listen to get the gist of the story, to find answers to specific questions, or to provide specific details about the story. When students know the purpose of the listening activity, they are more likely to be successful at it. Some strategies to teach listening comprehension follow.

- Use commands to teach basic listening skills. Use simple commands with beginning ELLs and more sophisticated instruction with more mature and advanced learners. The TPR uses this type of strategy to teach listening comprehension.

- Teach the intonation pattern and word stress, and explore how these can change meaning. Change statements to questions and vice versa to see if students can recognize the intonation pattern. For older learners, present words where word stress can change the meaning like *insert* (noun) and *insert* (verb) to see if students recognize the difference.

- Listen to taped stories, radio commercials, and announcements to guide children to get the main idea and details of the communication.

- Listen to a conversation without providing visuals, and answer questions about it. Students can listen more than once to listen for different purposes: to identify the speakers, to get the gist of the communication, to identify the tone and the purpose of the communication.

- Listen to routine activities, like the pledge of allegiance and morning announcements to answer comprehension questions.

- Listen to ballads (a song or a poem that tells stories), and guide students to answer questions. Country songs are ideal for this kind of activity because they are highly emotional and deal with love and family issues.

- Read a story to children and ask them to answer questions about it. For non-writers you can ask them to retell the story and to draw pictures representing the story. Guide more mature and advanced students to respond to specific comprehension questions.

- Ask students to call each other on the phone to practice listening skills. You might need to inform the parents of this activity to secure their support. In addition, ask students to call places like the movie theater to listen to information about movie schedules and time. One advantage of this type of activity is that they can hear the information more than once.

- Develop routine activities where children make oral reports while the other students listen for the information. Two examples follow:

  Weather forecaster: Teachers assign a different student to do the weather forecast for the day. The selected child will have to listen to the weather forecast the day before to present it in class.

  Family news: A second student can do family news, where he or she provides news about the family. Students listen to both reports and ask clarification questions of the presenters.

Teachers can be as creative as needed to be sure that they use authentic listening comprehension activities to teach the skills and help students practice the skills in situations that students will likely find in daily life.

Promoting Reading

Oral language development is acquired universally with minimum explicit instruction. Literacy instruction, on the other hand, is not universally acquired and requires substantial explicit instruction and practice (Peregoy, Boyle, and Cadiero-Kaplan, 2008). Two key questions have been researched in the area of literacy instruction:

How should language be studied and analyzed?
How is literacy acquired?

To address the first question: Literacy instruction has been conceptualized based on three models: the bottom-up, top-down, and balanced reading approach.

The ***bottom-up approach*** is an inductive and skill-based process based on the principles of behaviorist psychology. It analyzes language beginning with sounds, letters, words, sentences, paragraphs, and whole texts. This behaviorist approach is best represented by the phonics reading program. Teachers who practice a bottom-up approach emphasize the teaching of discrete skills sequentially and systematically. As a result of this sequential component, the concept of reading readiness gained momentum during the 1960s and became a prerequisite for formal reading instruction. Most basal readers contain strategies to teach reading readiness in an attempt to comply with the scope and sequence required in the bottom-up approach.

The ***top-down approach*** to reading relies on the schemata (prior knowledge) that readers bring to the text in their attempt to seek meaning from print. It is a deductive approach that proceeds from the whole to the parts. It begins with whole text, and it proceeds to smaller components of sentences and words and even sounds. Theories that stress top-down processing suggest that readers form hypotheses about the words they will encounter and take in only just enough visual information to test their hypothesis. In this approach, recognizing each word is not a prerequisite for comprehending the passage. Teachers generally advocate noninterference during oral reading and encourage students to use context or meaning of the passage to identify unrecognized words. The best representation of top-down models is the ***whole language approach***. The whole language approach began in the 1960s and was the program of choice in public schools during the 1980s and 1990s. After the 1990s, phonics instruction came back, and today teachers are using a combination of these two approaches: the ***balanced reading approach***. This approach combines the best of both models. Currently, the balanced reading approach is the model of choice to teach reading to children in the United States.

Reading Readiness and Emergent Literacy

To address the second question—How is literacy acquired?—two main models have emerged: reading readiness versus emergent literacy.

Reading readiness perspective was the dominant reading theory in the latter part of the twentieth century. In this perspective, reading was delayed until children had developed the speaking ability and were able to perform specific reading subskills linked to auditory and visual discrimination and visual motor skills. Traditionally, students develop these skills by age 6, which in theory delays formal reading instruction until first grade. However, researchers noticed that some children were able to read before entering first grade with a minimum or no formal reading instruction. To accommodate this kind of learner, a new view or perspective was conceptualized, the *emergent literacy* perspective.

In the emergent literacy perspective, literacy can emerge naturally among children without formal reading instruction. Literacy development is perceived as a process parallel to oral development, which emerges when children see adults engaging in meaningful literacy activities, such as reading newspapers, writing notes, and looking at environmental print. Children see these literacy activities and begin engaging and imitating the literacy process. Because this literacy development occurs mostly at home, family literacy practices become an important component of the literacy process. Family literacy programs encourage parents to involve children in meaningful literacy activities at home. At home and later in school, children go through predictable stages of literacy development.

STAGES OF READING

The process of literacy development in L1 and L2 is similar (Hudelson, 1984). Research shows that given the appropriate instructions, ELLs can benefit from literacy instruction in L2 before they have developed proficiency in L1 (Hudelson, 1984; Urzúa, 1987). Moreover, formal literacy instruction in L2 can also support the development of literacy in L1. Research also suggests that proficiency in L1 makes easier the development of proficiency in L2 because these skills are transferable (Cummins, 1981; Tragar & Wong, 1984). Despite the apparent contradictions on research in biliteracy, literacy in L1 and L2 is similar, and effective literacy instruction in both languages concurrently, or one before the other, can indeed promote biliteracy.

Lapp, Fisher, Flood, and Cabello (2001) suggested that children go through three stages of literacy development: emerging, early readers, and newly fluent readers. An analysis of these stages follows.

Emerging Readers

Children at the emerging stage of reading demonstrate curiosity for print and understand that print contains meaningful messages. They mimic the reading behaviors of adults and subconsciously acquire print conventions, such as directionality and print awareness. Children at this stage also begin developing phonemic awareness, that is, recognizing the connection between letters (graphemes) and the sounds (phonemes). Children use illustrations and other graphic representations to obtain meaning and to make predictions about the story. They are also able to retell a story that has been read to them. This type of metalinguistic awareness is a key factor in the development of reading and writing.

Early Readers

Early readers begin to connect words with their written representations and recognize a number of sight words. They begin to apply decoding skills to understand and confirm printed messages. Additionally, they are beginning to develop an awareness of features of print, such as punctuation, bond print, and text format. They can retell stories with specific details about plot and characters. They effectively use illustrations, prior experiences, sentence structure, and punctuation to make sense of print. Early readers rely on initial letter sound and phonic skills to decode words and to get meaning. They are also beginning to recognize the meaning of words in multiple contexts and the difference between narrative and nonnarrative texts. Children at this stage enjoy listening to narratives and begin choosing their favorite stories.

Newly Fluent Readers

Newly fluent readers are beginning to internalize the cuing or decoding system of the language and exhibit some degree of fluency. They use inferences, deduction, and prior experiences to infer meaning from text and to develop generalizations. They are able to discuss the point of view of the author and to identify similarities and differences between two stories. As the child becomes more fluent, reading independence emerges and many of the reading cuing systems of the language become automatic.

Instructional Implications of the Reading Stages

Children at the early stages of reading can be immersed in a variety of functional reading and writing experiences that display the purpose of literacy while demonstrating and modeling the process of reading and writing. At school, teachers can use routine activities to provide a rich print environment. For example, teachers can post classroom rules, read them to the children, and rehearse the meaning of each rule. They can also post signs identifying parts of the classroom, equipment, and guidelines for activities in the learning centers. Teachers can enrich dramatic play centers with functional print, including lists, phone books, and props to encourage children to experiment with reading and writing during play activities. Finally, it is important for teachers to guide children to be successful in their attempts to develop literacy; thus teachers should accept and celebrate the progress of ELLs in their gradual approximations to become biliterate.

Role of Environmental Print in Early Reading

Environmental print describes forms of written communication available to children in their community. Some of the most common print materials are road and store signs, magazines available in public areas, shopping guides, and announcements on billboards. Parents can use these high-profile written samples to motivate children to read and to guide them to discover meaning and information available in their environment.

HOME ENVIRONMENT AND EARLY LITERACY

At home, parents can model literacy through functional daily activities, such as reading newspapers and magazines, developing a grocery list, clipping coupons, posting notes on the refrigerator, labeling parts of the house, and posting rules. Parents can also read to their children and guide them to notice parts of a book. They can also read stories with simple and predictable story lines and ask children to predict the content of the story based on pictorial clues. They can also ask children to identify the parts of the story that they like the most or the parts they did not like. Parents can also use computer programs and interactive books to promote literacy in fun and relaxed ways. The use of captions on television can also be used to guide children to link spoken vocabulary with its written representation.

CLASSROOM ACTIVITIES TO PROMOTE EARLY LITERACY SKILLS

In the school environment, children get exposed to explicit instruction in reading, including reading conventions, the alphabetic principle, sound–symbol correspondence (graphophonemic awareness), and common sight words of the language (Peregoy, Boyle, & Cadiero-Kaplan, 2008). All these components are presented through whole texts like poems, songs, and short stories. Once students begin to make sense of simple text, instruction is supplemented with explicit phonics and sight-word instruction. Some of the key components of the early literacy are presented next.

Big books contain short repetitive stories that can be easily used to teach sight words and the sound–symbol correspondence. The size of the letters permits children to follow the story while the teacher reads and points to the words. This activity is ideal to promote interest in reading for students at the emergent stage of reading.

Sight words are high-frequency words in the language that are traditionally introduced to children visually for easy recognition. Traditionally, teachers use flash cards and games to teach sight words present in stories. They can organize whole group, small groups, or peer groups to practice word recognition and the meaning of words. To demonstrate the meaning of words, such as verbs and function words (prepositions, articles, conjunctions), teachers need to use them in a sentence. A strong foundation of sight words can support students in the emergent and early stages of reading. Edward W. Dolch (1948) identified 220 of the most frequently used words in the English language. He believed that if children were exposed to these words and learned to recognize them as sight words, they would become fluent readers. Some examples of these words are *a, an, am, at, can, had, has, ran, the, after, but, got,* and *away.* The introduction of these sight words can expedite the decoding process and develop fluency among early readers.

Phonics instruction is used to guide students to recognize words based on the way that they are pronounced. Students apply rules to sound out words, and based on the way that they sound, students are able to recognize and assign meaning to them. Phonics instruction is always introduced within a meaningful context. First, read the story and allow children to enjoy it; then, introduce the skills for word recognition. It is important to introduce phonics instruction together with other word recognition strategies or clues: syntactic, structural, and semantic.

Phonic instruction falls under the ***bottom-up*** reading model because it proceeds from the parts to the whole. It is generally introduced in a given sequence (Peregoy, Boyle, & Cadiero-Kaplan, 2008):

- Consistent single consonants in initial position: *m*at, *t*ag, *p*at

- Short and long vowels: *cat* (short) and *bay* (long)

- Word families or onset and rimes: *ake*, as in *lake, bake, take*

- Diagraphs, two consonants together producing one sound only: *ch*, *th*

- Blends, two or more consonants blending their sounds: *pl*, *cl*, *scr*

- Rules for syllabication

Classroom Routines

Daily classroom routines can enhance literacy development. Some examples of these activities follow.

- Write the schedule for the day, and guide students to follow the activities during the day.

- Post classroom rules and procedures and rehearse them, and guide students to refer to the written information during the day.

- Develop a dictionary wall containing vocabulary words that students can already read, and continue adding new words. Also create a word wall of new words or words that require special attention, such as deceptive cognates, or words that are difficult to spell or pronounce.

- Develop an attendance pocket chart with the date and two sections labeled, present and absent. Print cards with the names of students, and organize them alphabetically. In the morning, guide students to move their name from the section labeled absent to the section labeled present. At the end of the day, guide students to move back their name and place them in numeric and alphabetic order. Also guide students to change and read the date.

- Post students' writing samples inside and outside the classroom. Let them see what they and other students have written.

- Use language experience charts or the language experience approach. Dictate stories so students see the connection between speech and print.

Reading Narratives and Expository Writing

Narrative writing describes events or tells a story using context and often repetition to communicate ideas. It uses a predictable format containing three major components: beginning, middle, and ending. In the beginning part, the characters, the setting, and the problem are introduced. In the middle point, the topic is further developed creating a climax. In the ending, the problem is generally solved. Traditionally, these types of stories are given to teach reading skills. Children are generally able to identify this format and use it to make predictions and to obtain information. ELLs who are exposed to this format in L1 can easily transfer this information to L2. Narrative writing is relatively easy for ELLs when compared with expository writing, the type of reading skills and academic vocabulary that they need to master to read and get information in the content areas.

Expository writing provides an explanation of processes or concepts. It uses more technical vocabulary and is less redundant and contextualized than narratives are. In this kind of reading, students read to learn concepts, as opposed to learning to read, which is typical of narrative writing. This kind of technical writing is more succinct, linear, and hierarchical in its development than narrative writing is. The information in expository writing is structured topically, chronologically, or numerically. In the topic format, the information is organized in chapters divided among subtopics. For example: A chapter on the Native American groups can be divided among types of nations or tribes, location of the groups by regions, economic activities, and cultural features of each group. The information about the Native American groups can also be organized chronologically from the past to the present or based of a chronology of events that have shaped their history. The information can also be supplemented with charts, graphs, tables, and other graphic representation arranged numerically. ELLs need to have explicit instruction to use and interpret information in this writing format. Reading and interpreting information in expository format are vital for the future academic development of ELLs. Mastering the expository writing format will provide ELLs opportunities to catch up academically and compete with native English speakers.

Development of Writing

Writing is also a skill that that has to be taught explicitly. It requires a deep understanding of the connection between speech and print, and the grammar conventions used to represent speech in written form. Children go through several stages in an effort to eventually master the writing. For example: Children at the emerging and early stage of writing use several strategies to convey meaning in writing. Students in the emergent stage of literacy use drawing as a way to convey meaning, followed by scribbling and invented letters (pseudoletters) that they might or might not be able to read. Eventually, they use phonetic spelling to produce nonstandard words that they can read. Phonetic spelling represents an advanced degree of the emergent literacy stage and the beginning of the development of the ***alphabetic principle***: the idea that sounds are represented by letters and letter sequences (Peregoy, Boyle, & Cadiero-Kaplan, 2008). As part of the alphabetic principle, children notice the ***graphophonemic units***, sound–symbol correspondence of the language. Graphophonemic awareness leads the child to notice the sounds that comprise spoken words, which in turn leads to the development of ***phonemic awareness***. The development of phonemic awareness gets children ready to benefit from formal phonics instruction and the foundation to become fluent readers and writers.

Stages of Writing

It has been conceptualized that children go through three stages of writing: emerging writers, early writers, and newly fluent writers. A description of these stages follows (Lapp et al., 2001).

Emerging Writers

Children at the emerging stage of writing understand that writing symbolizes speech. They use a combination of drawings, scribbles, and conventional letters to convey written communication. They begin using the initial letter of conventional words to represent an entire word. This invented spelling represents a degree of phonemic awareness because children are actually connecting the sound of the word with its equivalent graphic representation.

Early Writers

Children at the early stages of writing are developing phonemic awareness and using this knowledge to progress through the stages of spelling development. Phonetic spelling is becoming more conventional as they begin to use rules for capitalization and punctuation. Despite the use of phonetic spelling, the writing is generally comprehensible.

Newly Fluent Writers

Newly fluent writers consistently use conventional grammar, spelling, and punctuation. They are beginning to use prewriting strategies to achieve a writing function (e.g., writing for a specific purpose or responding to a prompt). They are able to produce unique writing samples that contain a beginning, middle, and closing. With guidance, they can revise and edit their written work.

Activities for Children at Different Stages of Writing

Children at different stages of writing can benefit from real-life and functional writing activities. Some examples of activities to accomplish this kind of writing are labeling objects, note taking, writing about a drawing, and writing a list. These activities, together with the concepts and strategies that follow, can promote writing skills among ELLs.

Word families are words that have common spelling patterns in English. Knowledge about word families can help in the decoding process as well as spelling patterns. The main purpose of teaching English word families is to help students recognize frequently occurring letter patterns, which in turn can help in decoding and spelling. Word families are introduced through the use of *onsets* and *rimes*. Onset refers to the initial consonant or consonant clusters of a syllable. Rime, or *phonogram*, refers to the combination of vowels and consonants that follow the onset. The *p* in *pump* is called the onset and the *ump* is the rime (also called word family). Traditionally, onset and rimes are introduced with monosyllabic words. Examples of common word families are listed here.

ay: say, day, bay	**ing**: sing, ring, bring	**est**: best, rest, crest
out: shout, bout	**ank**: bank, sank	**ew**: few, dew, flew
ore: more, sore, bore	**ight**: sight, might	**eed**: deed, seed, weed

Knowledge of word families can definitely improve students' ability to write in English.

Journal Writing

Four kinds of journals guide students to write for meaningful purposes:

- *Personal journals* are used to guide students to conduct self-analysis of their experiences. Students write for self–expression, and teachers can be involved only when invited to be.

- *Dialogue journals* employ a type of functional writing where students communicate with the teacher, adults, or even students about topics of interest. Teachers respond to the content of the message by modeling standard language usage without overemphasizing corrections.

- *Reflective journals* are used to guide students to reflect on particular situations or content. This type of journal can be used for self-assessment.

- *Learning logs* are also a type of functional journal where students provide a summary of the elements that they have learned and an analysis of the difficulties they have experienced during the learning process. Teachers can use the information presented in learning logs to provide additional support or to reteach concepts.

Language Logic

Language logic in Standard English progresses linearly without allowing for digression. Speakers of English are expected to progress from point A to point B with minimal deviations from the topic. Russian, Arabic, Spanish, and other Romance languages in general have a linear structure, but the story grammar allows for a great deal of digression in formal and informal interactions. Native American and Semitic languages allow for even more flexibility and digression from the linear approach. When second-language learners or speakers of dialects of Standard American English impose the logic of their native language on the logic of Standard English, communication problems can occur. ESL teachers need to guide ELLs to use the linear logic of English. Through prewriting activities, teachers can guide students to organize their thoughts following the linear progression. Process writing can also guide children to organize ideas to write using the linear progression required in English.

Process writing is designed to guide students to write in the following specific steps:

- *Prewriting* activities are used to generate and organize the ideas. Once children identify the task, they are guided to develop an outline or a web to ensure the ideas are interconnected and follow a logical pattern. In this stage, the teacher can guide ELLs to organize their ideas following a linear progression.

- *Drafting* is used to put the ideas in writing. The main task is to address the purpose and audience intended.

- *Conference* with the teacher or peers is used to provide feedback to the writer.

- *Revising* is done based on input to emphasize mostly content and the clarity of ideas.

- *Editing* is done to correct for spelling, grammar, punctuation, and mechanics.

- *Publishing* represents that final step of the process where the document is presented in final form and can be shared with a general audience.

Integration of Language and Content

Teachers need to implement a variety of activities to teach the state or school district curriculum at the grade and level and complexity required of native English speakers. Some of the techniques to facilitate content mastery follow.

Scaffolding was originally used to describe the way in which adults support children in their efforts to communicate in L1. The same concept is used to facilitate language and content development for ELLs. The term alludes to the provisional structure established to support the construction of a building, which is eliminated upon completion of the structure. Following this analogy, ELLs receive support to make content cognitively accessible to them until they achieve L2 mastery, and once this is accomplished, the language support is eliminated.

Graphic organizers are used to show relationships using visuals. Following are some of the most common organizers:

- Semantic web or tree diagrams show relationship between main ideas and subordinated components.

- Time lines are used to present a visual summary of chronological events. This is ideal to show historical events or events in sequence.

- Flow charts are used to show cause-and-effect relationships. They can be used to show steps in a process, for example, the process for admission to a program.

- Venn diagrams use circles to compare common and unique elements of two distinct components. They can be used in mathematics to compare properties of numbers, in reading to compare two stories, and in social studies to compare two historical events.

The *SQ4R* is a study strategy where the learner is engaged during the whole reading process. The acronym stands for *survey, question, read, reflect, recite*, and *review* (Tomas & Robinson, 1972). During the survey (S) part, readers examine the headings, captions under pictures or graphs, and major components of the text to develop predictions and to generate *questions (Q)* about the topic. They are guided to examine how much they know about the topics and turn the titles, headings, and subheadings into questions. Through these questions, they establish the purpose for reading. During the third stage, *read (1R)*, students read the content looking for answers to the questions previously generated. They monitor their comprehension as they summarize and *recite (2R)* key terms and concepts. During the fourth stage, students *relate (3R)*, or link, concepts learned with prior learning. Finally, during the *review (4R)*, students skim back over the chapter, recite what they know, and evaluate how much they learned about the content.

Reciprocal teaching is an instructional activity designed for struggling readers where the teacher engages students in a dialogue about specific portions of a text (Palincsar, 1986). This dialogue is based on the use of the following four strategies:

- *Summarizing*: In the section, students present (summarize) the main content in their own words.

- *Questions generating*: Students identify the most significant content and design questions to test their own knowledge. Students can be guided to generate question at different levels of cognition (Bloom's taxonomy).

- *Clarifying*: Students are guided to identify specific parts of the text that might create comprehension problems, including the technical vocabulary, idiomatic expressions, and concept difficulty. Once students identify these problem areas, they are taught to seek support, ask questions, or use reference materials to be sure they understand the content.

- *Predicting*: Students are guided to predict the content based on prior knowledge and knowledge that they have accumulated from the reading. Then, students will read with the purpose of finding out if their predictions were accurate and to link new knowledge with the knowledge they already have.

Integrated Language Arts

The integrated language arts curriculum/classroom integrates reading, writing, speaking, and listening. It incorporates students' experiences with the aims of the curriculum.

Whole Language Approach (WLA)

The main principle of the WLA is that language should not be separated into discrete components or skills, but rather it should be treated as whole system of communication. Authentic text is preferred, especially literature and the use of language for personal communication. Following are some of the concepts and strategies associated with whole language:

- Reading aloud to children

- Journal writing

- Sustained silent reading

- Higher-order thinking skills

- Student choice in reading materials

- Frequent conferences between teachers and students

The Language Experience Approach (LEA)

The language experience (experience charts) is an approach to literacy based on the assumption that students' prior experiences need to be used as a bridge to new ideas and concepts. This approach was developed as an alternative to the use of basal readers to teach initial reading instruction to language-minority students. Proponents of the LEA felt that the vocabulary, topics, and ideas of the stories presented in basal readers did not match the schemata (background knowledge) and the vocabulary of language-minority students, and that this discrepancy created comprehension problems. To compensate for the discrepancy between the schemata needed to understand the story, students in the LEA share an activity or experience, such as a science experiment or an activity on the playground. After the initial activity, students are guided to talk about it and to dictate the story to the teacher. Once the story is written, the teacher reads the story while pointing to the words as they are read. Following this initial reading, students join the teacher in a choral reading. After the second reading, students copy the story and take it home. The next day the story is read again, and it is used for a variety of follow-up activities. For example, teachers can use a cloze activity (deletion of key words from the text) to check for comprehension. The text can also be used to teach grammar conventions and to promote vocabulary development.

Content-Based Language Programs

Content-based language programs are designed to meet the linguistic and cognitive needs of ELLs through the integration of language and content. Traditionally, these programs plan and introduce content area and language objectives concurrently. Some of the programs are presented next.

The CALLA Model

The *CALLA* model for ELLs was developed by Anna Chamot and Michael O'Malley. It was designed to promote English-language development through the content areas. It is based on cognitive psychology where students become active participants in the learning process—constructing knowledge. The model uses three main learning strategies for the goal of teaching language and content: metacognitive, cognitive, and social (Chamot & O'Malley, 1994).

Metacognitive strategies have been described as ways to conceptualize how learning takes place. It has been divided into two main components: organization and planning for learning, and self-monitoring and self-evaluating (Reiss, 2005).

Following are some strategies for organizing and planning for instruction:

- Keeping track of short- and long-term assignments with a due date

- Segmenting long tasks into smaller manageable parts

- Identifying specific strategies to facilitate learning of different kinds of content

- Organizing information to study for a test

The following are strategies for self-monitoring and self-evaluating:

- Assessing your weaknesses and strengths in the content

- Identifying the preferred and easiest strategy for learning content

- Conducting continuous self-assessment and progressing toward mastery of content

Cognitive strategies describes techniques to improve understanding, increase retention of information, and refine the ability to apply new information. Following are some of the specific strategies:

- Linking and making connections between current and new content

- Analyzing the interrelatedness and the elements that transfer from L1 and L2

- Fostering the ability to identify and isolate key concepts while reading or listening for comprehension

- Note taking to emphasize important concepts in a lesson

- Developing strategies for self-assessment of test content

- Visualizing information as a way to remember information

- Creating charts and graphs to synthesize and present content

- Classifying and organizing information as a way of remembering

Social strategies describe techniques in which students learn from each other or learn by interacting in groups. Following are some of these strategies:

- Working in pairs or in groups to complete projects and solve problems

- Asking questions for clarification or making requests

- Seeking support from peers to complete an assignment or to study for a test

- Observing and interacting with people from diverse backgrounds to learn about them

Most students can benefit from explicit instruction in learning strategies. ELLs need help to cope with dual demands of learning a new language and academic content. The CALLA approach is designed to assist ESL students to succeed in school by providing transitional instruction from ESL programs to grade-level English content instruction. The program is more effective for the three types of ELLs:

- Students who have developed the BICS but have not yet developed the academic skills appropriate to their grade level

- Students who have acquired academic language skills in their native language and initial proficiency in English but need assistance in transferring concepts and skills from L1 to L2

- Bilingual English-dominant students who have not yet developed academic language skills in either language

Sheltered English

Sheltered English (SE) is an instructional approach designed for ELLs at intermediate and advanced language proficiency. The main purpose of SE is to make content comprehensible to ELLs (Echevarría, Vogt, & Short, 2000). In this program, children are "sheltered" from the pressure of competing with native English learners. To deliver the comprehensible input, content instruction is linguistically simplified through contextualized instruction, visual aids, hands-on activities, and body language. Some of the strategies used to modify language to make it comprehensible are listed here.

- Control the length and complexity of the sentences. Children respond better to short and simple sentences.

- Introduce technical vocabulary before the lesson.

- Use repetition, restatement, and paraphrasing to clarify concepts.

- Control the speed of delivery, and use a different type of intonation to emphasize important concepts.

- Supplement oral presentations with diagrams, graphic organizers, and manipulatives to make content easier to understand.

- Guide students to use role playing to represent important concepts.

Like the CALLA approach, sheltered English is more effective for classrooms with students from multiple language groups who are at least at the intermediate level of English-language development (Schifini, 1985).

Cooperative learning is teaching strategy designed to create a low-anxiety learning environment where students work together in small groups to achieve instructional goals. As a result of this instructional arrangement, students with different levels of ability or language development work collaboratively to support each other, ensuring that each member masters the objectives of the lesson. This approach can easily be used to deliver content and language instruction. Traditionally, the strategy is delivered in the following specific steps (Arends, 1998)

1. Present goals: Teacher goes over objectives for the lesson and provides the motivation.

2. Present information: Teacher presents information to students either verbally or with text.

3. Organize students into learning teams: Teacher explains to students how to form learning teams and helps groups to make an efficient transition.

4. Assist teamwork and study: Teacher assists learning teams as they do their work.

5. Test students on the content: Teacher tests knowledge of learning materials as each group presents results of its work.

6. Provide recognition: Teacher finds ways to recognize both individual and group efforts and achievement.

To emphasize the cooperative nature of the strategy, specific strategies were developed to enrich the lessons. A list of these specialized strategies follows.

Student Teams Achievement Divisions (Adapted from Robert Slavin)

- Teacher presents new academic information to students.

- Students are divided into four- or five-member learning teams.

- Team members master the content and then help each other to learn the material through tutoring, quizzing one another, or carrying on team discussions.

- Each individual is given an improvement score to show the growth accomplished.

- Daily or weekly quizzes are given to assess mastery.

- Each week, through newsletters or short ceremonies, groups are recognized, as well as those students who have shown the most improvement.

Group Investigation (Adapted from Herbert Thelen)

- Students select a subtopic within a general area.

- The class is divided into small groups composed of two to six members. Group composition should be ethnically and academically heterogeneous.

- Students and teacher plan specific learning procedures, tasks, and goals (cooperative learning planning).

- Students carry out the plan using a variety of sources. Teacher follows the process and offers assistance as needed.

- Students analyze and evaluate information and plan how it can be summarized in some interesting fashion for possible display or presentation to the class as a whole (analysis and synthesis).

- The final product is presented.

- Individual or group evaluation is conducted.

Think-Pair Share (Adapted from Frank Lyman)

This activity was developed as a result of the wait-time research.

- *Thinking:* The teacher poses the question and asks students to spend a minute thinking alone about the answer. No talking or walking allowed.

- *Pairing:* Students pair off and discuss what they have been thinking about, sharing possible answers or information.

- *Sharing:* Share with the whole class. Go around the classroom from pair to pair and continue until a fourth or half of the class has had a chance to report.

Numbered Head Together (Adapted from Spencer Kagan)

This activity was designed to involve more students in the review of materials covered in class.

- *Numbering:* Divide students into teams of three to five members.

- *Questioning:* The teacher asks questions.

- *Heads together:* Students put their heads together to figure out the answer and to be sure everyone knows the answer.

- *Answering:* The teacher calls a number, and students from each group with that number raise their hands and provide the answer.

General Programs for Language-Minority Students

In addition to the language-specific program presented here, two other programs have been used effectively with language-minority students: accelerated learning and critical pedagogy.

Accelerated Learning

English-language learners begin schooling in the United States behind their native English-speaking counterparts. To improve their chances of catching up academically with monolingual English-speaking peers, a special type of program is required. One of the programs that can potentially achieve this goal is *accelerated learning*.

Accelerated learning is a concept that emerged from the work of Levin (1987). Its main purpose is to enhance and enrich the learning among students in at-risk situations to allow them to catch up academically with their peers. This approach relies heavily on enrichment strategies taken from the gifted and talented programs and uses effectively the strengths that children bring from home. The approach uses relevant and authentic applications, problem solving, and active learning as tools for instruction and cognitive development (Ovando, Combs & Collier, 2006). According to the North Central Regional Educational Laboratory, accelerated learning is based on the following cardinal principles:

- Learning environments with high expectations for all students

- Identification of achievement gaps and setting deadlines for eliminating identified gaps by the end of elementary school

- The implementation of an interdisciplinary curriculum that emphasizes hands-on activities, critical thinking, and problem solving using real-life situations

- Meaningful involvement of parents and empowerment of teachers

- Incorporation of the language and culture of minority students into daily school activities and used as teaching tools

Critical Pedagogy

Critical pedagogy is a concept that emerged from the work of the Brazilian educator Paulo Freire (1970). Freire believed that children are not exposed to a curriculum that reflects their reality and are not guided to analyze or question that reality. Critical pedagogy guides students to identify real-life problems, reflect on them, gather information, share it with peers, and collectively find solutions. In this approach, students become active learners and participants in their own reality. By exposing students to this approach, students develop a deep and relevant knowledge of life, develop problem-solving skills, and become protagonists in their quest for knowledge gathering and discovery. Critical pedagogy has the potential to empower ELLs and ethnic minorities in the United States.

Conclusions

This chapter presented a description of the learning and linguistic theories that have been used to develop methods to teach English as a second language. It also presented an overview of the language proficiency levels used to describe the development of L2 and the methods and the strategies used to teach the receptive and productive English skills. The chapter also summarized information about the integration of language and content, content-based language programs, and how teachers can use this information to promote second-language acquisition.

REFERENCES

Arends, R. 1998. *Learning to teach*, 4th ed. Boston: McGraw Hill

Asher, J. J. 1979. *Learning another language through actions*. San Jose, CA: AccuPrint.

Berlitz Method. Berlitz Official Website. http://www.berlitz.us/web/html/content .aspx?idTemplate=1.

Chamot, A. U., and J. M. O'Malley. 1994. *The CALLA handbook: Implementing the cognitive academic language learning approach*. New York: Addison-Wesley Publishing.

Chomsky, N. 1975. *Reflections on language*. New York: Pantheon Books.

Cummins, J. 1981. The role of primary language development in promoting educational success of minority students. In *Schooling and language minority students: A theoretical framework,* ed. California State Department of Education, 3–49. Los Angeles: Evaluation, Dissemination and Assessment Center, California State University.

Curran, C. A. 1976. *Counseling-learning in second languages*. Apple River, IL: Apple River Press.

Dolch, E.W. (1948). *Problems in reading*. Champaign, IL: Garrard Press.

Echevarría, J., M. Vogt, and D. Short. 2000. *Marking content comprehensible for English language learners: The SIOP model*. Needham Heights, MA: Allyn & Bacon.

Freire, P. 1970. *Pedagogy of the oppressed*. New York: Continuum.

Finocchiaro, M., and C Brumfit. 1983. *The functional-notional approach*. New York: Oxford University Press.

Gattegno, C. 1972. *Teaching foreign languages in school: The silent way*. New York: Educational Solutions.

Hudelson, S. 1984. Kan yo ret an rayt en ingles: Children becoming literate in English as a second language. *TESOL Quarterly* 18:221–38.

Kagan, S. 1985. *Cooperative learning resources for teachers*. Riverside, CA: Spencer Kagan.

Krashen, S. D. 1985. *The input hypothesis: Issues and implications*. London: Longman.

Krashen, S. D., and T. D. Terrell. 1983. *The natural approach: Language acquisition in the classroom*. Oxford: Pergamon Press.

Lapp, D., D. Fisher, J. Flood, and A. Cabello. 2001. An integrated approach to the teaching and assessment of language arts. In *Literacy assessment of second language learners*, eds. S. Rollins Hurley and J. Villamil Tinajero, 1–24. Boston: Allyn and Bacon.

Lenneberg, E. H. 1967. *Biological foundations of language*. New York: John Wiley & Sons.

Levin, H. M. 1987. Accelerated schools for disadvantaged students. *Educational Leadership* 44:19–21.

Lozanov, G. *Suggestology and suggestopedy*. http://lozanov.hit.bg/.

Ovando, C. J., M. C. Combs, and V. P. Collier. 2006. *Bilingual and ESL classrooms: Teaching in multicultural contexts*, 4th ed. Boston: McGraw Hill.

Palincsar, A. S. 1986. Reciprocal Teaching. In Teaching reading as thinking. OakBrook, IL: North Central Regional Laboratory.

Peregoy, S. F., W. F. Boyle, and K. Cadiero-Kaplan. 2008. *Reading, writing, and learning in ESL: A resource book for K–12 teachers*, 5th ed. New York: Pearson.

Quiocho, A. L., and S. H. Ulanoff. 2009. *Differentiated literacy instruction for English language learners*. Boston: Pearson.

Reiss, J. 2005. *Teaching content to English language learners: Strategies for secondary school success*. White Plains, NY: Pearson.

Schifini, A. 1985. *Sheltered English: Content area instruction for limited English proficiency students*. Los Angeles: Los Angeles County Office of Education.

Slavin, R. E. 1986. *Student learning: An overview and practical guide*. Washington, DC: Professional Library National Education Association.

Thelen, H. 1981. *The classroom society*. New York: Wiley.

Tomas, E., and H. Robinson. 1972. *Improving reading in every class: A Source book for teachers*. Boston: Allyn & Bacon.

Tomlinson, C. A. 2001. *How to differentiate instruction in mixed-ability classrooms*, 2nd ed. Alexandria, VA: Association for Supervision and Curriculum Development.

———. 2001a. *Differentiated instruction in the elementary grades*. ERIC Digest. Champaign, IL: ERIC Clearinghouse of Elementary and Early Childhood Education. ERIC Document No. ED443572.

Tragar, B., and B. K. Wong. 1984. The relationship between native and second language reading and second language oral ability. In *Placement procedures in bilingual education: Education and policy issues*, ed. C. Rivera, 152–64. Clevedon, England: Multicultural Matters.

Urzúa, C. 1987. You stopped too soon: Second language children composing and revising. *TESOL Quarterly* 21:279–305.

Assessment Techniques and Cultural Issues

FRAMEWORK FOR ASSESSING ENGLISH-LANGUAGE LEARNERS

Three major considerations have to be taken into account when designing and implementing assessment programs for English-language learners (ELLs): the expected levels or standards of performance from the students, the stages of development typical of learners learning English or another second language (L2), and the various cultural characteristics of the students. Information about the TESOL standards, the stages of language development, and consideration when assessing ELLs from diverse cultural backgrounds is discussed next.

Organization of TESOL Standards

In 1997, the organization Teachers of English to Speakers of Other Languages (TESOL) developed standards to describe the competencies and skills that ELLs ought to develop to be considered proficient English speakers (Boyd-Batstone, 2006). The standards of the organization described the skills that ELLs needed to function effectively socially, academically, and culturally. These standards are organized around three goals with three standards for each component. The TESOL goals and standards, as presented in the official TESOL website, follow (TESOL, 2006).

Area: Social language

Goal I: To use English to communicate in social settings
Standards: Students will

- Use English to participate in social interactions

- Interact in, through, and with spoken and written English for personal expression and enjoyment

- Use learning strategies to extend their communicative competence

> For additional information about the TESOL standards together with progress indicators and vignettes, go to the TESOL official website at www.tesol.org/s_tesol/seccss. asp?CID=113&DID=1583.

Area: Academic language

Goal II: To use English to achieve academically in all content areas
Standards: Students will use

- English to interact in the classroom

- English to obtain, process, construct, and provide subject matter information in spoken and written form

- Appropriate learning strategies to construct and apply academic knowledge

Area: Sociocultural Knowledge

Goal III: To use English in socially and culturally appropriate ways
Standards: Students will use

- The appropriate language variety, register, and genre according to audience, purpose, and setting

- Nonverbal communication appropriate to audience, purpose, and settings

- Appropriate learning strategies to extend their sociolinguistic and sociocultural competence

Description of language proficiency

Teachers need to have a clear understanding of the stages of L2 development and use these stages as a foundation for assessing language development and academic progress.

Krashen and Terrell (1983) identified five stages of L2 development: preproduction, early production, speech emergence, intermediate fluency, and advanced stage. TESOL (2006) also developed a similar framework to explain the development of second-language acquisition. The TESOL framework is described in Table 4.2.

NOTE: Intralingual (within the language) errors are caused by the complexity of the second language. These errors are generally developmental in nature. Interlingual errors (across languages) refer to those errors caused by interference from the native language.

Table 4.1 Stages of Second-Language Development

Stages of Second-Language Acquisition	Characteristics
Preproduction, or silent stage	• Communicate with gestures and actions • Lack receptive vocabulary and shows problems comprehending messages • Might experience frustration and anxiety • Rely heavily on nonverbal communication
Early speech production	• Increase listening comprehension • Communicate using yes or no and one-word statements • Expand receptive vocabulary • Understand language in contextualized situations
Speech emergence	• Communicate in phrases using words with high semantic context (verbs, adjectives. and nouns) • Continue gaining receptive vocabulary • Communicate more effectively in contextualized situations, face-to-face interactions • Understand more than able to communicate
Intermediate fluency	• Communicate using simple sentences. • Overgeneralizes due to intralingual and interlingual interference • Become more acculturated and feel more comfortable in school
Advanced stage	• Develop the academic language • Able to communicate with minimum difficulty • Are generally ready to participate in the all-English curriculum

Table 4.2 TESOL Standards (TESOL, 2006)

Levels	Characteristics
Level 1: Starting	• Has limited understanding of English • Rarely uses English for communication • Responds nonverbally to simple commands, statements, and questions • Begins to imitate the verbalizations of others by using single words or simple phrases and to use English spontaneously • Constructs meaning from text primarily through visuals and graphic representations
Level 2: Emerging	• Can understand phrases and short sentences • Can communicate limited information in simple everyday and routine situations by using memorized phrases, groups of words, and formulae • Can use selected simple structures correctly but still systematically produces basic errors • Begins to use general academic vocabulary and familiar everyday expressions • Makes errors in writing that often hinder communication
Level 3: Developing	• Understands more complex speech but still may require some repetition • Uses English spontaneously but may have difficulty expressing all thoughts because of a restricted vocabulary and a limited command of language structure • Speaks in simple sentences, which are comprehensible and appropriate, but frequently marked by grammatical errors • Proficiency in reading may vary considerably • Most successful constructing meaning from texts from which there is no background knowledge upon which to build upon
Level 4: Expanding	• English adequate for most day-to-day communication needs • Communicates in English in new or unfamiliar settings but will have occasional difficulty with complex structures and abstract academic concepts • May read with considerable fluency and be able to locate and identify the specific facts within the text; however, may not understand texts in which the concepts are presented in a decontextualized manner, the sentence structure is complex, or the vocabulary is abstract or has multiple meanings • Reads independently but may have occasional comprehension problems, especially when processing grade-level information
Level 5: Bridging	• Can express themselves fluently and spontaneously on a wide range of personal, general, academic, or social topics in a variety of contexts • Poised to function in an environment with native-speaking peers with minimal language support or guidance • Has a good command of technical and academic vocabulary as well of idiomatic expressions and colloquialisms • Can produce clear, smoothly flowing, well-structured texts of differing lengths and degrees of linguistic complexity • Commits few errors and generally corrects when they occurs

Krashen and Terrell's stages of development and the TESOL standards indicators are traditionally used around the nation to measure and label the performance of ELLs. Additionally, these standards are used as one of the components to determine if students are ready to be reclassified as fluent English speakers. However, when attempting to label language performance, we need to establish a distinction between social and academic language, and how these proficiencies can be assessed to develop a better understanding of the overall proficiency level of the learner. An analysis of these two components and the implications for the reclassification of students follow.

Social and Academic Proficiency

Students in bilingual and ESL programs have to demonstrate an advanced level of English-language proficiency to be reclassified as fluent English speakers. Traditionally, two types of proficiency are assessed, **basic interpersonal skills** (BICS) and **cognitive academic proficiency** (CALP) (Cummins, 1981). BICS describes the social language required to function in face-to-face communications in daily activities, whereas CALP describes the type of language required to function effectively in the classroom setting. BICS is commonly assessed informally and through the use of various commercial language proficiency tests available, such as the Woodcock-Muñoz Language Survey and the Language Assessment Scales (LAS). The CALP component is traditionally assessed through standardized, norm-referenced achievement tests or criterion-referenced tests available nationwide.

Traditionally, states and school districts require ELLs to master English language-arts basic skills examinations and norm-referenced tests to be considered for reclassification as fluent English speakers. For example, in Texas, state law requires that students in special language programs score at least at the 40th percentile in a norm-referenced achievement test to be considered for reclassification. Districts around the nation use tests like the Metropolitan Achievement Test (MAT), the Iowa Test of Basic Skills (ITBS), and the California Achievement Test (CAT) to comply with this requirement.

Formal and Informal Assessment

Assessment describes the process of gathering data to make instructional and programmatic decisions as well as for reporting purposes. Assessment can be performed formally or informally.

Formal Assessment

Formal Assessment is conducted using standardized norm-referenced and criterion-referenced tests. Norm-referenced tests are used to measure students' performance in a variety of skills and content. These tests are administered at set intervals using a professionally developed instrument. Norm-referenced tests compare the scores of students in other geographic locations using a ranking order based on their performance. Results are customarily reported based on percentiles on a normal curve. For example, a student who scored 1120 on a test with a possible maximum of 1600 would be in the 70th percentile, which means that 30 percent of the students who took the test on that day scored higher that the student did. The same student can retake the test and score lower but be in a higher percentile because the overall group did not do as well as the initial group did. Norm-referenced tests compare the performance of students, not necessarily the mastery of specific standards or objectives. Individual state education agencies or school districts generally determine the desired level of performance or the percentiles in these types of tests.

Standardized tests can produce three types of scores to indicate the relative strength and weaknesses of students:

- *Percentiles rank* indicates the percentage of the norm group that is at, over, or under the student's score. It does not indicate the percentage of correct items.

- *National curve equivalent* score is similar to the percentile, but it uses raw scores to produce the results. This measure is generally used in educational research because it represents a better view of the achievement of students.

- *Grade equivalent* measures how a child performed in regard to expectations based on grade level. Teachers have to use caution when interpreting this kind of score. For example, if a child in third grade scores 4.1 in the test, it does not mean that the child is ready to go to fourth grade. It means that the child is performing well above the third grade peers.

Criterion-referenced tests, on the other hand, are used to indicate the level of mastery attained on specific standards or instructional objectives. Most high-stakes examinations in the United States in K–12 measure the performance of students on specific standards or the state curriculum. Results are presented based on the percentage of questions answered correctly. Traditionally, a score of 70 percent is required to indicate mastery of the objectives or standards. Teacher-made tests and state-approved standard-based tests are criterion-based tests because mastery implies that the objectives or the standards have been met.

Informal Assessment

Informal assessment is often linked to *authentic assessment*, *ongoing assessment*, and *performance assessment*. Informal assessment is part of instruction, and it is generally done to assess students' progress. Results of informal assessment can be easily incorporated into teaching. Some of the most common types of informal assessments used in the language classroom are listed here (Peregoy, Boyle & Cadiero-Kaplan, 2008).

Observation is used to assess a student's use of language in a variety of instructional settings. In this type of assessment, teachers observe and record specific language features or behaviors. For example, the use of regular past tenses in places where the irregular version was required.

Checklists are used to track students' development by noting which skill or subsets of skills have become part of the linguistic repertoire of the child. Traditionally, developmental milestones and the stages of language development are used to develop such checklists.

Portfolio assessment is used to document students' progress in a variety of ways. Traditionally, teachers collect samples of students' work at different stages during the academic year. To assess language proficiency, teachers can collect taped oral performance in a variety of settings, and written samples in the student's native language (L1) and L2, including published writing.

Conferencing is used to provide opportunities for teachers and students to discuss individual language features to assess language development. Teachers meet with students to assess their performance and to identify activities and instruction needed to support student progress.

Peer review is a method that involves students in the evaluation process and gives them an opportunity to build their evaluative, critical-thinking, and interactive skills. For this type of assessment to be effective, teachers need to discuss with their students the purpose and the process to carry out the evaluation. Traditionally, the student's evaluation is taken into account when the teacher assigns the official grade.

Self-assessment is generally used to empower students by making them responsible and reflective of their performance in school. Teachers can guide students to self-assess using checklists, inventories, conferences, and portfolios. Self-assessment is one of the main components of student-centered practices and one of the foundations of constructivism learning theory.

Anecdotal records are helpful in capturing the process a group of students uses to solve a problem. This formative data can be useful during feedback to the group. Students can also be taught to write explanations of the procedures they use for their projects, such as science experiments or any kind of problem-solving projects. One advantage of the anecdotal record is that it can include a variety of information relevant to the purpose of the assessment. Disadvantages include the amount of time necessary to complete the record and difficulty in assigning a grade. If the anecdotal record is used solely for feedback, no grade is necessary.

Running record is a technique used to assess students' word identification skills and fluency in oral reading (Clay, 2002). As the teacher listens to a student read a page, the teacher uses a copy of the page to mark each word the child mispronounces. The teacher writes the incorrect word over the printed word, draws a line through each word the child skips, and draws an arrow under repeated words.

Miscue analysis is the process used to identify systematic errors that children make during oral reading. In this system, miscues are seen as important indicators of the current level of performance of the child.

The procedure to conduct a miscue analysis follows:

• Select reading material a little bit above the current reading level of the child. The complete story should be about 500 words.

• Provide a copy of the selection to the child.

• Type the selection triple spaced to allow space to write comments.

- Audiotape the reading.

- Provide instructions to the child. Tell the student that you cannot help during the reading.

- Ask questions about the story.

- Let the reader listen to tape recording and then analyze it.

Informal reading inventories (IRI) are normally used to determine reading level and to assess reading comprehension in general. Students are asked to read a set of graded passages aloud, and then the teacher asks a series of factual and interpretative comprehension questions (Peregoy, et al., 2008). Teachers listen to the reading performance looking for general miscue patterns, decoding strategies, and areas of strength. Students can also read the passages silently to have a better grasp of the content and to answer more in-depth comprehension questions. To determine the reading level using published IRI, students go through a series of passages until they fail to answer questions correctly. Using the performance of the child and through the use of formulas provided, reading specialist can identify the reading level of the child.

Performance-based assessment assesses students on how well they perform certain tasks. Students must use higher-level thinking skills to apply, analyze, synthesize, and evaluate ideas and data. For example, a science performance-based assessment might require students to read a problem, design and carry out a laboratory experiment, and write summaries of their findings. The performance-based assessment would evaluate both the processes students used and the output they produced. An English performance-based test might ask students to first read a selection of literature and then write a critical analysis. A mathematics performance-based test might state a general problem, require students to develop one or more methods of solving the problem, use one of the methods to arrive at a solution, and write the solution and an explanation of the processes they used.

Performance-based assessment allows students to be creative in solutions to problems or questions, and it requires them to use higher-level skills. Students work on content-related problems and use skills that are useful in various contexts. There are weaknesses, however. This type of assessment can be time consuming. Performance-based assessment often requires multiple resources, which can be expensive. Teachers must receive training on how to incorporate such types of assessment into their teaching. Nonetheless, convergent research suggests that performance-based testing is a more effective and authentic measure of student achievement than traditional tests are.

Assessment Data in Students' Permanent Record

A large amount of assessment data is recorded in the students' permanent record. Teachers can preview this valuable information about their students before the first day of class. Although this information should not be used to prejudge them, it can provide teachers with an idea of the needs and strengths of their students.

School records contain valuable information about the strengths and needs of children. Teachers can develop an overview of their students by examining grades from previous years, results of standardized tests, health records, and any other documents or descriptions of the students' background (McMillan, 2004).

School records should also contain a portfolio with documentation and the process used for admission and dismissal from the special language program, that is, bilingual, dual language, or ESL. Teachers have to pay close attention to the information about the results of English proficiency examinations, the performance of students in other required examinations, placement decisions, and testing accommodations approved by the Language Proficiency Assessment Committee.

Appropriate use of the information contained in school records can facilitate planning for the first days of class and address identified instructional, emotional, and medical needs of the children. However, as with any other kind of data, teachers have to be cautious when interpreting information about ethnic and linguistic minorities because the data can lead to inaccurate interpretations and stereotyping.

Diversity in the Classroom

Most classrooms in the United States are very diverse, and the responsibility of the teacher is to provide the best education possible to every learner. Students in a class may differ in their cognitive and language development, culture, religion, economic level, social class, racial and ethnic background, national origin, and learning modality. Determining the learning styles of individuals and teaching to those styles transcends cultural boundaries and recognizes that all people have distinct learning preferences and tendencies. Furthermore, this approach acknowledges that all preferences and tendencies are equally valid and that each style of learning has strengths. The teacher who understands and applies research on learning styles (auditory, visual, or tactile) can validate all students in the class. Moreover, these differences need to be taken into account when designing assessment instruments.

CULTURAL CONSIDERATIONS WHEN ASSESSING ELLs

When assessing ELLs, teachers have to take into account the stage of language development of the child to be sure that language does not interfere in the assessment of the intended concepts. Additionally, teachers have to take into account how culture can affect the performance of students in testing. Following are some assessment techniques that can be used to minimize the impact of language and culture:

- Use structured observation using a checklist to record the performance of students instead of requiring students to provide oral evidence of their growth.

- Allow students opportunities to demonstrate knowledge through dramatizations, such as role playing or readers theater.

- Use informal and ongoing evaluation to eliminate the pressure that students might feel during formal evaluations.

- Allow students opportunities for drawing, as opposed to speaking or writing, to represent ideas and to support demonstrations or explanations.

- When testing vocabulary development where students are required to provide specific words, allow access to a list of words from which they can choose the words to fill in the blanks.

- Explore the learning styles and cultural behaviors of students from diverse cultural backgrounds, and take their backgrounds into account when assessing them. Be aware that students from culturally diverse backgrounds might express knowledge and understanding differently.

- Be aware that ELLs might have an understanding of concepts but might not have the vocabulary to express the knowledge. Allow the option of expressing the knowledge nonverbally or through concrete objects.

- Organize individual or class demonstrations of key concepts to be sure that each student has a chance to master key concepts.

- Avoid the use of ineffective questions like *Do you understand? Do you have questions?* Most likely, students are not going to respond to these generic questions. Instead, ask specific questions about the topic, or ask them to perform activities to show content mastery.

- Be aware that some cultural groups follow a teacher-centered, or passive, approach in which students are not expected to ask clarification questions. Instead, they listen to the teacher and try to address the questions, even if it is not clear to them. Answering questions without having a clear understanding of them can definitely affect the validity of the instrument.

TESTING AND CLASSIFYING STUDENTS

Most school districts in the nation use some form of the Home Language Survey (HLS) to determine if a child should be tested for English proficiency. Traditionally, new students to the district are required to complete an HLS containing two basic questions:

> *What language is spoken in your home most of the time?*
> *What language does your child speak most of the time?*

If the answer to either of these questions is a language other than English, the child must then be tested for language dominance/proficiency.

Screening for Admission

Students in kindergarten to grade two are generally tested using oral language proficiency tests. Following are the three best known instruments that have an oral component:

The Woodcock–Muñoz Language Survey, Revised (Woodcock, Muñoz, Ruef, & Alvarado, 2001)

Language Assessment Scales (CTB McGraw-Hill, 1976)

The IDEA Oral Language Proficiency Test (Ballard & Tighe, 1991)

Using the results of these tests and the input of teachers and administrators, the district can make placement decisions. If a child qualifies for the program and the parents agree with the placement, the student can be officially admitted to the special language program. If the parents do not want to place a child in the program, they can complete a **parental denial form** or a sign a waiver to refuse program participation. Traditionally, students with parental denials are placed in the all-English program without any organized language support. Once students are admitted to the special language program, they will remain in it until they can be reclassified as fluent English speakers.

Testing for Reclassification as a Fluent English Speaker

To reclassify students as fluent English speakers, school districts in the nation administer a language proficiency examination to assess the development of the social and academic component of language (BICS and CALP). Most language proficiency tests now contain all four language components: listening, speaking, reading, and writing. These tests can used to assess both the social and academic language components; however, some school districts also require students to pass the language arts portion of a standardized achievement test to ensure that ELLs have the academic proficiency to perform well in the all-English classroom.

In making the final decision, a committee takes into account the results of the examinations, the overall academic performance of the child, teacher evaluations, and parental input. If the committee feels that the child is ready to be exited, the child is classified as a fluent English speaker and is officially exited from the program.

Two-Year Monitoring Services

The *No Child Left Behind Act* (NCLB) requires that upon reclassification as fluent English speakers, students are monitored for two years to be sure that they are successful in the English-only classroom. If a child experiences academic difficulties, the committee has the option of returning the child to the special language program or making the necessary changes to be sure the child is successful.

Testing to Comply with Federal Legislation

Title III of the NCLB legislation requires state education agencies to submit an assessment program to document the growth and development of ELLs. Beginning in 2001, state education agencies began submitting proposals to document the *adequate yearly progress* of ELLs. In June 2003, all 50 states, Puerto Rico, and the District of Columbia had complied with the mandate. Pre-service and in-service ESL teachers have to become familiar with the plan approved for their state and the instruments required for compliance. To see the approved plans approved for each state education agency, go to the USDP website at www .ed.gov/admins/lead/account/stateplans03/index.html.

For example, the state of Texas is required to submit evidence of the performance of students in various examinations:

The *Texas English Language Proficiency Assessment System* (TELPAS) was designed to comply with the accountability system required in the federal NCLB legislation. The legislation requires that ELLs are assessed yearly in all language skills listening, speaking, reading, and writing. Students begin taking TELPAS in Kindergarten and stop participating when they are exited from the bilingual/ESL program. TELPAS report results based on the following levels: Beginning, Intermediate, Advanced, and Advanced High. ELLs stop taking the TELPAS when they reach the *advanced high* level in the test.

In Georgia, state education agencies have developed a standards-based criterion-referenced English language proficiency examination to assess the social and academic language of ELLs (Georgia Department of Education, n.d.). It covers the content areas (math, social studies, science) and the areas of social and academic language. This test is used to document the progress of ELLs in language proficiency gains to meet NCLB requirements.

Assessing Speaking Ability

Intelligibility

A child's speaking ability is generally assessed informally in class as part of daily activities. First, teachers have to determine if the speech of the child is *intelligible* and can be understood by native speakers with minimum effort. Communication or intelligibility problems in native speakers can be caused by developmental issues, the use of dialectical variations, or speech disorders. To assess the speech of the child, teachers have to have an understanding of the developmental patterns that children follow in the process of language mastery, and use these patterns as a foundation for assessing their performance. Teacher should also develop an understanding of features from dialects spoken in the community to avoid confusion with contrasting features with Standard English. For example, speakers of African American vernacular English (AAVE) and some speakers of the New England area drop the /r/ after a vowel, as in the following typical statement: *Park the car in Harvard yard* [Pahk the kah in Hahvud yahd]. In these cases, the omission of the postvocalic /r/ cannot be identified as a pronunciation problem. Thus teachers have to have a working knowledge of features of the dialects used in the surrounding community to make accurate assessment of the children's speech.

Language Interference

For ELLs, teachers have to take into account how the first language interferes in the pronunciation of English. Phonologically, language interference can happen at the word or sentence level. The most noticeable form of language interference happens when students use the phonology of their first language to pronounce words in English. For example, most Spanish dialects do not use the /v/ sound; instead, they replace it with /b/. This feature creates semantic problems when native-Spanish speakers pronounce the English word *vowel* (letters of the alphabet) as *bowel* (gastrointestinal movement), which can create an embarrassing situation for the speaker. Korean, Vietnamese, Chinese, and Japanese ELLs might also experience language interference when using the English phoneme /r/. They have problems producing consonant cluster with /r/ as a component. Chinese speakers, specifically, have the tendency of substituting /r/ with /l/. This feature can create semantic problems when native Chinese, Korean, and Japanese speakers pronounce the English word *rice* as *lice*. A second type of interference can be caused by the application of incorrect **word stress** in English. For example, in Standard English, most speakers will place the primary stress of the word *com.po.**si**.tion* on the penultimate syllable but never in the last syllable. However, Spanish speakers and speakers of Caribbean English might place the primary stress on the ultimate syllable resulting in non-Standard English pronunciation. Language interference can potentially create communication problems and often embarrassing situations for ELLs. Thus teachers have to become aware of conflicting language sounds and provide appropriate language support to ELLs.

Communication Style and Culture

Culture plays an important role in the way people communicate orally and graphically. In oral communication, English uses a linear rhetorical pattern that allows little flexibility to deviate from the topic. Other languages—such as Spanish, Russian, and Arabic—allow for a more flexible progression to convey information. This flexibility is identified as a *curvilinear* or *associational* approach because it allows speakers the option of deviating from the main topic without being penalized. This cultural and linguistic difference can create problems when assessing the speaking capabilities of speaker of these types of languages because they might not produce the linear oral and written narrative required in Standard English. Teachers have to be vigilant to determine how L1 and culture affect the performance of children in L2.

Assessing Speaking Ability

Speaking ability can be assessed in the classroom with a structured checklist identifying specific features that teachers want to observe. Lapp, Fisher, Flood, and Cabello (2001) developed an instrument to assess the speaking ability: the **Speaking Checklist.** An adaptation of the instrument is presented here.

Speaking Checklist

✓ The communication is intelligible

✓ Speaks clearly with minimum language interference

✓ Presents a topical thesis and provides support for it

✓ Builds support for the subject

✓ Stays within the identified topic

✓ Presents information in an organized and interesting way

✓ Speaks with fluency

✓ Uses courteous language

✓ Takes turns and waits to talk

✓ Talks so others in the group can hear

✓ Ask questions for clarification and guidance

✓ Volunteers to talk and to answer questions

✓ Uses effective strategies to avoid breakdowns in communication

✓ Maintains the interest of the listeners

The speaking component of the ***Texas Observation Protocol*** (TOP), mentioned earlier, assesses the oral communication based on four language proficiencies: beginning, intermediate, advanced, and advanced high (TEA, 2006). This instrument is also an observation instrument that uses holistic scoring administered by teachers in the bilingual or ESL classroom. A performance at the advanced high proficiency level is generally required to be reclassified as a fluent English speaker. A description of the advanced high proficiency follows:

• Students are able to participate in extended discussion in a variety of social and grade-appropriate academic topics.

• Students are able to communicate effectively using abstract and concrete content-based vocabulary during classroom instruction.

• Students are able to use complex English grammar structures and complex sentences at a level comparable to native speakers.

- Students rarely make linguistic errors that interfere with overall communication.

- Students rarely use pronunciation that interferes with overall communication.

Communication Disorders

A *communicative disorder* occurs when a person's speech interferes with the ability to convey messages during interactions with community members. Four classifications of language disorders can be identified: voice, fluency, articulation, and language processing (Piper, 2003).

Voice Disorders

Voice disorders describe any type of distortion of the pitch, the timbre, and the volume of spoken communication. There are two type of voice disorders, phonation and resonance. *Phonation* describes any kind of abnormality in the vibration of the vocal folds. For example, hoarseness or extreme breathiness can interfere with comprehension. *Resonance* describes abnormalities created when sound passes through the vocal tract. The most typical example of resonance is caused when the sound passes through the nasal cavity changing oral sounds to nasal, hypernasal sounds. This type of disorder should not be confused with the nasal quality of Southern dialects.

Fluency Disorders

Fluency disorders refer to any kind of condition that affects the child's ability to produce coherent and fluent communication. The most common types of fluency disorder are caused by stuttering and cluttering. *Stuttering* is characterized by multiple false starts or inability to produce the intended sounds. *Cluttering* occurs when children try to communicate in an excessively fast mode that makes comprehension difficult.

Teachers have to be cautious when assessing ELLs who might experience temporary fluency dysfunction (hesitations, false starts, repetition) created by anxiety or confusion with the two languages. Often ELLs stutter because they cannot find or might not know the appropriate word in English. Allowing students to code switch from English to their first language can be used as a temporary remedy to stuttering. Additionally, children new to the language often use the intonation pattern and the speed of delivery of their native language. For example, when ELLs impose the intonation pattern and the speed of delivery of their native language to English, the delivery might become incomprehensible and it can be mistaken as cluttering.

Articulation Problems

Children may have problems with specific sounds of the language, which can cause unintelligibility and the production of esthetically displeasing sounds. The most common articulation disorder is the case of lisping. *Lisping* is a term used when children (or adults) produce certain sounds—/s/, /sh/, /z/, and /ch/—with their tongue between the upper and lower teeth. Some other sounds that can present challenges to children are the /w/, /l/, and /r/ sounds. Some of these problems might be developmental and eventually are eliminated, whereas others might require speech therapy. Elmer Fudd and Sylvester the Cat, two popular characters of animated cartoons, are well known for exhibiting these features: Sylvester's lisping and Elmer's difficulties with /r/, as in *wabbit*.

Language Processing

Language processing disorders are generally caused by a brain-based disturbance called *aphasia*. Three types of aphasia are known: receptive, expressive, and global.

- *Receptive aphasia*, or *sensory aphasia*, results from a lesion in the upper back part of the temporal lobe of the brain. It creates problems with listening comprehension and retrieval of words from memory. People affected with this condition have the tendency of repeating formulaic phrases and producing unintelligible sequences of words or sounds.

- *Expressive aphasia* results from damage to the lower back part of the frontal lobe. It affects the speaking ability with specific problems with articulation and fluency. The speech produced is often very slow, with multiple hesitations and problems with the suprasegmental features of language: intonation, rhythm, and stress. The sentences produced are generally very short and contain only the necessary features to convey the message. The speech of people with expressive aphasia resembles the speech of children at the telegraphic stage of first-language development.

- *Global aphasia* is also a brain-based disorder that affects both the receptive and expressive features of the language. Children with this kind of severe impairment of articulation and fluency produce minimal speech, and their comprehension is very limited. This type of language disorder is also known as *irreversible aphasia*, which suggests that little can be done to help children suffering from this condition.

Listening

Although there is no well-defined model of teaching listening skills, some theorists link listening skills to reading skills. They feel that reading and listening make use of similar language comprehension processes. Listening and reading both require the use of skills in phonology, syntax, semantics, and knowledge of the structure of text, and both language skills seem to be controlled by the same set of cognitive processes. Based on these assumptions, listening is generally assessed much the way reading comprehension is.

Following are some of the elements commonly assessed in listening comprehension:

- The main idea of a conversation

- The purpose of the communication

- The mood of the speaker

- Details and factual information presented orally

- The sequence of events as they appeared in the narrative

- The use of figurative language and implied meaning

- The ability to make inferences based on the communication presented

- Interpretation of idiomatic expressions used in the communication

In principle, the same assessment techniques used for reading comprehension can be used for listening comprehension. Some of the listening comprehension assessment strategies are presented next.

Listening Comprehension

Story retelling is a strategy used in early childhood to assess listening and reading comprehension. The strategy can also be used to assess sentence structure knowledge, vocabulary, speaking ability, and knowledge of the structure of stories.

An informal or structured checklist can be used to assess students' comprehension, sentence structure knowledge, and vocabulary development as they retell a story.

A checklist (Lapp et al., 2001) for listening comprehension should assess the ability of the child to

✓ retell the story with details;

✓ show evidence of comprehension of the story line and plot, including the characters, setting, author's intention, and literal and implied meaning;

✓ show evidence that the child understood major ideas and the details;

✓ bring background of information to the selection;

✓ analyze and make judgments based on facts;

✓ retell the selection in sentences that make grammatical sense;

✓ retell the story using sentences that include standard usage of verbs, adjectives, conjunctions, and compound sentences;

✓ use a rich and meaningful vocabulary with minimal use of slang and colloquial expressions;

✓ adapt spoken language for various audiences, purposes, and occasions;

✓ listen for various purposes: critical listening to evaluate a speaker's message, listening to enjoy and appreciate spoken language.

Assessing Comprehension

A frequent device for assessing comprehension is the use of oral or written questions. A question may be ***convergent***, which indicates that only one answer is correct, or ***divergent***, which indicates that more than one answer is correct. Most tests, however, include a combination of question types.

Another device for checking comprehension is a ***cloze test***, a passage with omitted words the test taker must supply. The test maker must decide whether to require the test taker to supply the exact word or to accept synonyms. Passing scores reflect which type of answer is acceptable. If meaning is the intent of the exercise, the teacher might accept synonyms and not demand the surface-level constructs or the exact word.

Assessing Writing

Language usage and writing skills are generally assessed through the analysis of specific grammar, language usage, and writing conventions. Writing can also be assessed though holistic scoring of writing samples. Language usage and the writing process can be assessed objectively through multiple-choice items. Some of the elements of language usage and the writing process that can be assessed objectively are

- the use of subject-verb agreement;

- sentence formation;

- verb usage;

- word choice;

- identification of the main idea;

- sequence of events;

- the use of implied meaning;

- organization of the paragraphs;

- main idea.

Scoring Compositions

Focused, holistic scoring is used to evaluate students' compositions. The whole story is scored based on specific writing objectives and the use of established criteria or rubrics. Rubrics may be designed based on the standards and expectations established by the national associations, such as TESOL. Some of the basic writing expectations for ELLs are listed here.

ELLs are expected to master the following writing objectives:

- To respond appropriately in a written composition to the purpose/audience specified in a given topic

- Organize ideas logically and coherently

- Demonstrate standard usage of the English language

- Generate written samples that develop/support/elaborate the central idea stated in a given topic

- Produce original writings that project the individuality and uniqueness of the writer

Rubrics in Holistic Scoring

Holistic scoring is a highly subjective way to assess writing samples. To minimize the subjectivity of the process, a *rubric* is commonly used. A rubric contains a description of the levels of writing performance expected. These descriptions are derived from the writing objectives and expectations for the intended population, like the ones listed for ELLs earlier. A commonly used rating scale is the 4-point scale, which represents four levels of proficiency:

Level 4—superior

Level 3—advanced

Level 2—intermediate

Level 1—novice or beginner

Raters read the writing samples and use the description of the levels to assign a score. Traditionally, a level of 3 or 4 is required to show mastery. Table 4.3 presents two examples of rubrics used to score compositions in English.

Linguistically Accommodated Testing for ELLs

The level of language mastery can affect the performance of English learners in content-area examinations. To minimize the impact of language and to increase the reliability of the instruments, districts are allowed to make linguistic accommodations for English learners. For example, the New York State Education Department (2002) provides translations of state tests in mathematics, social studies, and sciences for ELLs from the following language groups: Spanish, Haitian–Creole, Russian, Chinese, and Korean. They also provide glossaries for languages where translations are not available. New York State also provides glossaries in some additional languages and permits oral translations for those languages not available from the New York State Education Department.

Table 4.3 Criteria for Evaluation Compositions

Rubric I (TEA, 2005)	Rubric 2 (Lapp, et al., 2001)
4: An excellent paper that is well organized and displays facile use of language, content, and mechanics	4: Position statement is clearly stated. Lines of argument and evidence are presented in a systematic and convincing fashion.
3: A paper that demonstrates adequate organization, content, language use, and handling mechanics; may lack imagination and creativity	3: Position statement is both clearly stated and supported with several lines of argument. The lines of evidence and support are moderately well developed.
2: A lower-half paper that is weak in content, organization, style, and/or mechanics	2: Position statement is clear, but paper offers minimal evidence for support. The paper attempts to provide logical organization but falls short of presenting a unifying argument.
1: An unacceptable paper that addresses the topic but is weak in organization, content, and language use and is full of errors in mechanics	1: Position statement is unclearly or inappropriately stated. Evidence is illogical and/or emotional or nonexistent. Paper lacks any clear organization scheme.

Following are other considerations for linguistic accommodations for ELLs:

- Test administrators may be allowed to translate words, phrases, or sentences as requested by the student.

- Students may request that words, phrases, and sentences be read aloud to them.

- The test can be presented in two languages to enhance linguistic accessibility.

- Bilingual, monolingual, and ESL dictionaries may be used to find the meaning of appropriate words. However, these must not include explanations or definitions of content-area mathematical terminology, concepts, or skills that can provide undue advantage.

- Test administrators may prepare written bilingual glossaries of appropriate words.

- Test administrators may prepare written and pictorial ESL glossaries of appropriate words.

- Test administrators may simplify or clarify certain language used in test questions, as long as they do not refer to the content being tested.

- Pictures and gestures may be used by the test administrator to illustrate the meanings of appropriate words.

- Test administrators may provide extra time to complete the test.

Every state education agency has the option of selecting the linguistic accommodation for its ELLs. Teachers in charge of implementing these accommodations need to be sure that they comply only with the modifications allowed. Providing students more information or support can create an unfair advantage for the students, can have legal implications, and can result in civil penalties for teachers.

Some accommodations suggested have been challenged because they might provide an unfair advantage for the ELLs. For example, Abedi, Lord, Hofstetter, and Baker (2000) found that the use of a glossary and extra time to complete the examination tended to raise the performance of students in the English-only program, as well as of students learning English as a second language. The use of dictionaries in general—bilingual and English—

can also provide unfair advantages because they contain content-based information that can be used to complete the test (Stanfield & Rivera, 2001).

Assessing Special Education Students

The *Individuals with Disability Act* (IDEA) requires states to develop evaluation procedures to ensure accurate placement of students in the program. The law requires that the evaluation process for admission to special education programs contains instruments that are valid, reliable, and free of biases. Some of the other requirements to ensure that assessment process is fair and unbiased follow (cited in González, Brusca-Vega, & Yawkey, 1997):

- It is conducted using multiple instruments and techniques to evaluated suspected disability.

- It uses an assessment interdisciplinary team to interpret data.

- It uses the student's native language, if available.

- It includes all areas related to the suspected disability.

ELLs who are also receiving special education services can qualify for multiple testing accommodations to address their language and cognitive needs. The law also requires the creation of a committee to study assessment data and make appropriate placement decisions for students admitted to the program, known as admission review and dismissal (ARD). Once the child is admitted to the program, the ARD committee designs an *individualized education plan (IEP)* to address the identified needs of the child. Furthermore, the ARD committee identifies assessment accommodations based on the type of disability and the information provided in the IEP. If the child is also receiving special language services, both the ARD and the Language Proficiency Assessment Committee communicate to jointly determine language and other types of accommodations.

In addition to the appropriate linguistic accommodations previously presented, state education agencies and school districts have the options of offering the following testing modifications:

- To offer the same instrument with specific accommodations to address identified needs, that is, more time to complete the examination, reading the question out loud, modifying the testing environment, or spreading the examinations over several days

- To modify the official test or create a special test, using the same test standards, to address the needs of the group

- To exempt students from taking the examination

CONCLUSIONS

This chapter presented a description of the linguistic, developmental, and cultural components that have to be taken into account when designing and implementing assessment programs for ELLs. Some of the elements were the TESOL standards of performance, the stages of development typical of L2 learners, and the various cultural characteristics of the students. Taking into account these components, the chapter presented an analysis of assessment instruments available to assess and document language development and to gather data for reporting purposes. As a final point, it presented examples of linguistic accommodations used in the United States to improve the reliability of assessment instruments administered to special education children and ELLs.

REFERENCES

Abedi, J., C. Lord, C. Hofstetter, and E. Baker. 2000. Impact of accommodation strategies on English language learners' test performance. *Educational Measurement: Issues and Practice* 19:16–26.

Ballard, W. S., P. L. Tighe, and E. F. Dalton. 1991. *Examiner's manual IPT I, oral grades K–6, forms A, B, C, and D English*. Brea, CA: Ballard & Tighe, Publishers.

Boyd-Batstone, P. 2006. *Differentiated early literacy for English language learners: Practical strategies*. New York: Pearson.

Burt, M. K., H. C. Dulay, and E. Hernández-Chávez. 1976. *Bilingual Syntax Measure I: Technical Handbook*. San Antonio, TX: Harcourt, Brace, Jovanovich, Inc.

Clay, M. 2002. An observation survey of early literacy achievement, 2nd ed. Birkenhead, Auckland, New Zealand: Heinemann Education.

Cummins, J. 1981. The role of primary language development in promoting educational success of minority students. In *Schooling and language minority students: A theoretical framework*, ed. California State Department of Education, 3–49. Los Angeles: Evaluation, Dissemination and Assessment Center, California State University.

Georgia Department of Education. *Assessing comprehension and communication in English state to state for English language learners (ACCESS for ELLs)*. www.doe.k12.ga.us/ci_testing.aspx?PageReq=CI_TESTING_ACCESS.

González, V., R. Brusca-Vega, and T. Yawkey. 1997. Assessment and instruction of culturally and linguistically diverse students. Boston: Allyn and Bacon.

Krashen, S. D., and T. C. Terrell. 1983. The natural approach: Language acquisition in the classroom. Hayward, CA: Alemany Press.

Lapp, D., D. Fisher, J. Flood, and A. Cabello, A. 2001. An integrated approach to the teaching and assessment of language arts. In Literacy assessment of second language learners, eds. S. Rollins Hurley and J. Villamil Tinajero, 1–24. Boston: Allyn and Bacon.

McMillan, J. H. 2004. Classroom assessment: Principles and practice for effective instruction, 3rd ed. Boston: Pearson.

New York State Education Department. 2002. Accountability peer review: New York State. Albany, NY: www.ed.gov/admins/lead/account/stateplans03/nycsa.doc.

Peregoy, S. F., O. F. Boyle, and K. Cadiero-Kaplan. 2008. Reading, writing and learning in ESL: A resource book for K–12 teachers, 5th. ed. New York: Pearson.

Piper, T. 2003. Language and learning: The home and school years, 3rd ed. Columbus, OH: Merrill Prentice Hall.

Stanfield, C., and C. Rivera. 2001. Tests accommodations for LEP. College Park, MD: ERIC Clearinghouse on Assessment and Evaluation. ED458289.

TEA. Texas Education Agency. Student Assessment Division. www.tea.state.tx.us/student.assessment/taks/booklets/index.html.

TESOL revises preK–12 English language proficiency standards. 2006. TESOL (March). www.tesol.org/s_tesol/sec_document.asp?CID=1186& DID=5349#levels. USDE. 2003. President Bush, Secretary Paige celebrate approval of every state accountability plan under No Child Left Behind. www.ed.gov/news/pressreleases/2003/06/06102003 .html.

Woodcock, R. W., A. F. Muñoz-Sandoval, M. Ruef, and C. G. Alvarado. 2001. Itasca, IL: Riverside Publishing Company.

CHAPTER 5

Professional Issues

This chapter addresses the historical development, major court cases, and significant events that have affected the development of English-language learners (ELLs) in the United States. It also describes federal, state, and local policies and the development of various program models to address the needs of ELLs.

ENGLISH AS A SECOND LANGUAGE AND BILINGUAL EDUCATION

English as a second language (ESL) is a system of instruction designed to teach language to children whose native language is other than English. The term *English as a second language* evolved from foreign language instruction as part of the Americanization efforts of immigrants in the late nineteenth and early twentieth centuries (Crawford, 2004). In 1941, English as a foreign language became a field of study under the leadership of researchers at the University of Michigan (Ovando, Combs & Collier, 2006). As part of its research effort, the University of Michigan began preparing teachers to teach English abroad. In the 1960s, the field shifted its emphasis and began preparing teachers to teach English to American immigrants. With this new emphasis, the field of English as a second language was created. Following the creation of the field of study in 1966—and under the leadership of the Center for Applied Linguistics, the National Council of Teachers of English, and other organizations—the organization Teachers of Speakers of Other Languages (TESOL) was founded (Alatis, n.d). Currently, the terms *English as a second language* and *English for speakers of other languages* (ESOL) are used to describe a system of instruction used in schools to meet the needs of English language learners (ELLs).

TESOL is an international organization with more than 14,206 members representing 162 countries worldwide. The website of the organization is www.tesol.org/s_tesol/index.asp.

The National Association for Bilingual Education (NABE) is another organization that provides support to bilingual and ESL teachers in the United States and abroad. NABE is an international organization with more than 6,000 members representing the United States, Canada, the Virgin Islands, and Puerto Rico. The website of the organization is www.nabe.org.

ESL and the Curriculum

ESL is part of the curriculum in most school districts in the United States. The field is perceived as compensatory and transitional. Currently, ESL is used in two main educational settings.

It is a component of bilingual education and dual-language programs where students receive native-language instruction and language development through ESL. In transitional early-exit bilingual education models, ESL is the bridge used to move students from native-language instruction to instruction in English. In late-exit programs, like the one-way and two-way dual language, ESL is used to develop the English proficiency needed to receive instruction in a dual-language format.

ESL is also used as a program where bilingual education is not feasible because of the large number of foreign languages spoken in the district. In this case, the program is designed to scaffold instruction while students develop the English proficiency to function in the all-English classroom.

In middle school and high school, ESL can also be used as an independent course designed to promote English development or a course to comply with grade promotion and graduation requirements.

Merging Bilingual and ESL Program Models

Several programs that merge native-language instruction with ESL help meet the language needs of ELLs. A summary of these programs and a description of the role of English as a second language follow.

Early-Exit Programs (Two to Three Years)
Transitional Bilingual Education

Early-exit transitional bilingual education is the program of choice for most school districts in the United States. The main goal of the program is to move students from the bilingual to the English program (mainstreaming) as quickly as possible. This program promotes literacy and content-area instruction in the native language in grades K–2, with at least 45 minutes of ESL instruction. Traditionally, in third grade, the transition to English begins officially, and by fourth grade, students are reclassified as fluent English speakers and mainstreamed or placed in sheltered English classes. In a sheltered English class, students are placed in the English classroom with a teacher certified to teach ESL and who can provide language support as needed.

Transitional bilingual education may be implemented as an early-exit or late-exit program, depending on the time in the program. However, the term *late-exit* has also been linked to nontransitional programs identified as developmental/maintenance, bilingual-bicultural, or one-way bilingual education.

Late-Exit Dual-Language Programs (Four to Six Years)

The late-exit model describes programs that offer four or more years of dual-language support. These were originally designed for K–12; however, the programs are being implemented mostly from kindergarten through fifth or six grade. Two models are presented in this section: developmental/maintenance, or one-way dual language, and two-way immersion programs.

Developmental/Maintenance

Developmental/maintenance bilingual education is a program that emerged in the 1970s as an alternative to the transitional bilingual education (TBE) model (Crawford, 2004). The program is also known as **bilingual-bicultural education** and more recently has been labeled **one-way bilingual education**. In this model, students from the same language group learn their native language and English. In this program, children are encouraged to maintain their native language and add English to be able to function academically and socially in both languages. Opponents of bilingual education have attacked the program, alleging that it does not place sufficient emphasis on English-language development. However, research has shown that the one-way dual-language program is superior to any other form of ESL program alone (Thomas & Collier, 2002).

Two-Way Dual-Language Immersion

The two-way bilingual education program is a form of developmental bilingual education because it promotes the maintenance of both languages. The program serves language-majority (English speakers) and language-minority students in an instructional setting where both groups learn from each other in a peer-teaching situation. In addition to the language benefits of peer instruction, it contributes to a better cultural understanding among children in the group (Christian, 1994). In this program, students are perceived as gifted, as opposed to the compensatory and deficient nature of the early-exit model. The positive view of the program and the participation of language majority students in the program make funding and support more palatable to the general public.

Implementation of Dual-Language Programs

The one-way and two-way programs are implemented in a variety of ways throughout the United States. The different programs are structured based on language usage by content, teacher formats, and percentage of instruction by language.

Content

In one model, part of the content areas is delivered in the student's native language (L1) and the others in English, or the second language (L2). For example, one day social studies and sciences can be delivered in L1, and mathematics, art, and music can be presented in L2. Switching the language of instruction is often done to expose students to the content areas in both languages. Traditionally, ESL teachers are hired to deliver the English component of the program.

Teacher Formats

Teachers are generally organized in one of two ways.

Two teachers (mixed) or team teaching: In this approach, there are two separate classrooms, with one teacher delivering instruction in the minority language, and the second teacher teaching in the majority language (English). At a specific point in the day or during the week, students switch teachers. One of the benefits of this system is that students identify the teacher with a given language, and *code switching* (mixing languages) is discouraged. Traditionally, a teacher certified in ESL and with preparation in dual-language programs, delivers the English component of the program. This teacher also uses ESL techniques to be sure students are able to comprehend instruction in the majority language.

Single teacher format: In this design, one teacher alternates the use of languages across disciplines. In this model, the teacher must be fully bilingual and must guide students to separate the two languages. Because students know that the teacher is bilingual, they often switch from one language to the other; however, teachers have to make an extra effort to communicate in the language of instruction.

Percentage of Instruction

In the two-way model, a specific percentage of the instructional time is assigned to each of the two languages.

Balanced programs: the 50/50 model: In this model, students receive equal instructional time in L1 and L2. This percentage is maintained through the duration of the program. This is the second most popular model in the United States. Some 33 percent of the programs in the United States use this model (Howard & Sugarman, 2001).

Minority/majority language program: the 90/10 or 80/20 model: In this model, the largest percent of instruction is done in the minority language, which means that language-majority students (English-speaking students) are placed in an immersion format. This is the type of program used in Canada with English speakers learning French as a second language. As in the French immersion program, the amount of instruction in the majority language increases to a point where balance instruction is achieved (50/50) by third or fourth grade. This is the most popular model in the United States. About 42 percent of the programs in the United States follow this model (Howard & Sugarman, 2001).

Program Organization

The two most common formats for program organization are the *half-day* and the *one-day* alternate.

Half-day alternate bilingual program: In the half-day organization, morning lessons are delivered in one language and then switched to the second language in the afternoon. To cover all content areas in both languages, the program switches the language of the morning to the afternoon.

One-day alternate bilingual program: One full day is delivered in a given language, and the following day the content is delivered in the second language.

One-way and Two-Way Programs

The one-way and two-way programs are designed to develop bilingualism. The key distinction between the programs is the type of population they serve. The one-way program serves language-minority students with a common L1. The two-way dual-language program serves both language-minority and language-majority students.

Special Considerations

Alternate approaches to bilingual content area avoid the repetition of lessons in each language within the class period. For students with very limited proficiency in one of the languages of instruction, the alternate model may not be appropriate because such students may miss too much content during the time that teaching is in L2.

Special ESL Programs

ESL or ESOL is a component of bilingual education programs in the elementary classroom. In middle school and high school, ESL can function as an independent course or as a medium to deliver content-based instruction. A description of these programs follows.

ESL PULLOUT

One of the first approaches used in public schools to teach English to ELLs was the pullout system. In this system, students spend most of the day in mainstream (English-only) classes and are pulled out of their classes for one or two periods per day to receive English instruction. This approach is perhaps the most expensive and least effective of the ESL methods currently used (Crawford, 2004; Thomas & Collier, 1997). Although schools with a large number of ESL students may have a full-time ESL teacher, some districts employ an ESL teacher who travels to several schools to work with small groups of students scattered throughout the district. This program has been criticized for its cost and for its shortcomings. Some of the limitations of this approach are listed here (Crawford, 2004; Ovando, Combs, & Collier, 2006):

- When ELLs are pulled out, they miss classes and can fall behind academically.

- Students do not receive support in their native language; thus they are not guided to transfer knowledge from L1 to L2.

- Children might feel embarrassed for being pulled out from the mainstream program to a program viewed as remedial and compensatory.

Structured English Immersion

Structured English immersion (SEI) was conceptualized in the 1980s under the auspices of the U.S. Department of Education (USDE), the leadership of conservative members of the congress, and the English-only movement (Crawford, 2004). The origin of this method goes back to 1981 with the publication of the Baker-de Kanter report, a USDE-commissioned study on the effectiveness of TBE programs in the United States. In this report, the researchers argued that TBE programs did not provide consistent evidence of their effectiveness. Despite the multiple flaws of the study (Crawford, 2004; Ovando, Combs, & Collier, 2006), it convinced legislators to search for a different way to address the language needs of ELLs. They studied the French–English immersion programs in Canada. After analyzing the success of these programs, the researchers proposed a program similar to the Canadian model to replace TBE. The model is today known as the *structured English immersion* program. Contrary to the additive nature of the Canadian bilingual immersion programs, the SEI is a subtractive program designed to teach English only. In the self-contained ESL classroom, the teacher delivers instruction in English to ELLs. To ensure comprehension, teachers use techniques to simplify and contextualize instruction. Through the use of sheltered instruction, children learn content and language concurrently.

Sheltered English or ESL Content

This model, developed in the 1980s, represents a shift from programs that emphasize English-language development only to a more content-based ESL instruction (Crawford, 2004). This instructional approach attempts to make academic instruction in English understandable to ELLs while at the same time promoting English-language development. In this approach, teachers use hands-on activities, concrete objects, simplified speech, and physical activities to teach concept development in the content areas. Before this model, ESL teachers taught language development at the expense of content-area instruction; thus students usually fell behind academically. The approach is used mostly at the secondary level, and it is more effective for students with intermediate and advanced proficiency in English.

The program focuses on the delivery of content in contextualized situations with the addition of language objectives. Two of the better known commercial programs that emphasize content and language development are the CALLA model, developed by Chamot and O'Malley (1994), and the SIOP model developed by Echevarría, Vogt, and Short (2000). The former was developed for secondary students, and the latter addressed both the elementary and secondary levels. (See chapter 3.)

Newcomer Centers

The term *newcomer* refers to a program that addresses the needs of recent immigrants or students who are new to the English language. In this program, ESL is used to support ELLs in their linguistic and cultural adjustment to life and schooling in the United States. The program provides linguistic and psychological support to unschooled and other non-traditional ELLs. It was designed mostly for students in middle and high school; however, today it is also used at the elementary level.

The instructional language approach and methods used in newcomer programs vary by district and state. Some provide intensive English-language development, whereas others adopt a sheltered English approach where students can keep up academically while developing proficiency in English. Traditionally, students remain in the program for as little as six months or as long as three years before they are moved to mainstream classrooms.

Legal Documents and Court Cases

Three main documents provide the foundation for litigation seeking support for language minority students: Title VI of the Civil Right Act of 1964; the 1970 memorandum of the Office of Civil Rights (OCR), Department of Health, Education, and Welfare; and the Equal Education Opportunity Act (EEOA) of 1974.

Title VI of the Civil Rights Act: Title VI prohibits discrimination on the basis of race, color, or national origin in any program receiving federal financial assistance.

The OCR Memorandum: In 1970, the secretary of the Department of Health, Education, and Welfare sent a memorandum to school officials in the nation requiring districts to offer appropriate instruction to address the educational needs of language-minority students. The document also prohibited the use of data relying strictly on language as the key reason for assigning students to special education programs. Based on the historical value of the document, the OCR incorporated its content into the compliance procedure for Title VI of the Civil Rights Act of 1964 (Castro Feinberg, 1990).

Equal Educational Opportunities Act of 1974: The EEOA is a federal law that prohibits states from denying equal educational opportunity to individuals based on race, color, sex, or national origin. It also prohibits segregating students based on the same characteristics. This civil rights statute provided additional support for the Lau ruling and put more pressure on districts to offer meaningful education to ELLs. Contrary to Title VI of the Civil

Rights Act of 1964, the EEOA applied to all schools not only those receiving federal funding. Using the OCR memorandum, the Equal Opportunity Act, and the Lau ruling, the Office of Civil Rights instituted the Lau Remedies.

The three documents cited here were used as a foundation for seeking programs to support ELLs. An analysis of key federal court cases that paved the way to bilingual and ESL education follows.

Federal Court Cases

Current bilingual education program came as a result of political activism and court mandates. Some of the most important court cases that shaped bilingual education follow.

Serna v. Portales (1972 & 1974) in New Mexico was the first successful court case seeking support for bilingual education. In 1972, a federal court mandated the Portales School District in New Mexico to implement a bilingual-bicultural curriculum, revise assessment procedures to monitor Hispanic students' academic achievement, and recruit bilingual personnel. The Portales Municipal Schools appealed the decision in 1972, and in 1974, as a result of the *Lau v. Nichols* ruling, the Tenth U.S. District Court of Appeals upheld the original decision.

In ***Lau v. Nichols*** (1974), Kinney Lau, representing 1,790 Chinese students, initiated a class action suit against the San Francisco Unified School District seeking support for Chinese students who were failing school because they could not understand English. In 1974, the U.S. Supreme Court, citing the Equal Education Opportunity Act of the Civil Rights Act and the OCR Memorandum of 1970, found in favor of the plaintiffs. However, the court did not specify the remedy. It was left up to the district as how to comply with the mandates of providing "meaningful education" to ELLs. Later, in the consent decree that followed, the San Francisco School District agreed to provide bilingual/bicultural education. Despite the fact that in the Lau ruling the court did not provide a specific a remedy, this landmark case provided the momentum and foundation for other litigations in progress, and it became the de facto tool for the implementation of bilingual education in the United States.

Lau Remedies (1975): The Lau ruling received little attention until 1975 when the former Department of Health, Education, and Welfare introduced a document to guide districts in the implementation of the Lau ruling: the Lau Remedies. In this document, the federal government described the process for identification and evaluation of students in the program. It further established the criteria that school districts must not assign national-origin minorities to classes for the mentally retarded on the basis of criteria that measure language development in English. The document also mandated bilingual education for elementary schools and ESL instruction for older students. It also described the guidelines for exiting students from the program and the professional standards required for teacher participation in the program. The Lau Remedies evolved into the de facto compliance standards of the OCR. The role of the Lau Remedies ended in 1980 when President Ronald Reagan withdrew the guidelines (USDE, 1985).

Aspira v. New York (1974): Aspira, a community-based organization, sued the city of New York seeking relief for the large number of ELLs in the city. While the case was being heard, the Lau ruling was handed down, and the litigation ended in a consent decree; that is, the district agreed with the demands of the plaintiffs. The court mandated a citywide assessment and identification of students in need of special language services, and the implementation of a districtwide bilingual education program to addressed identified needs.

Rios v. Read (1977): In 1977, the issue of program quality to meet the needs of ELLs was put to the test. In this litigation, a federal court ruled that the Patchogue–Medford school district in New York had violated the rights of ELLs by providing a "half-hearted" (Crawford, 2004, p. 11) bilingual program that relied mostly on ESL and did not include a bicultural component. The court upheld the importance of teaching English to students but also indicated the need to provide meaningful education while accomplishing the language goal. This ruling clearly called for the use of L1 instruction for the content areas while developing English proficiency. The *Rios v. Read* decision provided the foundation for the development of the multiple bilingual education programs founded later in the 1980s and beyond.

Castañeda v. Pickard (1981): In 1981, the issue of program quality was addressed again in *Castañeda v. Pickard* when the school district of Raymondville in Texas was charged with violating the Equal Educational Opportunity Act of 1974. As a result of this litigation, the Fifth Court of Appeals mandated a three-step process to develop quality bilingual education programs. The court ruled that program implementation must be based on sound research background, with adequate resources, and with opportunities for students to have access to the full curriculum. The Castañeda guidelines were used as the model implementation process to enforce the Lau Remedies.

U.S. v. the State of Texas (1981/1982): As a result of this case, U.S. District Judge William Wayne Justice ordered the state of Texas to offer a bilingual education program for Mexican American students in grades K–12. In his ruling, the judge indicated that the state had segregated children to inferior schools and had "vilified" the language and culture of the Mexican American children. The ruling was reversed a year later, but as a result of the litigation, the governor of the state appointed a bilingual education task force to draft a state plan for bilingual education. The work of the task force was instrumental in the drafting of Senate Bill 477, the current bilingual education law in Texas.

Plyler v. Doe (1982): The ruling in this court case guarantees the rights of undocumented immigrants to free public education. Public schools were prohibited from denying children of undocumented workers admission to school, requiring parents of students to disclose their immigration status or requiring social security numbers. *Proposition 187* (1994): this was a ballot measure passed by California voters in 1994 as an attempt to slow down immigration. It required school personnel to report to law enforcement agencies and the U.S. Immigration Services children or personnel unable to prove their legal immigration status. Based on *Plyler v. Doe*, the reporting requirements of Proposition 187 were declared unconstitutional. The judge ruled that immigration is a federal responsibility, and states do not have the option of establishing their own system.

EVENTS THAT SHAPED THE DEVELOPMENT OF PROGRAMS FOR ELLs

The Elementary and Secondary Education Act

In 1965, the U.S. Congress enacted the Elementary and Secondary Education Act (ESEA) to provide financial support for public education. Chapter, or Title, I, one of the key components of the legislation, provided support for children from low socioeconomic backgrounds. In 1968, the legislation added Title VII, which provided funding to support programs to address the needs of ELLs. Both Title I and Title VII remained major components of the ESEA until 2001 when the law was replaced with NCLB. For 31 years, the ESEA legislation regulated the types of services and programs to address the needs of language-minority students in the nation.

English-Only Movement

In 1981, Senator S. I. Hayakawa initiated a campaign to declare English the official language of the United States and to eliminate bilingual education. This movement gained momentum during the 1980s and remains strong today. To date, 24 states have passed English-only legislation and have banned dual-language instruction.

English-Plus Movement

In 1985, the English-plus movement was founded by the League of United Latin American Citizens (LULAC) and the Spanish American League Against Discrimination (SALAD) as a reaction against the English-only movement. The influence of these groups resulted in the increase of funding for bilingual education in 1994 and propelled interest in the growth of developmental and two-way dual-language programs in the nation.

Official Endorsement of Dual-Language Instruction

In 2000, the outgoing secretary of the Department of Education, Bill Riley, officially endorsed dual language education.

> Proficiency in English and one other language is something that we need to encourage among all young people. That is why I am delighted to see and highlight the growth and promise of so many dual-language bilingual programs across the country. . . . That is why I am challenging our nation to increase the number of dual-language schools to at least 1,000 over the next five years, and with strong federal, state, and local support we can have many more. www.ed.gov/Speeches/03-2000/000315 .html.

Unfortunately, this official endorsement of dual language did not help the development of these programs. Instead, with the new Republican administrations, early exit programs and ESL became the program of choice to serve the needs of ELLs.

The No Child Left Behind Act (NCLB)

The NCLB legislation replaced ESEA of 1965. The legislation contains two components that affect directly the education of language-minority students, Title I and Title III (formerly known as Title VII). Title I requires school districts to hire highly qualified teachers. This regulation was fully enforced in 2006 when school districts were required to provide evidence that teachers serving poor language-minority students were fully certified and proficient in the languages used for instruction.

The Bilingual Education Act was renamed *the English Language Acquisition, Language Enhancement, and Academic Achievement Act* (Title III). The aim of the legislation is to promote English-language development, but it allowed for local flexibility in the implementation of programs. In the legislation, the terms *bilingual education* and *dual-language education* were systematically replaced by *English-language acquisition and development*. This action suggests that the main purpose of the legislation was to promote English-language development and to rapidly move children to the English-mainstream classroom.

Following are some of the key components of the legislation:

- Consolidated services and funding for language-minority students with the Emergency Immigrant Education Program

- Made local education agencies (LEAs) responsible for the English-language growth of ELLs

- Allowed LEAs the flexibility to choose the method of instruction to teach ELLs

- Provided funds to the states based on a formula using the number of ELLs and immigrant students identified in the state and reported to the federal government.

- Provided that funds be sent to state education agencies, which in turn distribute funds to LEAs

- Recognized the important role of parents in the education of their children

- Required LEAs to inform parents of the rationale for placing students in special language programs

- Granted parents the right to agree or disagree with LEA decisions

- Required school districts to use 95 percent of the funding for direct instruction for ELLs

- Required mandatory testing in English for reading and language arts for ELLs who have attended school in the United States for at least three consecutive years

- Mandated federal accountability systems to ensure that school districts provide effective instruction to ELLs

Based on the accountability system, districts are required to develop annual measurable achievement objectives to monitor progress in attaining English proficiency, and to notify parents if the program fails to meet objectives for two consecutive years. The legislation also established that after four years of failing to meet the objectives, the state will require LEAs to modify their curriculum, program, and methods of instruction. If the situation is not solved, the entity can lose federal funding. Furthermore, entities receiving funding are required to conduct an evaluation every year on the progress students are making toward mastery of English and achieving the same levels of academic achievement as other students are.

The Presidential Election of 2008

During one of his speeches in 2008, then-candidate Barack Obama endorsed bilingualism as one of the best alternatives to teach not only immigrants but also American children in general.

> I agree that immigrants should learn English. . . . But instead of you worrying about whether immigrants can learn English . . . you need to make sure that your child speaks Spanish. You should be thinking about how can your child become bilingual. We should have every child speaking more than one language. (Obama, July 8, 2008, Powder Spring, GA)

The election of Barack Obama to the presidency of the nation brings high hopes for the development of new programs for language-minority students. His endorsement of bilingualism suggests that dual-language instruction will take center stage as a program to meet the needs of ELLs in the United States.

For a comprehensive list of terminology related to linguistically diverse students and bilingual and ESL education, go the OELA's website:

www.ncela.gwu.edu/expert/glossary.html#developmentalbilingual.

CONCLUSIONS

This chapter addressed the historical development, major court cases, and significant events that affected the development of ELLs in the United States. It also described the federal, state, and local policies and the development of the various program models to address the needs of ELLs. Finally, it presented an analysis of major events that shaped the development of program for ELLs in the United States, including the presidential election of 2008.

REFERENCES

Alatis, J. E. *The early history of TESOL*. TESOL website. www.tesol.org/s_tesol/sec_document.asp?CID=674&DID=2728.

Castro Feinberg, R. 1990. Bilingual education in the United States. A summary of Lau compliance requirements. *Language, Culture and Curriculum* 3:141–52.

Chamot, A., and J. M. O'Malley. 1994. *The CALLA handbook: Implementing the cognitive academic language learning approach*. Reading: MA: Addison-Wesley Publishing Company.

Christian, D. 1994. *Two-way bilingual education: Students learning through two languages*. Education Practice Report 12. Washington, DC: Center for Applied Linguistics.

Crawford, J. 2004. *Educating English learners: Language diversity in the classroom*, 5th ed. Los Angeles: Bilingual Education Services, Inc.

Echevarría, J., M. Vogt, and D. Short. 2000. *Marking content comprehensible for English language learners: the SIOP model*. Needham Heights, MA: Allyn & Bacon.

Howard, E. R., and J. Sugarman. 2001. *Two-way immersion programs: Features and statistics*. Washington, DC: Center for Applied Linguistics. www.cal.org/resources/digest/0101twi.html.

Ovando, C. J., M. C. Combs, and V. P. Collier. 2006. *Bilingual and ESL classrooms: Teaching in multicultural contexts*, 4th ed. Boston, MA: McGraw-Hill.

Palincsar, A. S. 1986. Reciprocal teaching. In *Teaching reading as thinking*. Oak Brook, IL: North Central Regional Educational Laboratory.

Riley, R. W. 2000. *Excelencia para todos—Excellence for all: The progress of Hispanic education and the challenges of a new century*. Speech delivered March 2000 at Bell Multicultural High School, Washington, D.C. www.ed.gov/Speeches/03-2000/000315.html.

Thomas, W., and V. Collier. 1997. *School effectiveness for language minority students*. NCBE Resource Collection Series No. 9. Washington, D.C.: National Clearing-house for Bilingual Education.

Thomas, W., and V. Collier. 2002. *A national study of school effectiveness for language minority students' long term academic achievement*. Santa Cruz, CA: Center for Research on Education, Diversity, and Excellence.

USDE. 1985. *Developing programs for English language learners: Guidance document*. U.S. Department of Education. www.ed.gov/about/offices/list/ocr/ell/december3.html.

Practice Test 1

Praxis English to Speakers of Other Languages (0360)

1. Ⓐ Ⓑ Ⓒ Ⓓ
2. Ⓐ Ⓑ Ⓒ Ⓓ
3. Ⓐ Ⓑ Ⓒ Ⓓ
4. Ⓐ Ⓑ Ⓒ Ⓓ
5. Ⓐ Ⓑ Ⓒ Ⓓ
6. Ⓐ Ⓑ Ⓒ Ⓓ
7. Ⓐ Ⓑ Ⓒ Ⓓ
8. Ⓐ Ⓑ Ⓒ Ⓓ
9. Ⓐ Ⓑ Ⓒ Ⓓ
10. Ⓐ Ⓑ Ⓒ Ⓓ
11. Ⓐ Ⓑ Ⓒ Ⓓ
12. Ⓐ Ⓑ Ⓒ Ⓓ
13. Ⓐ Ⓑ Ⓒ Ⓓ
14. Ⓐ Ⓑ Ⓒ Ⓓ
15. Ⓐ Ⓑ Ⓒ Ⓓ
16. Ⓐ Ⓑ Ⓒ Ⓓ
17. Ⓐ Ⓑ Ⓒ Ⓓ
18. Ⓐ Ⓑ Ⓒ Ⓓ
19. Ⓐ Ⓑ Ⓒ Ⓓ
20. Ⓐ Ⓑ Ⓒ Ⓓ
21. Ⓐ Ⓑ Ⓒ Ⓓ
22. Ⓐ Ⓑ Ⓒ Ⓓ
23. Ⓐ Ⓑ Ⓒ Ⓓ
24. Ⓐ Ⓑ Ⓒ Ⓓ
25. Ⓐ Ⓑ Ⓒ Ⓓ
26. Ⓐ Ⓑ Ⓒ Ⓓ
27. Ⓐ Ⓑ Ⓒ Ⓓ
28. Ⓐ Ⓑ Ⓒ Ⓓ
29. Ⓐ Ⓑ Ⓒ Ⓓ
30. Ⓐ Ⓑ Ⓒ Ⓓ

31. Ⓐ Ⓑ Ⓒ Ⓓ
32. Ⓐ Ⓑ Ⓒ Ⓓ
33. Ⓐ Ⓑ Ⓒ Ⓓ
34. Ⓐ Ⓑ Ⓒ Ⓓ
35. Ⓐ Ⓑ Ⓒ Ⓓ
36. Ⓐ Ⓑ Ⓒ Ⓓ
37. Ⓐ Ⓑ Ⓒ Ⓓ
38. Ⓐ Ⓑ Ⓒ Ⓓ
39. Ⓐ Ⓑ Ⓒ Ⓓ
40. Ⓐ Ⓑ Ⓒ Ⓓ
41. Ⓐ Ⓑ Ⓒ Ⓓ
42. Ⓐ Ⓑ Ⓒ Ⓓ
43. Ⓐ Ⓑ Ⓒ Ⓓ
44. Ⓐ Ⓑ Ⓒ Ⓓ
45. Ⓐ Ⓑ Ⓒ Ⓓ
46. Ⓐ Ⓑ Ⓒ Ⓓ
47. Ⓐ Ⓑ Ⓒ Ⓓ
48. Ⓐ Ⓑ Ⓒ Ⓓ
49. Ⓐ Ⓑ Ⓒ Ⓓ
50. Ⓐ Ⓑ Ⓒ Ⓓ
51. Ⓐ Ⓑ Ⓒ Ⓓ
52. Ⓐ Ⓑ Ⓒ Ⓓ
53. Ⓐ Ⓑ Ⓒ Ⓓ
54. Ⓐ Ⓑ Ⓒ Ⓓ
55. Ⓐ Ⓑ Ⓒ Ⓓ
56. Ⓐ Ⓑ Ⓒ Ⓓ
57. Ⓐ Ⓑ Ⓒ Ⓓ
58. Ⓐ Ⓑ Ⓒ Ⓓ
59. Ⓐ Ⓑ Ⓒ Ⓓ
60. Ⓐ Ⓑ Ⓒ Ⓓ

61. Ⓐ Ⓑ Ⓒ Ⓓ
62. Ⓐ Ⓑ Ⓒ Ⓓ
63. Ⓐ Ⓑ Ⓒ Ⓓ
64. Ⓐ Ⓑ Ⓒ Ⓓ
65. Ⓐ Ⓑ Ⓒ Ⓓ
66. Ⓐ Ⓑ Ⓒ Ⓓ
67. Ⓐ Ⓑ Ⓒ Ⓓ
68. Ⓐ Ⓑ Ⓒ Ⓓ
69. Ⓐ Ⓑ Ⓒ Ⓓ
70. Ⓐ Ⓑ Ⓒ Ⓓ
71. Ⓐ Ⓑ Ⓒ Ⓓ
72. Ⓐ Ⓑ Ⓒ Ⓓ
73. Ⓐ Ⓑ Ⓒ Ⓓ
74. Ⓐ Ⓑ Ⓒ Ⓓ
75. Ⓐ Ⓑ Ⓒ Ⓓ
76. Ⓐ Ⓑ Ⓒ Ⓓ
77. Ⓐ Ⓑ Ⓒ Ⓓ
78. Ⓐ Ⓑ Ⓒ Ⓓ
79. Ⓐ Ⓑ Ⓒ Ⓓ
80. Ⓐ Ⓑ Ⓒ Ⓓ
81. Ⓐ Ⓑ Ⓒ Ⓓ
82. Ⓐ Ⓑ Ⓒ Ⓓ
83. Ⓐ Ⓑ Ⓒ Ⓓ
84. Ⓐ Ⓑ Ⓒ Ⓓ
85. Ⓐ Ⓑ Ⓒ Ⓓ
86. Ⓐ Ⓑ Ⓒ Ⓓ
87. Ⓐ Ⓑ Ⓒ Ⓓ
88. Ⓐ Ⓑ Ⓒ Ⓓ
89. Ⓐ Ⓑ Ⓒ Ⓓ
90. Ⓐ Ⓑ Ⓒ Ⓓ

91. Ⓐ Ⓑ Ⓒ Ⓓ
92. Ⓐ Ⓑ Ⓒ Ⓓ
93. Ⓐ Ⓑ Ⓒ Ⓓ
94. Ⓐ Ⓑ Ⓒ Ⓓ
95. Ⓐ Ⓑ Ⓒ Ⓓ
96. Ⓐ Ⓑ Ⓒ Ⓓ
97. Ⓐ Ⓑ Ⓒ Ⓓ
98. Ⓐ Ⓑ Ⓒ Ⓓ
99. Ⓐ Ⓑ Ⓒ Ⓓ
100. Ⓐ Ⓑ Ⓒ Ⓓ
101. Ⓐ Ⓑ Ⓒ Ⓓ
102. Ⓐ Ⓑ Ⓒ Ⓓ
103. Ⓐ Ⓑ Ⓒ Ⓓ
104. Ⓐ Ⓑ Ⓒ Ⓓ
105. Ⓐ Ⓑ Ⓒ Ⓓ
106. Ⓐ Ⓑ Ⓒ Ⓓ
107. Ⓐ Ⓑ Ⓒ Ⓓ
108. Ⓐ Ⓑ Ⓒ Ⓓ
109. Ⓐ Ⓑ Ⓒ Ⓓ
110. Ⓐ Ⓑ Ⓒ Ⓓ
111. Ⓐ Ⓑ Ⓒ Ⓓ
112. Ⓐ Ⓑ Ⓒ Ⓓ
113. Ⓐ Ⓑ Ⓒ Ⓓ
114. Ⓐ Ⓑ Ⓒ Ⓓ
115. Ⓐ Ⓑ Ⓒ Ⓓ
116. Ⓐ Ⓑ Ⓒ Ⓓ
117. Ⓐ Ⓑ Ⓒ Ⓓ
118. Ⓐ Ⓑ Ⓒ Ⓓ
119. Ⓐ Ⓑ Ⓒ Ⓓ
120. Ⓐ Ⓑ Ⓒ Ⓓ

120 QUESTIONS
120 MINUTES

SECTION I. ANALYSIS OF STUDENT LANGUAGE PRODUCTION

Directions: In this part of the test you are asked to read and answer questions regarding problems with the student's use of grammar or vocabulary reflected in their speech. We begin with a short recording of the English spoken by a non-native speaker. We encourage you to follow along with the transcript in your book to help you remember what you hear. After listening to the student's speech, please read and answer the questions about the student's grammar or vocabulary in the time allotted; mark them on your answer sheet. We suggest that you make notes on the printed transcripts as you listen to the recordings.

Part A: Grammar and Vocabulary

Approximate time — 10 minutes

For Question 1, listen as a student talks about a visit to the Statue of Liberty.

Um, because, uh, it was . . . a . . . second time in, uh, I, I walk around very, uh, um, interesting and take a . . . a . . . picture.

1. The speech sample does NOT contain an error in the use of

   (A) articles.
   (B) past tense.
   (C) adjectives.
   (D) sentence structures

For Question 2, listen as a student answers the question: "When did you move here?"

About two months.

2. Based on the student's reply to the question, which of the following can be said?

(A) The student is in the telegraphic stage.
(B) The student does not understand the question.
(C) The student fails to use "ago" to follow expressions of time.
(D) The student has no knowledge of word order.

For Question 3, listen as a student talks about visiting an interesting place.

Um, I went to a place called Jeju Island, and it's part of Korea's island.

3. The error in the student's statement involves

   (A) redundancy.
   (B) ambiguity.
   (C) subject-verb agreement.
   (D) irrelevance.

For Question 4, listen as a student describes an activity yesterday after school.

I swam three times, so I'm not . . . I'm really sensitive with my fat, so when I was young I was <u>overweighted</u>, so I kept exercising, exercising, and I like to swim.

4. The underlined word shows an error that is a result of

    (A) simplification.
    (B) overgeneralization.
    (C) code-switching.
    (D) transfer.

For Question 5, listen as a student talks about the advantages of studying abroad.

And studying here is we're advantage because oh, I can learn American history and, um, other things, like science of volcano or earthquake.

5. In this speech sample, the student has difficulty using the word "advantage"

    (A) in a meaningful way.
    (B) in a grammatical way.
    (C) in a logical way.
    (D) with an intelligible pronunciation.

For Question 6, listen as a student describes what occurs on her first day of school.

My grandmother came to me, and she send me some flower.

6. This speech sample does NOT contain errors in

    (A) past tenses.
    (B) pronoun-antecedent agreement.
    (C) parallelism with tenses.
    (D) plural forms.

For Question 7, listen as a student answers a question that asks, "Describe what you did yesterday after school."

I went here.

7. The student's reply indicates

    (A) a failure to comprehend the question
    (B) an error in the choice of the verb
    (C) that the student does not want to answer the question
    (D) an error in the tense

For Question 8, listen as a student confirms that there is a Disneyland in El Salvador.

Yeah, but not many people get to go since it's kind of a poverty country.

8. The speech sample indicates that the student has not mastered which of the following?

    (A) Modification of a noun
    (B) Modification of a verb
    (C) Construction of comparative
    (D) Use of negation

For Question 9, listen as a student is asked to describe her activities yesterday after school.

Um, almost went to our . . . <u>can I do of today</u>?

9. The underlined sentence presents an error with

    (A) the use of modals
    (B) an addition of a preposition
    (C) verbs
    (D) the placement of the time

For Question 10, listen as a student describes events after school.

Um, I went to library and, uh, Halloween costume store.

10. The speech sample indicates that the student has not mastered whch of the following?

(A) Forms of regular verbs
(B) Forms of irregular verbs
(C) Uses of articles
(D) Noun modifiers

This is the End of Part A.

Go to Part B on the Next Page.

SECTION I. ANALYSIS OF STUDENT LANGUAGE PRODUCTION

Part B: Pronunciation
Approximate time — 10 minutes

Directions: In this part of the test you will listen to more speeches by English speakers of other languages. First, you will hear a short speech. To help you remember what you heard a transcript of the recording is printed in your test book. Then, you will read the question about the student's problem with pronunciation. To help you answer each question, the recorded speech will be played a second time. Then you will be asked to answer the question and mark it on your answer sheet.

Again, it is strongly recommended that you make notes on the printed transcripts as you listen to the recordings.

For Question 11, listen as a student reads from a passage about bilingualism.

We have to support and establish political organizations to pressure our <u>legislators</u> to change this archaic policy of our education system.

11. Which of the following represents the student's pronunciation of the "g" sound in the underlined word?

    (A) [g]
    (B) [k]
    (C) [ʤ]
    (D) [d]

For Question 12, listen as a student reads from a passage about the linguistic development of immigrants.

The United States was established by people who spoke different languages, and this linguistic pluralism did not affect the development of the country.

12. The repetition of the word "pluralism" in the speech sample indicates the student's attempt to

(A) create sound effect.
(B) self-correct.
(C) emphasize the word.
(D) seek help.

For Question 13, listen as a student reads the following sentence.
This <u>policy</u> has not affected their political integrity.

13. Which of the following shows the student's pronunciation of the underlined word?

    (A) [ˈpɑləsi]
    (B) [pəˈlaɪsi]
    (C) [ˈpaɪləsi]
    (D) [poˈlosi]

For Question 14, listen as a student reads from a passage about a language policy of the U.S.
The United States needs to adopt a more proactive linguistic policy for the teaching and maintenance of <u>foreign</u> languages in the nation's public schools.

14. Which of the following shows the student's pronunciation of the underlined word?

    (A) [ˈfɔrɪn]
    (B) [ˈfɔren]

(C) [´fɔrgən]

(D) [´fɔrʤən]

(C) [ə´blot]

(D) [ə´baʊt]

For Question 15, listen as a student reads from a passage about language policy.

The policy that <u>prohibits</u> the teaching foreign languages in some states is archaic and lacks vision.

15. Which of the following occurs when the student pronounces the underlined word?

(A) Insertion of a syllable

(B) Deletion of a syllable

(C) Deletion of a consonant sound

(D) Repetition of a syllable

For Question 16, listen as a student reads from a passage about a language policy of the U.S.

The United States is one of the few countries in the world with a policy that restricts the development of <u>bilingualism</u>.

16. In the speech sample, the underlined word illustrates the student's problem with

(A) producing the /r/ sound

(B) consonant clusters

(C) placing of stress

(D) word final /s/ sounds

For Question 17, listen as a student reads the following passage.

Sometimes when Americans travel <u>abroad</u>, they don't make an effort to speak the language of the nation visited.

17. In which of the following ways does the student pronounce the underlined word?

(A) [ə´brɔd]

(B) [ə´bɔrd]

For Question 18, listen as a student reads the following passage.

We need to get organized and <u>pressure</u> our legislators to change this linguistic policy.

18. Which of the following occurs when the student utters the underlined word?

(A) Substitutes [i] for [ɛ]

(B) Substitutes [ʒ] for [ʃ]

(C) Substitutes [i] for [ə]

(D) Shifts the word stress

For Question 19, listen as a student reads the following sentence.

A lot of people think that the maintenance of foreign languages in the United States can <u>lead</u> to political fragmentation.

19. Which of the following indicates how the student pronounces the vowel of the underlined word?

(A) [ɛ]

(B) [o]

(C) [i]

(D) [æ]

For Question 20, listen as a student reads the following sentence.

The United States needs to adopt a more proactive linguistic policy for the teaching and <u>maintenance</u> of foreign languages in the nation's public schools.

20. In the underlined word, the student demonstrates

(A) a substitute of synonyms.
(B) an avoidance of unfamiliar words.
(C) a stylistic variation.
(D) a misplacement of word stress.

STOP
This is the End of the Recorded Portion of the
Test.
Go To Part C Below.
END OF RECORDING

SECTION I. ANALYSIS OF STUDENT LANGUAGE PRODUCTION

Part C: Writing
Approximate time — 7 minutes

Directions: The questions in this part refer to a number of excerpts from writings by ESOL students. Choose the best answer to each question and mark it on your answer sheet.

Question 21 is based on the following message from a student's comments on an exam.

There were three essay questions. Some students had a hard time and took a long time to finish it. I finished it in a rush because I had prepared the exam and practiced a lot. The exam was a piece of pie.

21. Based on the writing sample, the student needs to focus on the use of

   (A) past tense
   (B) idiomatic expressions
   (C) plurals
   (D) prepositions

Question 22 is based on the following passage from a student's essay about English learning experience.

I arrived to the United States one year ago. I am interest to study English. I am learning English at school, but I also listen to music and watch English TV programs. I think I am good to listening, but not good to speaking.

22. This writing sample contains errors of

   (A) prepositions
   (B) past tense
   (C) pronouns
   (D) progressive

Question 23 is based on the following excerpt from a student's essay about a career plan.

When I was 7 years old, my mother took me went to a concert. The pianist played beautiful. I decided to learning piano after listened to music. My mother brought me a piano. My teacher came to my house taught me played every Sunday. I dreamed I will play very good in the future.

23. The writing sample shows that the student needs instruction on which two of the following areas?

   I. Subject-verb agreement
   II. Use of adverbials
   III. Past tense forms
   IV. Use of an infinitive

   (A) I and II
   (B) I and III
   (C) III and IV
   (D) II and IV

Question 24 is based on the following excerpt from a student's essay about family.

My big brother studies in a university. He is in the fourth grade. He will finish his studies and will become a graduate student in May. He hopes he can find a good job soon.

24. In this writing sample, the most prevalent errors include

(A) verb tense
(B) vocabulary
(C) use of prepositions
(D) use of adverbials

Question 25 is based on the following excerpt from a student's shopping experience.

I like to go window shopping because I don't like to spend too much money. One day I saw a very cute doll when I passed by a store. The store is very big and has many furnitures. I went in and asked how much the doll cost. The lady told me it was two fifty. I was very happy and gave her the exact amount—two dollars bills and fifty cents. The lady stared at me and said it was two hundreds and fifty dollars.

25. On the basis of the writing sample, this student has not mastered

(A) American culture
(B) how to haggle
(C) how to count
(D) the use of plurals

Question 26 is based on the following excerpt from a student's account getting a book.

Last week my younger sister called me and telled me that she needed a good grammar book. I finded a good book yesterday. So, I buyed the book and sended it to her this morning. The person at the post office sayed that the book will get to my sister in a week.

26. Based on this sample, this student does not appear to have mastered the concept of

(A) past tense
(B) placement of adverbs of time
(C) past-tense forms of irregular verbs
(D) prepositional phrases

Question 27 is based on the following excerpt from a student's essay about cultural differences.

In my country, you can see many homeless dogs on street. Most people don't care and they run around on street and look scary. Here, many people have dogs and they walk with dogs. They don't run around and they don't look scary.

27. Based on the weakness in the above excerpt, which of the following might be the first step to improve the student's writing?

(A) Correcting the errors for the student.
(B) Not pointing out the problem but assigning a low grade.
(C) Reading the essay to the class and allowing the fellow students to correct the errors.
(D) Reading the essay to the student and allowing the student to identify the problem.

Question 28 is based on the following excerpt from a student's essay about books.

I think the most interesting books are novels that they are terrifying. I know many people who they like to read terrifying novels. Sometimes, it is scary to read a story by myself. I will read together with my friends who they also like to read.

28. This writing sample shows several errors in the construction of

(A) relative clauses
(B) comparison
(C) superlatives
(D) prepositional phrases

Questions 29–30 are based on the following excerpt from a student's essay about a telephone call.

Someone called and I didn't ask who was because I thought she was my classmate Nancy. She didn't ask me who was I because she thought I was my sister. She asked me where was I going this weekend and we talked about an interesting movie. I asked when did she want to see the movie and she said now. So I went to the movie theater, but I didn't see Nancy. I went home and called her, but she was not home. I thought she was waiting for me. So, I went to the movie theater again.

29. Based on the writing sample, the student has not mastered

   (A) relative clauses.
   (B) wh-interrogatives.
   (C) embedded questions.
   (D) subject-verb inversion.

30. The student's errors are instances of

   (A) simplification.
   (B) overgeneralization.
   (C) code-switching.
   (D) transfer.

This is the End of Section I.

**Go On To Section II,
Read the Directions and
Begin Work On The
Questions In That Section.**

SECTION II: LANGUAGE THEORY AND TEACHING

Approximate Time: 60 minutes

31. The key feature of linking verbs is that they

   (A) receive the action of the verb.
   (B) link the subject of the sentence with a direct object.
   (C) cannot take objects.
   (D) can take a direct object.

32. Identify the phonetic symbol of the International Phonetic Alphabet (IPA) used to represent the following sound

   Oral, voiceless, fricative and interdental

   (A) /t/
   (B) /θ/
   (C) /ð/
   (D) /z/

33. What makes the following three sets of phonemes different from each other?

   /k/ and /g/; /s/ and /z/; /f/ and /v/

   (A) Voicing
   (B) Place of articulation
   (C) Manner of articulation
   (D) Oral vs. Nasal

34. The terms *stop*, *fricative*, and *affricate* are terms used to describe

   (A) the place of articulations for vowels.
   (B) the manner of articulation for consonants.
   (C) the place and manner of articulation for English phonemes.
   (D) the types of English morphemes.

35. How many voiced sounds does the word *although* contain?

    (A) 3
    (B) 1
    (C) 8
    (D) 4

36. Identify the number of voiced phonemes in the word *jumping*.

    (A) two
    (B) four
    (C) five
    (D) six

37. What does the International Phonetic Alphabet (IPA) use to represent the initial sound of the word *job*?

    (A) /ʃ/
    (B) /ʒ/
    (C) /tʃ/
    (D) /dʒ/

38. A child having problems with labio-dental sounds might have problems pronouncing the following set of minimal pairs.

    (A) very—berry
    (B) fine—vine
    (C) park—spark
    (D) tank—bank

39. How are the vowels in the words *feet* [fit] and *fool* [ful] classified?

    (A) The first /i/ is classified as a high, back, unrounded and the /u/ is classified as a mid, front unrounded.
    (B) The first /i/ is classified as a high, front, unrounded and the /u/ is classified as a high, back rounded.
    (C) Both the /i/ and /u/ are classified as high, back, unrounded sounds.

    (D) Both the /i/ and /u/ sounds are classified low, back, rounded sounds

40. What is the term *high back* describing when referring to vowels?

    (A) It describes how high is the tongue in the mouth and the part of the tongue involved in the production of the sound.
    (B) It describes how tense is the sound and the vibration of the tongue in the production of the sound.
    (C) It describes how high is the pitch and the length of the sound.
    (D) It describes the level of obstruction and friction required to produce the sounds.

41. The vowel sounds of the following three words represent examples of

    Boy /ɔj/, cow /aw/, by /aj/

    (A) fricative sounds
    (B) diphthongs
    (C) unstressed vowels
    (D) voiceless consonants

42. Tonal languages like Chinese, Thai, and Burmese use _____ to change word meaning.

    (A) context
    (B) tone at the syllable level
    (C) intonation patterns
    (D) allophones

43. English homographs can use _____ to change the meaning of words.

    (A) context
    (B) word stress
    (C) rhythm
    (D) phonemes

44. Traditionally, content words are stressed in sentences more frequently than function words. What is the rationale for this practice?

    (A) Function words are more frequently used in English than content words.
    (B) Content words are usually more sophisticated than function words.
    (C) Function words are not native of the English language.
    (D) Content words can convey more information than function words.

45. Identify the statement that best summarizes the research findings associated with the development of proficiency in L2 and age of initial exposure to the language.

    (A) Children exposed to the second language before puberty develop native-like pronunciation in the second language.
    (B) Children who are exposed to a second language after puberty will develop a similar language proficiency level as children who came in contact with the L2 at an earlier age.
    (C) Children exposed to L2 after puberty master pronunciation, grammar and reading better than younger children.
    (D) Children may have advantages over adults in the mastery of pronunciation, but adults might have an advantage in the acquisition of the abstract components of language.

46. ELLs go through specific stages of second language acquisition. These stages are pre-production, early production, speech emergence, and intermediate and advanced fluency. Identify the stage where students begin to understand written information accompanied by concrete objects and based on prior experiences.

    (A) Pre-production
    (B) Early production
    (C) Speech emergence

    (D) Intermediate Fluency

47. The development of second language proficiency is best achieved when

    (A) the language of instruction leads to the development of functional communication skills in L2.
    (B) the language is taught deductively by involving students with activities in which they use language and derive language principles in a conscious manner.
    (C) instruction is contextualized and presented together with meaningful memorization drills.
    (D) students are exposed to idiomatic expressions and tongue twisters to facilitate communication.

48. Mary is a middle school ELL without prior schooling in L1. She is having problems with the graphophonemic cuing system of English. She can recognize the name and logos of stores and a few sight words, but she cannot decode written communication. Based on this information, Mary is having problems with the

    (A) grapheme-morpheme correspondence.
    (B) alphabetic principle of L1 and L2.
    (C) letter-sound correspondence.
    (D) sound system in L2.

49. Second language learners often experience problems with the semantic and cultural components of the English language. What language component will most likely be impacted by this situation?

    (A) The use and understanding of figurative language or idioms.
    (B) The application of phonological analysis.
    (C) The use of syntactic and phonological components.

(D) The application of the lexical and structural components.

50. The alphabetic principle describes children's ability to understand that

(A) English and other European languages are alphabetic languages.

(B) letters and letter combinations represent specific sounds.

(C) children need to memorize the alphabet prior to the introduction of formal reading.

(D) learning the alphabet is a prerequisite for the introduction of dictionary skills.

51. Knowledge of common cognates between L1 and L2 can support reading comprehension. What are cognates?

(A) Words with similar or identical spelling and meaning in two languages.

(B) Homophones in the two languages.

(C) Homographs in the two languages.

(D) Words that are spelled similarly in two languages but have different meaning.

52. Speakers of Russian, Italian and Spanish have a tendency to follow an associational approach in oral and written communication. Based on this feature, identify the components of a "speaking checklist" that might penalize speakers of these languages.

(A) provide support for the subject

(B) answer questions effectively

(C) stay within the given topic

(D) volunteers to answer questions

53. Identify the number of syllables and the number of phonemes present in the word *thought*.

(A) Two syllables and three phonemes

(B) One syllable and three phonemes

(C) Three syllables and six phonemes

(D) Two syllables and three phonemes

54. Identify the number of morphemes present in the word *subconsciously*.

(A) Three morphemes

(B) Two morphemes

(C) Four morphemes

(D) Five morphemes

55. Identify the syntactic structure that represents the following sentence: Mary gave me a dollar.

(A) Noun + Intransitive Verb + Predicative Nominative

(B) Noun + Intransitive Verb + Predicative Adjective

(C) Noun + Transitive Verb + Indirect Object + Direct Object

(D) Noun Transitive Verb   Direct Object

56. Syllabic writing systems are more efficient than purely pictographic writing systems because

(A) pictographic representations are no longer used in modern society.

(B) syllabic writing systems can represent an infinite number of words with a finite number of syllables.

(C) Syllabic writing systems are easier to understand than pictographic writing systems.

(D) Pictographic writing systems represent an evolution of the concept of writing and its simplicity can interfere with the delivery of messages.

57. Identify the set of words that best represents the concept of consonant diagraphs.

(A) Blue and blew

(B) write and gnat

(C) scream and first

(D) cat and bag

Read the scenario below and answer Question 58.

Elizabeth, an advanced ESL learner from Puerto Rico, is experiencing adjustment problems in school. Since she learned academic English in Puerto Rico, her vocabulary is always very formal. Students say that she uses "book English." Her peers often make jokes vocabulary choice during social gatherings. They call her "the professor."

58. What type of communicative competence is Elizabeth lacking?

   (A) Grammatical
   (B) Sociolinguistic
   (C) Discourse
   (D) Strategic

59. Prior to reading a story, Mr. Sherman introduces key vocabulary of the story and explains the idioms used in the story. What is the main benefit of this pre-reading activity for ELLs?

   (A) Children develop reading fluency and comprehension faster.
   (B) Children are exposed to the schemata needed to understand the story.
   (C) Children learn and apply decoding skills in reading in a subconscious manner.
   (D) Children develop reading and writing skills concurrently.

60. One of the key advantages of using learning logs in the ESL classroom is to

   (A) provide a comprehensive list of elements learned during a grading period.
   (B) guide students to synthesize the content learned in class and identify areas in need of further support.
   (C) develop an advanced organizer to communicate orally with teachers and peers.

   (D) guide students make oral presentations describing elements that they have learned in class.

61. Prior to teaching the science concepts of the day, Mr. Panetta uses a KWL chart to explore the knowledge that children bring to the lesson as a foundation for lesson of the day. What is the purpose of this activity?

   (A) To compare the vocabulary that the child brings to the lesson and the one required to understand it.
   (B) To expand the schemata needed to comprehend new contents.
   (C) To facilitate the process of second language acquisition.
   (D) To provide students with the vocabulary needed to understand the lesson.

62. Mr. Panetta, a high school teacher in Virginia, notices that ESL students are having problems understanding the concept of "global warming." To address the problem, he developed a semantic map. He uses semantic maps to

   (A) teach science concepts to ELLs.
   (B) identify critical features of a given concept.
   (C) establish connections between concepts in L1 and L2.
   (D) present a graphic representation of a process.

63. Marisela developed a study guide to be sure that she can synthesize content knowledge and to check how much she knows about the content of a given class. What strategy is she using?

   (A) cognitive
   (B) social
   (C) metacognitive
   (D) memory

64. Joe is literate in his native language and he possesses a strong background in mathematics, social studies and science. Once he arrived in the United States he automatically began using the knowledge that he acquired in his native language as a foundation for learning new concepts in English. What strategy is he using?

   (A) metacognitive

   (B) cognitive

   (C) social

   (D) mnemonic

65. One of the most important strategies to help students gather information from textbooks is to

   (A) teach the technical vocabulary needed to understand the content.

   (B) teach the format used in textbooks and discuss how information is presented.

   (C) teach cognates in L1 and L2 and explain how this knowledge can facilitate the understanding of new concepts.

   (D) provide a glossary of terms related to the content areas.

66. Effective approaches for teaching English as a second language are

   (A) student-centered and communication driven.

   (B) sequenced based on the complexity of the grammatical structures and teacher-controlled.

   (C) geared toward grammaticality with little emphasis on communication.

   (D) teacher-centered and multicultural in nature.

67. Identify examples of appropriate linguistic test adaptations for ELLs.

   (A) Allow more time to complete the test, provide a practice test, and allow the student to take the test orally.

   (B) Provide fewer items, translate the test, and include items that address some of the learning targets covered in class.

   (C) Substitute testing for other activities, guide students to the correct answer, and provide practice tests.

   (D) Avoid testing that requires higher-order thinking skills, simplify items and reduce the number of them.

68. When planning for assessment accommodations for ELLs in special education, the first element the teacher should consider is

   (A) the cost associated with the proposed adaptations.

   (B) the legality of the proposed adaptations.

   (C) the feasibility of time and resources available for such accommodation.

   (D) the type of disability of the child.

69. Why is the final sound of the word *has* a voiced /z/?

   (A) English requires that the grapheme s at the end of a word is always voiced.

   (B) Because the grapheme ve in have is also voiced.

   (C) Typically, the [s] verbal ending is voiced when it follows a vowel or a voiced consonant.

   (D) Because children pronounce it that way.

70. Identify the theoretical framework that best describes how a native language is learned.

   (A) Language learning appears to be the result of some combination of innate ability, environmental influences, and social interactions.

   (B) Language is learned through imitation of older siblings, parents and caregivers.

   (C) Humans learned languages in meaningful contexts and reinforced with direct corrections.

(D) Humans are innately endowed with fully developed language which is stored in the left hemisphere of the brain.

71. Informal reading inventories are used to

(A) to measure reading proficiency.

(B) read short stories and poems.

(C) motivate children to enjoy reading

(D) create an inventory of new words learned daily.

72. English language learners (ELLs) might develop and demonstrate intelligence and capabilities differently from children from mainstream groups. When ELLs are not performing well academically, teachers have a tendency to refer students for special education services. What is the best strategy to deal with this situation?

(A) Place the students in the special education program in an inclusion model.

(B) Test students using a simpler and less demanding adaptation of the instrument used with mainstream students.

(C) Delay assessment because these problems can be cause by lack of development in L2.

(D) Provide special education services in a pull-out format until the child learns English.

73. Identify the rationale for promoting literacy development in the students' native language.

(A) It facilitates and accelerates literacy development in the second language.

(B) It facilitates the acquisition of a second language in a fun and relaxed environment.

(C) It promotes the acquisition of academic language.

(D) It guarantees that English language learners (ELL) will maintain their native language.

74. Knowledge of the students' native language can provide teachers with valuable informa-

tion about the _____ that ESL students develop in the process of L2 mastery.

(A) idioms

(B) interlanguage

(C) levels of bilingualism

(D) dialect

75. Ms. Obama introduced a list of Greek and Latin prefixes common to French, German, Italian, Spanish and English. She explained the spelling patterns and the meaning of each of these prefixes. She presented examples of words that contain the prefixes, and led students to decode them based on the meaning of the prefixes. What decoding strategies is Ms. Obama promoting?

(A) Contextual

(B) Structural

(C) Pictorial

(D) Syntactical

76. What was the main purpose of emphasizing common prefixes in L1 and L2 in Ms. Obama's class?

(A) to present the idea that English has been influenced by other languages

(B) to present the idea that English has many foreign words

(C) to present the idea that elements from the first language can transfer to English

(D) to present the idea that English is not a difficult language

77. Healthy young children acquire their first language in natural settings with little or no direct language instruction. In the formal classroom environment, these conditions might be difficult to replicate. However, there are ESL methods that have made an attempt to replicate the language acquisition process. These methods are

I. The Language Experience Approach

II. Community Language Learning Method

III.   The Total Physical Response
IV.   Audio Lingual Method
V.   The Natural Method
VI.   The Grammar Translation Method
VII.   Direct Method

(A)   I and II
(B)   III and IV
(C)   VI and VII
(D)   II and VII

78. Children learn their first language in an environment in which risk-taking is encouraged and errors are allowed. Identify the ESL method that best incorporates these principles in the teaching of a second language.

(A)   The Audio Lingual Method
(B)   The Natural Method
(C)   Suggestopedia
(D)   Direct Method

79. Marcus is able to separate words into their individual phonemes and put them back together to recreate the original word. However, he has problems separating words into syllables and identifying the syllable with the primary stress. Based on this scenario, Marcus needs additional support with

(A)   phonological awareness.
(B)   phonemic awareness.
(C)   syllabication.
(D)   word stress.

80. The spelling patterns of high frequency words are generally taught through

(A)   word analysis.
(B)   sight word or holistic word recognition.
(C)   the use of contextual clues.
(D)   the use of phonics skills.

81. One of the key advantages of using the Language Experience Approach (LEA) to teach reading to language minority students is it

(A)   links the language produced by the children with the way it is written.
(B)   links the experiences of the children with the experiences of the teachers.
(C)   uses the components of L1 as a foundation for teaching reading in L2.
(D)   uses the standard grammar of L1 and L2 as a foundation.

82. The Total Physical Response (TPR) is used to promote listening comprehension for students at the _____ stage of second language development.

(A)   fluent
(B)   intermediate
(C)   advanced
(D)   pre-production

83. Chants used for instructional purposes are

(A)   choral renditions of religious nature used to promote listening skills.
(B)   repetition of sounds of a given language to promote phonological awareness.
(C)   oral renditions of highly repetitive and rhythmic content used to promote fluency.
(D)   choral renditions of folk songs used to teach listening and speaking skills.

84. Identify the statement that best represents the connection between reading and writing.

(A)   Reading and writing skills develop concurrently rather than sequentially.
(B)   Formal reading instruction should precede writing.
(C)   Reading and writing develop sequentially and in a structured manner.

(D) Reading and writing should be postponed until children are completely fluent in the second language.

85. Dung is a jovial and outspoken Vietnamese ELL student assigned to your sixth grade class. He lives in an all-Vietnamese neighborhood where English is rarely spoken. In school, he likes to interact with native speakers of English, but often has problems understanding them. What strategy(ies) can we use to address Dung's language needs?

(A) Introduce activities to promote listening comprehension and activities that simulate real-life situations in the classroom.

(B) Introduce direct activities to polish pronunciation and use readers' theater to enhance her knowledge of the language.

(C) Introduce idiomatic and colloquial expressions in contextualized situations.

(D) When the purpose of the task is communication, focus the attention on the message and avoid over-correcting the child.

86. Farideh is an advanced middle school English language learner from Iran. She is an advanced English speaker, but has specific problems with English sounds. These problems often make her pronunciation difficult to understand. She tells the teacher that she can conceptualize the standard pronunciation in her mind, but when it comes out, it comes out all wrong. What strategy can the teacher use to address this pronunciation problem?

(A) Ask the student to spend more time in the language laboratory, listening to authentic discourse.

(B) Develop a list describing all the pronunciation problems typical of Farsi speakers and share the list with her.

(C) Isolate key pronunciation problems, identify the sounds, and describe how the sounds are produced.

(D) Describe the articulators involved in the production of each English phoneme.

87. Identify the most appropriate strategies to promote oral language development among kindergarten English language learners.

(A) Use dramatic play, songs, and rhymes

(B) Introduce games and activities where students listen for comprehension.

(C) Lead students to memorize and recite poems and composing short stories

(D) Help students in the preparation of formal presentations using technology

88. During the pre-reading activities of the shared-book experience with ELLs, teachers

(A) introduce children to parts of the book, and additional books written by the same author.

(B) encourage students to draw a picture representing the main idea of the story.

(C) introduce the book and guide students to make predictions based on the title and the pictures.

(D) introduce children to the biography and other books with similar themes.

89. During the first reading of the shared-reading activity, the teacher reads the whole story in an enthusiastic and dramatic manner. What is the main purpose of this activity?

(A) To make the content understood to the children so they can enjoy it and corroborate predictions of the story.

(B) To introduce decoding skills and main idea.

(C) To introduce vocabulary unknown to the children, practice decoding skills, and identify the main idea of the story.

(D) To review the parts of the book and contextual clues.

90. Right after the initial shared reading, the teacher reads the story again. Which of the following activities should the teacher conduct?

    (A) Ask individual students to read orally one page per student.

    (B) Use oral cloze by pausing and encouraging students to orally fill-in the missing words.

    (C) Guide students to write their own stories using the same characters of the original story.

    (D) Stop frequently for discussions and clarification, and to allow students opportunities to ask questions and make comments about each page.

91. The main purpose for using interactive journals with ELLs is to allow

    (A) children opportunities to practice their speaking and writing skills.

    (B) children opportunities to communicate freely in a written form.

    (C) students opportunities to receive corrective feedback from peers.

    (D) students opportunities to practice listening, speaking, reading and writing.

92. One of the main principles of the "Schema Theory" and the importance of prior knowledge is

    (A) students learn best when they enjoy the content being taught.

    (B) students learn best when the content is developmentally appropriate to their cognitive level.

    (C) students' background experiences and knowledge impact their ability to understand new and related content.

    (D) students' educational backgrounds have a direct impact in the development of effective learning strategies.

93. Identify the option that best describes the steps in process writing.

    (A) Develop an outline of the intended writing project, complete the initial draft, edit for content.

    (B) Complete the initial draft, revise for the accuracy of content and publish

    (C) Brainstorm for ideas, develop an outline, complete initial draft, edit, and publish.

    (D) Write initial draft, share it with peers, review for grammaticality, and publish.

94. The main purpose of family literacy programs is to

    (A) teach ESL to Spanish-speaking parents and to provide training in cross-cultural communication.

    (B) keep children busy while parents attend ESL classes.

    (C) empower parents to help and be involved in the education of their children.

    (D) empower children and adult English language learners by providing meaningful education.

95. Ms. Ramos believes that culturally and linguistically diverse Learners (CLDL) must be assessed with instruments designed specifically for them. She refuses to allow CLDL to be tested using the traditional instruments used for native English speaking students. Mr. Hart, her colleague, believes that they should be tested using the instruments currently used by the district. What compromise can they work out?

    (A) Administer the usual diagnostic battery but take into account the students' linguistic background in interpreting the test profile.

    (B) Delay assessment until the student is exited from the language development program.

    (C) Administer only nonverbal measures.

(D) Administer first-language assessment instruments until the child is exited from the special language program.

96. In preparation for high-stakes summative examinations, students should be introduced to

    (A) test-taking skills and the format of the test.
    (B) filling in the blanks and forced answers format.
    (C) multiple-choice test and matching type of format.
    (D) relaxation techniques and scoring rubrics.

97. Identify the statement that best describes portfolio assessment.

    (A) Portfolio provides information about academic progress in the core courses like mathematics, science and social studies.
    (B) Portfolio assessment is a collection of the student's work that helps in tracking student progress.
    (C) Data from portfolio is confidential and should be used for official purposes only.
    (D) Portfolio assessment provides students with opportunities to practice with the assessment process used in the United States.

98. Based on the developmental characteristics of children in kindergarten-first grade, teachers should develop tests that

    (A) are challenging and comprehensive.
    (B) are culturally responsive and easy to grade.
    (C) can be scored in 5–10 minutes.
    (D) can be answered in 5–10 minutes.

Read the passage below and answer Question 98.

The purpose of grading is to identify what students have learned. However, in special educa-tion, grading accommodations are needed to obtain a realistic picture of performance. There are several grading accommodations for special education students. These include IEP grading, share grading, and contract grading.

99. Identify the statement that best describes the individualized education plan (IEP) grading system for special education children in an inclusion model.

    (A) The grade is based on the objectives and the criteria for mastery stated in the IEP.
    (B) The grade is based on the mastery of the state curriculum.
    (C) The grade is based on a previously agreed contract between the child and the teacher.
    (D) The grade is based on an agreement between the mainstream and special education teachers.

100. Using non verbal testing can minimize the impact of language in testing; however, the use of non verbal instrument has an intrinsic limitation that can its effectiveness. Identify the statement that best explains the main problem of using a non-verbal to assess with students from diverse cultural backgrounds.

    (A) Non-verbal communication is confusing and threatening to students.
    (B) Non-verbal communication can be confusing due to linguistic differences
    (C) Non-verbal communication is a culturally-bound process
    (D) Non-verbal communication should not be allowed in the classroom.

101. Assessing ELLs using instruments designed for mainstream students might create problems because these instruments might contain _____ that can affect the results.

    (A) wrong information
    (B) cultural bias

(C) hateful and ignorant information

(D) classified information

102. Identify the problems with the use of translated assessment instruments.

(A) It can lead to a false sense of security about the validity of the instrument.

(B) It can be understood as a way to "water down the curriculum."

(C) It can affect the development in L2.

(D) It can affect the integrity of the assessment process.

103. Identify one of the key advantages for using on-going assessment as part of instruction.

(A) Students get adjusted to formal assessment instruments used in schools.

(B) Students develop interest in the testing instruments.

(C) The stress associated with testing is minimized.

(D) The stress associated with testing increases with the frequency of testing.

104. From the district's administrative point of view, formal assessment is used mostly

(A) for diagnostic purposes and for accountability purposes.

(B) to make instructional decisions at the classroom level.

(C) for accountability reporting, to teach test-taking skills and content.

(D) to promote analytical and reading skills among students

105. When analyzing and interpreting assessment data from ELLs from diverse cultural and linguistic backgrounds, assessors must take into account that

(A) the main objective of assessment is to make students feel valued and wanted in school.

(B) students go through different stages of development and these stages should not affect the way that children are assessed.

(C) the students might express potential differently due to linguistic and cultural influences.

(D) students may have culture and language deficits which, which can preclude them from effective participation in the testing process.

106. Effective assessment practices for ELLs and for children in general share which of the following guiding principles?

(A) They are child-centered, ongoing and collected as part of daily instruction.

(B) They are summative in nature and collected with instruments approved by the state.

(C) They use competent bilingual diagnosticians.

(D) They emphasize student weaknesses and promote self-monitoring

107. Rubrics are commonly used in holistic scoring of writing samples. In this context, holistic scoring is best defined as a system designed to

(A) determine if the students are following process writing.

(B) determine if the students are using the logic of the language in writing.

(C) obtain assign scoring based on broad descriptions of writing.

(D) evaluate writing based on mechanics, capitalization and punctuation.

108. Cloze reading is a technique to assess

(A) writing skills.

(B) comprehension skills.

(C) spelling and punctuation skills.

(D) receptive language skills.

109. Story retelling inventories are generally used to assess students'

(A) listening comprehension, speaking and vocabulary development.

(B) oral language development and writing skills.

(C) listening skills, speaking, reading and writing skills.

(D) the writing style used in the story, and the point of view of the author.

110. Checklists and structured teacher observation are examples of

(A) effective teaching strategies.

(B) informal teaching strategies.

(C) formal assessment strategies.

(D) informal assessment strategies.

111. Running records is an assessment component of the Reading Recovery method. What is the key advantage of using this component in the assessment for English language learners?

(A) It allows teachers the opportunity to compare features of L1 and L2.

(B) It provides teachers with continuous information about students' progress.

(C) It allows teachers the opportunity to measure how fast students are adapting to the new culture.

(D) It provides teachers with records of each student, on-demand.

Read the scenario below and answer Question 112.

Mary Clinton is a pre-service teacher seeking initial teacher certification in ESL. As part of her residency (student-teaching), she is required to demonstrate her expertise in teaching English to ESL students. As part of the process, she submitted and received approval to teach a lesson on American idioms. To assess her teaching perfor-

mance, her supervisor uses the state-approved assessment instrument—a checklist of effective teaching indicators.

112. What type of assessment is Ms. Clinton's supervisor using?

(A) Informal assessment

(B) Summative assessment

(C) Norm-referenced achievement examination

(D) Authentic assessment

113. Effective approaches for teaching English as a second language are

(A) student-centered and communication driven.

(B) sequenced based on the complexity of the grammatical structures and teacher-centered.

(C) geared toward grammaticality with little emphasis on communication.

(D) teacher-centered and multicultural in nature.

114. Identify the techniques that best represent the concept of Sheltered English Instruction (SEI).

(A) Speaking slowly in English and provide support in L1 as needed to promote comprehension.

(B) Using non-verbal communication to promote comprehension.

(C) Evaluate the mastery of the content taught at least once per week.

(D) Use visuals, hands-on activities and contextualize instruction to ensure comprehension.

115. What was the key contribution of the Lau Remedies to the education of ELLs in the United States?

(A) It initiated English as a second language (ESL) programs to address the needs of English language learners.

(B) It forced the U.S. Congress to enact dual language legislation.

(C) It established the criteria and enforced the implementation of special language programs for ELLs.

(D) It guided state legislators to enact English-only legislation.

116. In the last few years, the two-way dual language programs have received public support in the United States. What is the main reason for the popularity of this language program?

(A) The program allows for the maintenance of L1 and L2.

(B) It allows the inclusion of children from mainstream groups.

(C) The program has been endorsed by the U.S. Department of Education.

(D) It is grounded in solid scientific research.

117. Identify the similarities between the Language Proficiency Assessment Committee (or equivalent body) and the Admission Review and Dismissal (ARD).

(A) Both are mandated by the federal bilingual legislation.

(B) Both are mandated by the Individuals with Disability Education Act (IDEA).

(C) The committees regulate admission and dismissal to the bilingual and special education programs, respectively.

(D) The membership of both committees must be composed of the parents of the child along with teachers and an administrator.

118. The key distinction between the one-way and the two-way dual language program is the

(A) language goal of the programs.

(B) academic goal of the programs.

(C) type of student population served.

(D) percentage of language distribution in the programs.

Read the scenario below and answer Questions 119–120.

Marian is a middle school Latino student who was born and raised in the city of Chicago. She spent three years in the bilingual/ESL program, and was exited at the end of fifth grade. She grew up in the barrios (Latino enclaves), where Spanish and English are used constantly. She functions and communicates well in a bilingual and bicultural environment. However, during her year in middle school, she is experiencing problems with her courses. The student complains that the language used in books is different from the language that she knows.

119. What component of the language is she lacking?

(A) Basic interpersonal communication skills (BICS)

(B) Cognitive academy linguistic proficiency (CALP)

(C) Phonology and syntax

(D) English for special purposes (ESP)

120. The LPAC met to discuss her situation and to find possible solutions. Since the school does not have dual language instruction for middle school students, the only possible solution is to offer ESL instruction. What type of ESL program or approach should best meet the needs of the student?

(A) Pull-out ESL

(B) Grammar-based ESL

(C) Sheltered English Instruction (SEI)

(D) Newcomers group for socialization

Detailed Explanations of Answers for Practice Test 1

Praxis English to Speakers of Other Languages

Question Number	Correct Answer	Content Category
1	C	Analysis of Student Language Production; Linguistic Theory: Syntax
2	C	Analysis of Student Language Production; Linguistic Theory: Syntax
3	A	Analysis of Student Language Production; Linguistic Theory: Syntax
4	B	Analysis of Student Language Production; Linguistic Theory: Psycholinguistics
5	B	Analysis of Student Language Production; Linguistic Theory: Syntax
6	B	Analysis of Student Language Production; Linguistic Theory: Syntax
7	B	Analysis of Student Language Production; Linguistic Theory: Syntax
8	A	Analysis of Student Language Production; Linguistic Theory: Syntax
9	B	Analysis of Student Language Production; Linguistic Theory: Syntax
10	C	Analysis of Student Language Production; Linguistic Theory: Syntax
11	A	Analysis of Student Language Production; Linguistic Theory: Phonology
12	B	Analysis of Student Language Production; Linguistic Theory: Phonology
13	B	Analysis of Student Language Production; Linguistic Theory: Phonology
14	D	Analysis of Student Language Production; Linguistic Theory: Phonology
15	B	Analysis of Student Language Production; Linguistic Theory: Phonology
16	B	Analysis of Student Language Production; Linguistic Theory: Phonology
17	B	Analysis of Student Language Production; Linguistic Theory: Phonology
18	A	Analysis of Student Language Production; Linguistic Theory: Phonology
19	A	Analysis of Student Language Production; Linguistic Theory: Phonology
20	D	Analysis of Student Language Production; Linguistic Theory: Phonology
21	B	Analysis of Student Language Production; Linguistic Theory: Syntax
22	A	Analysis of Student Language Production; Linguistic Theory: Syntax
23	D	Analysis of Student Language Production; Linguistic Theory: Syntax
24	B	Analysis of Student Language Production; Linguistic Theory: Syntax
25	D	Analysis of Student Language Production; Linguistic Theory: Syntax
26	C	Analysis of Student Language Production; Linguistic Theory: Syntax
27	D	Analysis of Student Language Production; Teaching Methods and Techniques
28	A	Analysis of Student Language Production; Linguistic Theory: Syntax
29	C	Analysis of Student Language Production; Linguistic Theory: Syntax
30	B	Analysis of Student Language Production; Linguistic Theory: Psycholinguistics
31	C	Linguistic Theory: Syntax
32	B	Linguistic Theory: Phonology
33	A	Linguistic Theory: Phonology
34	B	Linguistic Theory: Phonology
35	D	Linguistic Theory: Phonology
36	C	Linguistic Theory: Phonology

Question Number	Correct Answer	Content Category
37	D	Linguistic Theory: Phonology
38	B	Linguistic Theory: Phonology
39	B	Linguistic Theory: Phonology
40	A	Linguistic Theory: Phonology
41	B	Linguistic Theory: Phonology
42	B	Linguistic Theory: Phonology
43	B	Linguistic Theory: Phonology
44	D	Linguistic Theory: Phonology
45	D	Linguistic Theory: Psycholinguistics
46	C	Linguistic Theory: Psycholinguistics
47	A	Linguistic Theory: Psycholinguistics
48	C	Linguistic Theory: Psycholinguistics
49	A	Linguistic Theory: Syntax
50	B	Linguistic Theory: Phonology
51	A	Linguistic Theory: Morphology
52	C	Linguistic Theory: Sociolinguistics
53	B	Linguistic Theory: Phonology
54	C	Linguistic Theory: Phonology
55	C	Linguistic Theory: Syntax
56	B	Linguistic Theory: Psycholinguistics
57	B	Linguistic Theory: Phonology
58	B	Linguistic Theory: Sociolinguistics
59	B	Teaching Methods and Techniques
60	B	Teaching Methods and Techniques
61	B	Teaching Methods and Techniques
62	B	Teaching Methods and Techniques
63	C	Teaching Methods and Techniques
64	B	Teaching Methods and Techniques
65	B	Teaching Methods and Techniques
66	A	Teaching Methods and Techniques
67	A	Teaching Methods and Techniques
68	D	Teaching Methods and Techniques
69	C	Linguistic Theory: Phonology
70	A	Linguistic Theory: Syntax
71	A	Teaching Methods and Techniques
72	C	Teaching Methods and Techniques

Question Number	Correct Answer	Content Category
73	A	Teaching Methods and Techniques
74	B	Linguistic Theory: Psycholinguistics
75	B	Teaching Methods and Techniques
76	C	Teaching Methods and Techniques
77	B	Teaching Methods and Techniques
78	B	Teaching Methods and Techniques
79	A	Teaching Methods and Techniques
80	B	Teaching Methods and Techniques
81	A	Teaching Methods and Techniques
82	D	Teaching Methods and Techniques
83	C	Teaching Methods and Techniques
84	A	Teaching Methods and Techniques
85	A	Teaching Methods and Techniques
86	C	Teaching Methods and Techniques
87	A	Teaching Methods and Techniques
88	C	Teaching Methods and Techniques
89	A	Teaching Methods and Techniques
90	D	Teaching Methods and Techniques
91	B	Teaching Methods and Techniques
92	C	Teaching Methods and Techniques
93	C	Teaching Methods and Techniques
94	C	Teaching Methods and Techniques
95	A	Assessment Techniques and Cultural Issues: Evaluation and Assessment
96	A	Assessment Techniques and Cultural Issues: Evaluation and Assessment
97	B	Assessment Techniques and Cultural Issues: Evaluation and Assessment
98	D	Assessment Techniques and Cultural Issues: Evaluation and Assessment
99	A	Assessment Techniques and Cultural Issues: Evaluation and Assessment
100	C	Assessment Techniques and Cultural Issues: Cultural Issues
101	B	Assessment Techniques and Cultural Issues: Cultural Issues
102	A	Assessment Techniques and Cultural Issues: Cultural Issues
103	C	Assessment Techniques and Cultural Issues: Evaluation and Assessment
104	A	Assessment Techniques and Cultural Issues: Evaluation and Assessment
105	C	Assessment Techniques and Cultural Issues: Cultural Issues
106	A	Assessment Techniques and Cultural Issues: Cultural Issues
107	C	Assessment Techniques and Cultural Issues: Evaluation and Assessment
108	B	Assessment Techniques and Cultural Issues: Evaluation and Assessment

Question Number	Correct Answer	Content Category
109	A	Assessment Techniques and Cultural Issues: Evaluation and Assessment
110	D	Assessment Techniques and Cultural Issues: Evaluation and Assessment
111	B	Assessment Techniques and Cultural Issues: Evaluation and Assessment
112	D	Assessment Techniques and Cultural Issues: Evaluation and Assessment
113	A	Professional Issues: Curriculum and Materials
114	D	Professional Issues: Programs and Models
115	C	Professional Issues: Legal Foundations
116	B	Professional Issues: Programs and Models
117	C	Professional Issues: Legal Foundations
118	C	Professional Issues: Programs and Models
119	B	Professional Issues: Curriculum and Materials
120	C	Professional Issues: Programs and Models

PRACTICE TEST 1 (0360): DETAILED EXPLANATIONS OF ANSWERS

Section I: Part A–Oral Grammar and Vocabulary

1. (C)

This question tests your ability to identify grammatical errors in a student's speech. First, the student makes an error with articles: a definite article should be used, rather than an indefinite article in the utterance "it was a second time." Second, the past tense –*ed* form is missing in "I walk around." Third, the student's utterance tails off into sentence fragments. Therefore, the correct answer is (C).

2. (C)

This question is to test your ability to identify a specific grammatical error in a student's utterance. The fact that the student is able to provide the time indicates that she understands the question. The question does not require a response in a complete sentence. The answer would be perfect if the student added "ago" to follow the time expression. Therefore, the correct answer is (C).

3. (A)

This question asks you to identify a grammatical error in an utterance. Since Jeju Island is part of Korea, it is redundant to say that it is "Korea's island." Therefore, the correct answer is (A).

4. (B)

This question tests your knowledge of language learning theory. The –*ed* form used for the word "overweight" indicates that the student is aware the form required for a past tense. However, the student overgeneralizes the rule and incorrectly applies the rule in which it is incorrect. Therefore, the correct answer is (B).

5. (B)

This question tests your ability to identify grammatical errors in a student's utterance. The student shows understanding of the question and gives a relevant answer. The problem is that the student needs to use the word "advantage" in a grammatical way. Therefore, the correct answer is (B).

6. (B)

This question asks you to identify grammatical errors in a student's utterance. The students fails to use the past tense in the second verb, which also result in an error with parallelism: the first verb is in past tense. In addition, the student omits the plural ending –s for "flower." Therefore, the correct answer is (B).

7. (B)

This question tests your ability to identify a grammatical error in a student's utterance. In the utterance, the student correctly uses a past tense and gives a relevant reply to the question. Nevertheless, the verb should be "came" since the place is "here." Therefore, the correct answer is (B).

8. (A)

This question asks you to identify a grammatical error in a student's utterance. The student incorrectly uses a noun, "poverty," to modify "country," which is also a noun. Therefore, the correct answer is (A).

9. (B)

This question asks you to identify a grammatical error in a student's utterance. The utterance would be acceptable if the preposition "of" were deleted from the utterance. Therefore, the correct answer is (B).

10. (C)

This question asks you to identify a common error in a student's utterance. The student fails to use the appropriate articles that are required to precede the nouns. Therefore, the correct answer is (C).

Section I: Part B–Pronunciation

11. (A)

This question asks you to identify a specific error of pronunciation and recognize the phonetic alphabet. The student incorrectly pronounces the "g" sound in the word "legislators" as [g]. Therefore, the correct answer is (A).

12. (B)

This question tests your familiarity with some common features in students' speech. In the speech sample, the student incorrectly pronounces the word "pluralism" twice before she gets it right. The student does not stop to ask for help, but tries to correct herself. Therefore, the correct answer is (B).

13. (B)

This question tests your ability to identify a student's phonetic errors and your knowledge of phonetic transcriptions. Option (A) is how "policy" should sound, but the student incorrectly pronounces the word as (B) indicates. Therefore, the correct answer is (B).

14. (D)

This question tests your ability to analyze speech sounds and recognize their phonetic transcriptions. Option (A) is how the word should sound. The "g" in the word "foreign" is silent, but it is incorrectly pronounced as [dʒ] in the speech sample. In addition, the student inserts schwa (ə). Therefore, the correct answer is (D).

15. (B)

This question tests your ability to describe student speech errors. In the speech sample, the student does not pronounce the "bi" in the word "prohibits." Therefore, the correct answer is (B).

16. (B)

This question tests your ability to recognize student speech errors. The student has trouble with the "str" consonant cluster in the word "restricts."

Specifically, the student omits the "s" in the "str" cluster in the speech sample. Therefore, the correct answer is (B).

17. (B)

This question tests your ability to analyze student speech sounds and recognize their phonetic transcriptions. Option (A) indicates how the word "abroad" should be pronounced, but the student incorrectly shifts the [r] sound. Therefore, the correct answer is (B).

18. (A)

This question tests your ability to describe a student's problems with pronunciation and recognize phonetic transcriptions. The stressed vowel in the word "pressure" is [ɛ], but the student incorrectly pronounces it as [i]. Therefore, the correct answer is (A).

19. (A)

This question tests your ability to identify a student's errors in pronunciation and recognize their phonetic transcriptions. The vowel of the word "lead" as a verb should be pronounced as [i]. In this speech sample, the student incorrectly pronounces it as [ɛ]. Therefore, the correct answer is (A)

20. (D)

This question tests your ability to determine and describe a student's errors in pronunciation. The word "maintenance" is stressed on the first syllable, but the student incorrectly places the stress on the second syllable. Therefore, the correct answer is (D).

Section I: Part C–Writing

21. (B)

The sample clearly demonstrates errors in idiomatic expressions. In the context, the use of "in a rush" is incorrect. Further, "a piece of cake" is the correct expression, not "a piece of pie." Therefore, the correct answer is (B).

22. (A)

This question asks you to identify common grammatical errors. The student incorrectly uses prepositions throughout the sample. The student shows no problems with use of past tense or pronouns in the sample. The only instance of progressive also shows no errors. Therefore, the correct answer is (A).

23. (D)

This question asks you to identify grammatical errors at the sentence level. There is no indication that the student has a problem with subject-verb agreement. The student does not show an awareness of the use of adverbials: "played beautiful," "played very good." The forms of past tense are used correctly. However, the student does not demonstrate the knowledge of using an infinitive to combine two verbs. Therefore, the correct answer is (D).

24. (B)

This question tests your ability to identify errors in vocabulary. Since the student's brother is a college student, the use of "the fourth grade" is incorrect even though we can infer that the brother is a senior. From the context, the student does not plan to go to a graduate school. The use of "a graduate student" is incorrect. Therefore, the correct answer is (B).

25. (D)

This question asks you to identify errors in using plurals. From the description of the writing sample, the student might be surprised by the high price, which has little to do with American culture. After all, even the same merchandize can have various different prices, which is not unique to the culture. To haggle is a common practice in many cultures, but not in American stores. "Two fifty" can mean either two hundred and fifty dollars or two dollars and fifty cents. The writing sample shows that the student has the knowledge of the plural form –s. Nevertheless, the student uses the plural form where it is not appropriate. Therefore, the correct answer is (D).

26. (C)

This question tests to see if you can identify errors in the past-tense forms of irregular verbs. From the writing sample, the student demonstrates an awareness of the past tense. However, the student applies the –ed form to regular verbs as well as irregular verbs. The student does not seem to have trouble using adverbs of time or prepositional phrases. So, the correct answer is (C).

27. (D)

This question asks you to identify an appropriate way to improve a student's writing. In this sample, several uses of pronouns might not correctly link to the intended reference. This type of ambiguity can often be self-corrected if the teacher lets students listen to their own writing. Therefore, the correct answer is (D).

28. (A)

This question asks you to identify errors in relative clauses. From the writing sample, the student incorrectly uses pronouns when only relative subject pronoun is permitted. There are no errors with comparison, superlatives or prepositional phrases in the sample. Therefore, the correct answer is (A).

29. (C)

This writing sample contains no instances of relative clauses. So, the student's knowledge of relative clauses cannot be judged here. There are no uses of *wh-* questions. It seems that the student is aware of subject-verb inversion for wh-questions but is not aware that the inversion is not needed for indirect questions, when *wh-* questions are embedded in a sentence. The first four sentences of the writing sample include four errors where the student inverts subject-verb in embedded questions. Therefore, the correct answer is (C).

30. (B)

This question tests your knowledge of errors associated with terms used for second language acquisition. Following up on the above explanation, we see that the student incorrectly extends the rule of subject-verb inversion for *wh-* interrogatives to indirect questions. That is, the student overgeneralizes the rule. The correct answer, therefore, is (B).

SECTION II: LANGUAGE THEORY AND TEACHING

31. (C)

Linking verbs are intransitive verbs; thus, they cannot take objects. Their function is to connect the subject with a predicate adjective or predicate nominative. (A), (B), and (D) are incorrect because they describe features of transitive verbs. Transitive verbs can take direct and indirect objects.

32. (B)

The sound /θ/ is generally represented by the diagraph, *th*, in words like "think" and "path." This sound is produced when the tip of the tongue is placed between the upper and lower teeth and producing a continuous sound creating friction (fricative). In the production of the sounds, the vocal cords are not engaged (voiceless). (A) is incorrect because it describes an alveolar, voiceless, stop sound, the /t/. (C) is incorrect because it represents the voiced counterpart of the th sound. That is, the sound /ð/ is produced in the same way as the /θ/, and the only difference is the /ð/ is voiced and the /θ/ is voiceless. (D) is incorrect because the /z/ represents a voiced, fricative and alveolar sound.

33. (A)

All three sets of words have a voiceless sound followed by its voiced counterpart. (B) is incorrect because the place of articulation refers to the articulators involved in the production of the sounds, and the three sets words are produced using different articulators. (C) is incorrect because the manner of articulation describes how the sounds are produce. In the examples provided, the first set of sounds are stop (/k/ and /g/, and the second (/s/ and /z/) and third sets (/f/ and /v/) are fricative sounds.

(D) is incorrect because all three sets of words are oral sounds.

34. (B)

The terms "fricative," "stop" and "affricate" describe the way in which the sounds are produced. (A) is incorrect because vowels are described based how high is the tongue in the mouth (high low), the shape of the lips (rounded unrounded), and whether they sounds are produced in front or on the back of the vocal tract. (C) is incorrect because the terms are not used to describe the place of articulation used to produce English consonants. (D) is incorrect because the descriptors are used to classify sounds, as opposed to units of meaning (morphemes).

35. (D)

The word contains four sounds, and all of them are voiced sounds—[ɔlðo]. (A), (B), and (C) are incorrect based on the previous explanation.

36. (C)

The word contains six sounds. Notice that the ng, represents one nasal sound /ŋ/. Out of the six sounds, only the /p/ is voiceless, the remaining five sounds are voiced. Based on this analysis options (A), (B), and (D) are incorrect.

37. (D)

The initial sound of the word "job" is one of the only two affricates of the English, /ʤ/. Based on this explanation, options (A), (B), and (C) are incorrect.

38. (B)

The /f/ and /v/ sounds of the minimal pairs, "fine" and "vine," are both interdental sounds. (A) is incorrect because the /b/ of the word berry is a bilabial sound. (C) is incorrect because the /p/ of park and the /s/ of spark are bilabial and alveolar sounds, respectively. (D) is incorrect because the /t/ of tank, and the /b/ of bank are alveolar and bilabial sounds, respectively.

39. (B)

The /i/ and the /u/ vowel sounds are produced in opposite part of the vocal tract—front vs. back. Vowel sounds produced in front are also unrounded, and those produced on the back are classified as rounded. Based on this explanation, options (A), (C), and (D) are incorrect.

40. (A)

Vowels are described based on the relative height of the tongue in the vocal tract, and the part of the tongue raised to produce the sounds. (B) is incorrect because the tongue does not necessarily vibrate to produce vowel sounds. (C) and (D) are incorrect because the concept of pitch (level of a sound) is not used to describe the production of vowel sounds.

41. (B)

A diphthong occurs when two joined vowels are pronounced in one syllable. The words "boy," "cow," and "by" contain the three diphthongs identified in English. (A) is incorrect because the term "fricative: refers to the manner of articulation used to describe consonants. (C) is incorrect because monosyllabic words, like the ones presented in the examples, technically do not contain unstressed

vowels. (D) is incorrect because by definition all vowels are voiced.

42. (B)

Tonal languages use different levels of pitch at the syllable level to change the meaning of words. Speakers of a tonal language can pronounce a word using different tones—low, mid, high, falling tone, and rising tones—to communicate multiple meanings using the same word. (A) is incorrect because context by itself will not convey the meaning without the use of the appropriate pitch. (C) is incorrect because the term intonation describes the high and low points of words in sentences. (D) is incorrect because the term "allophone" is use to describe English phonemes that appear in complimentary distribution.

43. (B)

English contains multiple homographs—words with identical spelling that can be pronounced differently to create two distinct words, e.g., PROject (noun) and proJECT (verb). Based on the explanation, options (A), (C), and (D) are incorrect.

44. (D)

Content words like nouns, adjectives, and verbs can convey more information than function words. Function words are generally used to comply with grammaticality. Some examples of function words are articles and prepositions. Based on the explanation provided, options (A), (B), and (C) are incorrect.

45. (D)

Children who get exposed to the second language before puberty generally develop native-like pronunciation. On the other hand, adults generally rely on their native language as a foundation for the development of L2; this reliance often leads to language interference at the phonological level. Adults are generally better at handling the grammar and the abstract components of the language. Therefore, children have advantages over adults at the phonological level, but adults might have advantage in all other areas. (A) is a true statement but addresses only the phonological component of the language. (B) is probably a true statement, but there is not empirical research to support it. (C) negates research findings in the acquisition of a second language. Children exposed to the language after puberty might develop a better understanding of the abstract component of the language but might lag behind in the development of pronunciation.

46. (C)

Students at the speech emergence communicate in phrases using words with high semantic value. They are also beginning to understand the print concept. They can understand speech and written communication presented in contextualized situations and accompanied with visuals. In the pre-production stage (A) students lack basic language skills and might have to rely on non-verbal communication to get their point across. Thus, it is highly unlikely that they can understand written communication at all. In the early production (B), students begin to communicate using language at the social level in everyday situations. Print awareness is taking place but the main emphasis at this stage is the development of basic oral communication. The intermediate fluency (D) represents a higher level of proficiency where students communicate using simple sentences; however, the language is not fully developed and their speech might experience language interference together with overgeneralizations. Their literacy development is beyond the basic recognition skills alluded in the question.

47. (A)

Second-language development is best achieved when instruction is geared toward meaningful and functional tasks in the language. This kind of approach can facilitate and increase the motivation for L2 learning. (B) presents a convoluted and contradictory explanation involving inductive and deductive teaching. Deductive and inductive teaching can be used to teach a second language. However, inductive or indirect teaching seems to be more effective with young learners than direct instruction. (C) looks fine until the term "meaningful memorization" was introduced. Memorization is not the best tool to promote proficiency in L2. (D) is incorrect because idiomatic expression and tongue twisters are useful activities to promote pronunciation and basic communication skills but fail to go beyond that.

48. (C)

Mary is having problems connecting the letter (grapheme) and sound (phoneme) correspondence that will allow her to begin decoding written communication (reading). (A) is incorrect because the grapheme-morpheme correspondence describes the connection between a specific letter and letter strings that represent units of meaning in English--morphemes. The alphabetic principle (B) is a related concept that describes the ability to understand that the letters of the alphabet represent the sounds of the language. The graphophonemic correspondence of the language goes beyond the understanding of the connection of letters in the alphabet and the sounds that they produce. The sound system in L2 (D) is not specific enough to describe the connection between letters and sounds of the language.

49. (A)

English uses multiple figures of speech and idioms to convey meaning (semantics). Understanding the connotative nature of this figurative language requires students to have knowledge and experience with the target culture. Students new to the culture will take these kinds of communication literally resulting in miscommunications. The application of neither phonological analysis (B), nor the syntax (C) will be directly impacted by lack of cultural knowledge.

50. (B)

The alphabetic principle suggests that letters of the alphabet represent the sounds of the language. It also implies that speech can be represented in print and it can be reversed back to speech. (A) presents a fact, but does not describe the concept of the alphabetic principle. (C) presents an opinion not supported by research; memorizing the alphabet will not hurt, but it does not guarantee that children will understand the alphabetic principle. (D) presents a plausible statement, but unrelated to the actual question. The introduction of dictionary skills is a concept unrelated to the development of the alphabetic principle.

51. (A)

Cognates are words with similar meaning in two or more languages. Most of these words come from the Greek and the Latin, and they constitute the key vocabulary of the content areas (social studies, mathematics, science, music and the arts). Homophones (B) are words pronounced in a similar fashion but they can be spelled differently, and they have different meaning (hare and hair). Homographs are words that are spelled in the same way, but can have more than one meaning, depending on the location of the stress in the word (INsert (noun)-inSERT (verb). (D) presents a definition of homonyms, words that can have the same pronun-

ciation or spelling, but which have two entirely different meanings (e.g.,bear (animal)—bear (carry).

52. (C)

Speakers who follow an associational or curvilinear communication pattern have the tendency to deviate from the main topic of the conversation. They deviate to provide more details about a component of the conversation, and then return to the main topic. Since they do not follow the linear progression typical of Standard English, they get penalized for it. They provide support for the subject (A), but not in the linear fashion, which makes the information difficult to follow and document. Answering (B) and asking (D) questions might be affected by this communication style, but they will not effectively affect the ability to stay within the topic.

53. (B)

The word "thought" is a very long word but it is monosyllabic. It has three phonemes—the word contains two consonant diagraphs, the *th* and the *ght* and a vowel diagraph ou representing one sound each for a total of three sounds. (A), (C), and (D) are incorrect based on the previous explanation.

54. (C)

The word contains a prefix (sub), the root word (consci), the morpheme that calls for an adjective (ous), and the morpheme that defines the word as an adjective (ly) for a total of four units of meaning. (A), (B), and (D) are incorrect based on the previous explanation.

55. (C)

The sentence contains a noun (Mary), a transitive verb (gave), an indirect object (me) and a direct object (dollar). The key clue in this question is the type of verb used in the sentence—a transitive verb. Transitive verbs by definition can take objects. To determine if the sentence contains a direct object or an indirect object, we ask the following two questions: Mary gave what?—the answer is the director object—a dollar. The second question is, Mary gave it to whom?—the answer is me—the indirect object. (A) and (B) are incorrect because both contain intransitive verbs. (D) is incorrect because it does not contain an indirect object.

56. (B)

Through the combination of syllables, languages like Japanese can meet their communication needs. (A) is incorrect because pictorial languages are currently used to represent ideas in road signs and in most public facilities in the world. For example, a picture of a circle with a crossed line is commonly used to indicate that something is prohibited—smoking, swimming, use of bicycles, etc. (C) is incorrect because there is no evidence to suggest that syllabic languages are easier to understand than pictographic languages. (D) is incorrect because current pictographic representations (ideograms) are relatively easy to understand.

57. (B)

The initial sound of the words "write" and "gnat" represents a diagraph because the first two graphemes in the words represent only one sound /r/ and /n/. (A) is incorrect because the homophones blue and blew do not contain consonant diagraphs, they contain the consonant blend (bl). (C) is incorrect because both letters contain consonant clusters or blends, i.e., individual sounds are blended to

create a unique sound combination. (D) is incorrect because all letters in the words are pronounced.

58. (B)

The learner is unable to switch registers (communication styles) based on the context of communication. This language feature is identified as sociolinguistic competence. The concept of communicative competence has been defined based another three components: grammatical, discourse, and strategic. The grammatical component (A) describes the ability of the learner to apply grammar of the language. Discourse competence (C) refers to the ability of the learners to present an argument in a cohesive fashion. And strategic competence (D) describes the ability of the child to maintain the flow of communication to achieve the communicative purpose.

59. (B)

ELLs generally lack the background knowledge to understand stories written from diverse cultural points of view. When the teacher explains the vocabulary and idiomatic expression used in the story, students are able to fill in the gaps needed to understand and enjoy the story. Pre-reading activities can enhance comprehension but they are not generally designed to promote reading fluency (A). Traditionally, decoding skills (C) are not emphasized in pre-reading activities; thus, children will not necessarily apply these skills in a subconscious manner. (D) has a commonly acceptable statement, children develop reading and writing concurrently; however, this information does not address the question.

60. (B)

Learning logs are used to guide students to summarize elements learned and identify those where additional support is needed. By guiding students to summarize or synthesizing the information, students strengthen their understanding of the concepts learned. Learning logs provide a list of elements learned (A), but its value goes beyond a mere list of concepts. A learning log can be used as an advanced organizer to communicate with teachers and peer (C) and as a guide for oral presentations (D), but these are not the main objectives of learning logs.

61. (B)

English language learners often have problems understanding academic content because they might not have the background information needed to internalize new concepts. By examining the knowledge that children bring to the lesson and providing the content missing, children are able to link current knowledge with new ones. The KWL chart (know, wants to know, learn) provides an ideal tool to assess prior knowledge and their interest. It is important to assess the vocabulary the child brings and the one needed to understand the lesson (A); however, the KWL charts are not designed to gather this kind of information. I can explore it superficially, but not at the level required to make an accurate assessment of the vocabulary that the child brings to the lesson. The question deals with getting students to understand new academic content, not necessarily dealing with language development (A). Second language acquisition (C) and vocabulary development (D) will be definitely help the child, but the question does not address language development by itself.

62. (B)

Semantic mapping is a visual representation of interconnected characteristics or features of a given concept. This interrelatedness can be represented with words or visuals. For example the concept of landscape can be linked to pictures of lacks, rivers, mountains, grass, threes and other features that represent possible attributes of the concept. Through semantic mapping students will learn science concepts (A), however, the question calls for a technical definition of the concept. People can use semantic mapping to contrast concepts in L1 and L2 (C), but the process was not designed to accomplish that. (D) describes a possible type of mapping but does not represent the specific type of mapping required in the question—semantic.

63. (C)

Metacognitive strategies describe ways to conceptualize how learning takes place. This type of strategy is divided into two classifications: organization and planning for learning, and self-monitoring and self-evaluating. *Cognitive strategies* (A) describes techniques to improve understanding, increase retention of information and the ability to apply new information. It refers to the ability to link knowledge acquire in L1 to knowledge in L2. *Social strategies* (B) describes techniques used to learn from each other in social situations--peer or group format. (D) describes strategies to promote rote memorization of facts. Some typical examples of this type of strategy are the use songs, acronyms, and mnemonics to remember facts or rules.

64. (B)

Cognitive strategies uses techniques to improve retention of content and the use of prior knowledge like information acquired in L1 as a foundation for acquiring new concepts. Metacognitive (A) describes the ability of conceptualizing how learning takes place, not the actual transfer of information from L1 to L2. Social strategies (C) describe ways to acquire new knowledge in social settings. The use of mnemonic devices is part of rote memory strategy which has no correlation with transferring content from L1 to L2.

65. (B)

Information in textbooks is organized following a specific layout that provides information different from the traditional narrative format used in children's literature. Students need to make use of things like glossaries, indexes, text boxes, highlighted areas, graphics and visuals to increase comprehension. Teaching technical vocabulary (A), the use of cognates (C), and the use of glossaries (D) are good strategies to help students gather information from textbooks, but individually they do not constitute the best answer.

66. (A)

Effective methods to teach a second language should evolve around the child and his/her communication needs. The statement "student-centered and communication driven" describes an effective approach to teach a second language. (D) calls for the opposite, teacher-centered, and does not represent best teaching practices. (B) and (C) call for the teaching of a second language following a grammatical syllabus. Research does not support a grammar-based approach to teach languages.

67. (A)

Linguistic accommodations are designed to minimize the impact that language can have in testing. Through the selected accommodations, the validity of the test increases and it can yield a better view of the performance of the students. ELLs should be exposed to the same learning target as native English speakers; thus addressing part of learning target only (B) is not an acceptable approach. Substituting testing for other activities (C) might work for a while, but eventually, ELLs will have to be assessed like the other students. Avoiding testing that requires high order thinking skills (D) constitute an attempt to "water down the

curriculum," a strategy is contra productive and not fair for ELLs.

68. (D)

Accommodations are designed to compensate for specific characteristics or limitations that can interfere with the assessment process. With ELLs, teachers have to take into account not only the language but the specific disability of the child. Cost of the adaptation (A) should not be the primary concern in the identification of the accommodation. The legality of the modification (B) and the resources available (C) have to be taken into account when planning accommodations, they should not be the first element that teacher ought to consider to address the need of the child.

69. (C)

(C) is correct; just think of examples like pick/picks, dig/digs, buy/buys, and you should see this sound pattern for verbs. (A) is wrong because the grapheme *s* is not always devoiced at the end of a word; example: *sis* for sister. (B) is just plain wrong. (D) The fact that children pronounce it that way is an observation, not a reason.

70. (A)

Nativists believe that humans are born with a mechanism that they call the Language Acquisition Device (LAD), which gives humans the capability to acquire languages. However, in order to for this mechanism to work, children must be exposed to speakers of the language. Healthy children, who are exposed to language in natural settings during the early years, develop language. Yet children who are socially and linguistically isolated during the formative years can experience language delay or might not be able to develop adult-like language. Initially, children learn language through imitation with little direct corrections, but after age two children generally develop language creativity and other techniques to improve language acquisition; thus, option (B) and (C) are incorrect. (D) is incorrect because children are not born with language; they rather have the mechanism to acquire it.

71. (A)

Informal reading inventories are used to assess reading proficiency and to determine reading levels. They are called informal because teachers can administer the instrument. Based on this explanation, options (B), (C), and (D) are incorrect.

72. (C)

Language plays a determinant role in assessment; if the child is not fluent in the language used for assessment, results might not be valid and/or reliable. Thus, if the effect of language cannot be controlled, it is better to postpone the referral and assessment for special education until a reliable instrument can be found or the child exhibits the required linguistic development to take the test. Students cannot be placed in the special education program (A) or receive services (D) until the assessment process is completed, and the Admission, Review and Dismissal (ARD) committee makes the appropriate placement decision. Less demanding adaptations (B) of the instruments can be used, but these might not yield reliable data to make placement decisions.

73. (A)

A strong literacy background in L1 facilitates the transferring of skills to the second language, which will indeed expedite the development of literacy in the second language. A strong L1 development will facilitates the acquisition of a second language (B), but it will not guarantee that it will

be done in a "fun and relaxed environment." The transfer of literacy skills from L1 to L2 (C) goes beyond the transfer of academic language (C). Children also transfer metacognitive strategies and grammar concepts to the second language. A strong background in L1 can help in the preservation of the language (D), but is cannot guarantee it, especially if instruction in L1 is discontinued.

74. (B)

In an effort to make sense of the new language, ELLs develop a temporary form of the language called an interlanguage. This construction combines features of L1 and L2, and it contains numerous systematic performance errors. Teachers that have knowledge of the student's native language and English can predict problems faced when learning the language. (A) is incorrect between every language have its own idiomatic expression, and most of the time these do not transfer literally from one language to the other. (C) is incorrect because it provides information about the current levels of performance, but it does not provide information on how this information can affect future development in the language.

75. (B)

Teachers can guide ESL students in the identification of the units of meaning in a sentence (morphemes) to facilitate the decoding and comprehension of written discourse. This structural analysis can help decoding since most of the Greek and Latin prefixes are common among the content areas taught in school. The term "contextual" (A) makes reference to another decoding strategy that uses context and pragmatics to obtain meaning from text. Pictorial analysis (C) uses pictures and graphic material to obtain information from text. This strategy is commonly used at the beginning stages of reading. Syntactic clues uses the position of the words in a sentence to determine the syntactic classification of the word, and to narrow the possible meaning of words in text.

76. (C)

When students realize that a large number of prefixes and suffixes are common to L1 and L2, they become more confident in their ability to use L1 as a foundation to L2. They also begin to notice that these affixes also create similar words in the two languages (cognates) that can also be transferred to the second language. Teachers can use affixes to identify the influence of other languages (A) in English and the resulting foreign words used in the language (B), but these are not the primary reason for using affixes in the classroom. When students see all the elements that can be transferred from L1 to L2 might develop the idea that English is not a difficult language (D); however, soon they will realize that English has unique features and that not all the components from L1 can transfer to L2.

77. (B)

The Natural Method and the Total Physical Response (TPR) are both direct methods; that is, they attempt to replicate the way that children acquire a first language in natural settings. These methods generally avoid the students' native language to teach the target language (English). The Community Language Learning Method (A) is a communicative method that uses L2 to support students in their attempt communicate in the second language. The Audio Lingual Method (B) uses repetition drills and memorization of dialogues, which are not typical of direct methods. The grammar translation (D) does not address the first two language components that children acquire in natural settings, listening and speaking.

78. (B)

The Natural Methods uses a student-centered approach, where performance errors are seen as surface manifestations of the actual level of linguistic competence of the learner. These are generally used to re-teach and support students in their attempt to master L2. The Audio Lingual (A) is a teacher-centered method that uses direct error corrections in class. This lack of tolerance for errors can discourage risk-taking in class. Suggestopedia (C) does not present a clear idea of how errors are used in the method. Their main concern is to create a relaxed learning environment where direct error corrections are avoided; however, they correct errors through modeling. The Direct Method (D) is traditionally delivered through teacher-centered practices, which leaves the door open for direct corrections.

79. (A)

Syllabication and word stress are part of the concept called phonological awareness. (B) is incorrect because the child is able to connect the letters with the corresponding sounds (phonemic awareness). He has mastered the ability to separate phonemes and blends them back to recreate the word. (C) and (D) are incorrect because none of them individually explain the needs of the child. The reality is that the child needs support in both components; thus (C) or (D) individually cannot be the correct answer.

80. (B)

Sight words are those words that you can recognize visually without using specific decoding strategies. Words that appear frequently in sentences, like prepositions, forms of the verb "to be" and articles are generally taught as sight words. Word analysis (A), contextual clues (B), and phonics (D) are decoding strategies used to teach other than sight words.

81. (A)

In the LEA, students share an activity and then come back to the classroom to talk about and dictate it to the teacher. Teachers generally write the story verbatim, which allow students the opportunity to see their own words in a written form. LEA attempts to link the experience of the children with the experience presented in stories, but the methods is not necessarily used to link their experiences with the experiences of the teacher (B). LEA does not attempt to use grammar (D) of L1 as a foundation (D) for teaching reading in L2.

82. (D)

The TPR is traditionally used to engage students in the silent stage of second language acquisition or the preproduction stage. It can be used for the intermediate level (B), but it is more appropriate for the beginning levels. Based on this explanation, options (A) and (C) are incorrect.

83. (C)

Chants used for academic purposes are oral performance of a repetitive and rhythmic nature used to promote oral fluency. The original chants are choral renditions of religious nature (A) that monks use for prayer. Based on the information share in C and A, options (B) and (D) are incorrect.

84. (A)

The process of reading and writing complement each other, and these skills can be taught concurrently. In the 70s reading was conceptualized as system that progresses sequentially (C), where

reading (B) development was supposed to precede writing. Following this sequential process, often reading and writing were postponed (D) until students mastered the speaking ability. These views are no longer supporter by research, and today's researchers agree that language skills can be taught concurrently.

85. (A)

The student needs to be exposed to classroom activities that resemble real-life situations so that he can practice listening and speaking skills in meaningful situations. Exposing students to activities to polish pronunciation can support ELLs; however, the readers' theater (B) is not a strategy to polish pronunciation. Instead, readers' theater is designed to introduce literature in a dramatic form. Teaching idioms and colloquial expressions (C) in isolation does not address the specific communication needs identified in the scenario. (D) presents a good suggestion, focus attention on the message and avoid over corrections; however, the suggested strategy does not address the communication needs presented in the scenario.

86. (C)

When older ESL students have problems with specific English sounds, the best strategy is to isolate them, and provide explicit instruction to produce the sounds. This instruction includes the manner of articulation and the articulators involved in the production of the sounds. Spending time in the language laboratory (B) and identifying pronunciation errors typical of Farsi speaker can help, but students need specific information to deal with troublesome sounds. A mere description of the articulators involved (D) will help, but ESL students need information on way the sounds are produced in the vocal tract (manner of articulation).

87. (A)

Oral language development for young learners is best introduced inductively or indirectly through fun and inviting activities. Through the modeling presented in language play and in songs, young ESL learners can easily master English pronunciation. Listening for comprehension activities (B) is part of the strategies to conceptualize the sound system of the language, but we need to guide children to practice oral communication. Leading children to memorized poems and composing short stories (C) and developing formal presentation (D) might be challenging, developmentally inappropriate, and ineffective with young learners.

88. (C)

Teachers present the title, the author, illustrator, and visuals representation of the story to guide students to make prediction of the content of the story. Introducing children to other books from the same author (A), or drawing pictures to represent the main idea (B), presenting books with similar themes (D) are generally done as post reading activities.

89. (A)

The main purpose of the first reading is to get students engaged in the reading process, and to present the content of the story so children can corroborate their predictions. The introduction of decoding skills (B), including contextual clues (D), or the introduction of new vocabulary (C) are not generally done either before the reading or after the initial reading.

90. (D)

The second reading is designed to engage students in the reading process, and to enhance their comprehension of the story. Guiding students to read aloud (A) in a round-robin format (different students taking turns to read) is not a strategy commonly used in shared reading. Forcing all students to read out-loud can be counterproductive, since some of them might not have skills to model reading fluently. The cloze activity (B) is done to check for comprehension, and it is traditionally done as an assessment strategy right after the second reading. Guiding students to write their own stories (C) can be done as a follow up activity, only when students have developed a clear understanding of the story presented in class.

91. (B)

Interactive journals allow opportunities for children to communicate orally in real and purposeful activities. Learners communicate freely in a written form with other students or the teacher and indirectly they are practicing writing and reading skills. No direct corrections (C) are expected as part of the written interaction. If corrections are needed, these are generally done indirectly through modeling. The speaking (A) and the listening (B) abilities are not emphasized in interactive journals.

92. (C)

The main principle of the schema theory is that students develop a better understanding of new concepts when they can link them to concepts and experiences that they already have. Options (A) and (C) are true statements, but they are not directly related to the schema theory. The schema theory is not directly related to the development of learning strategies (D).

93. (C)

Brainstorming and the development of an outline are the first and most important components of process writing. Without an adequate outline, it is difficult to comply with the linear progression required in English writing. Once the initial draft is written, reviewing for content and grammaticality are also very important to complete a good essay. Based on this explanation, options (A), (B), and (D) are incorrect.

94. (C)

In the emergent literacy perspective, literacy emerges naturally among children without formal reading instruction. Literacy development is perceived as a process parallel to oral development which emerges when children see adults engaging in meaningful literacy activities like reading newspapers, writing notes, and looking at environmental print among others. Since this literacy development occurs mostly at home, family literacy practices become an important component of the literacy process. Family literacy programs encourage parents to involve children in meaningful literacy activities at home. Based on this explanation, options (A), (B), and (D) are incorrect.

95. (A)

In the absence of instrument design specifically for ELLs, it is appropriate to administer the instrument used for the general English population; however, it is very important to sure that results are evaluated based on the specific language and cognitive development of ELLs. Delaying assessment (B) can be done to a certain point, but it cannot be postponed until the student is exited (D) from the special language program. The use of non verbal examinations (C) might be effective for the early grades; however, for older students it might be impractical.

96. (A)

Schools in the United States traditionally use forced answer format in a form of multiple-choice examinations in summative evaluations. These tests have a specific format that might be foreign for students from the international community; thus, it is important to provide direct instruction in test-taking skills and the format used in these examinations. The format for filling in the blanks (B) or matching (C) are not generally used in high stakes examinations in the United States. Introducing relaxation techniques and the scoring rubric (D) can be used to support students, but they need to know the format of the actual examination.

97. (B)

Like the portfolio of an artist, a portfolio is a collection of the work that best represents the capabilities of the student. Since it is collected systematically through a given period, it provides teachers and parents with information about the development of the students. Portfolio can be used not only for the basic content areas (A), but for any area of the curriculum, including reading and writing. Portfolio data is not designed to be used for confidential purposes (C) only; instead, it can be shared with parents and teachers. Portfolio assessment is an informal component of the total assessment process, and it is not design to exposed people to the total assessment program (D) used in schools nationwide.

98. (D)

Since the attention span of five- and six-year-old students is limited, teachers need to develop tests that they can answer is a relatively short period of time—5 to 10 minutes. Tests should be challenging, but not all of them have to be comprehensive (A). The content of the test can be segmented to be sure that students can handle the components being assessed. It is important to develop culturally responsive tests (B), but the facility and time needed to grade them (C) should not be a major concern with developing these instruments.

99. (A)

The IEP contains the objectives and the assessment components for the grading period. These components have to be used when assigning grades using the IEP grading system. Depending on the disability, special education students exhibit a certain degree of mastery of the state curriculum (B). However, the degree of mastery might be different from the mastery required from students in the mainstream classroom. Based on the explanation given, options (C) and (D) are incorrect.

100. (C)

All language groups have developed some form of nonverbal communication. Some of the features are common among languages, but there are others that are culture-specific. Thus, the use of nonverbal means does not guarantee that the intended communication is being delivered. Based on the explanation provided, options (A), (B), and (D) are incorrect.

101. (B)

When tests for ELLs are designed based on the experiences of middle class, European American groups, it is safe to say that the test might contain cultural bias. Asking ELLs to respond to questions that do not represent their reality or experiences can place students at a disadvantageous position. Cultural bias does not have to contain wrong information (A), or hateful and ignorant (C); the key problem with biases is that they can affect the reli-

ability of the instrument, and are ultimately unfair. (D) is incorrect because cultural bias does not have to contain classified information.

102. (A)

Translated material can provide teachers and administrators with a false sense of security about the value of the instrument. A translated document does not guarantee that the cultural and conceptual frameworks of the test have been preserved. Translated materials might address the superficial meaning of the word, but it might fail to interpret how the hidden components of one language are communicate in the second language. Based on this explanation, options (B), (C), and (D) are incorrect.

103. (C)

When assessment is done informally as part of daily instruments, students get adjusted to the process, and do not experience as much anxiety as with formal assessment. Based on this explanation, option (D) is incorrect. Ongoing assessment can provide students with an idea of the type of instrument used in formal assessment (A), but this a by-product of ongoing assessment, but not the intended purpose of this type of assessment. Students might develop interest (B) in the assessment process, but this by-product of assessment is not the primary reason for using ongoing assessment.

104. (A)

Districts commonly use assessment to determine readiness for major examinations (benchmark examinations), and to report results to the public and governmental entities. Traditionally, districts do not use formal assessment to make direct changes at the classroom level (B). They present the information to the building principals, and it is they who will implement the necessary programmatic changes at the school level. Official high-stakes examinations are not designed to teach test-taking skills or concepts (C); preparation for taking a test, including reading skills (D), is done prior to the official examinations.

105. (C)

Culture shapes the way that children behave and perform in school. Linguistic limitations can also affect the ability of children to demonstrate capabilities and potential. The option of making students feel valued and wanted (A) is a noble cause, but it should not be the main concern when assessing ELLs. (B) presents a true statement when indicating that students go through different stages of development, but invalidats the answer by saying that these should not affect the way in which they are assessed. The term "cultural deficit" used in (D) invalidates the answer because ELLs cannot be considered as culturally deficient since they already bring with them their language and culture.

106. (A)

Effective assessment practices are generally part of instruction, on an ongoing basis and interpreted based on the developmental and cultural characteristics of the child (student-centered). It can be formative as well as summative (end product) (B), but its data collection cannot be restricted to documentation collected using state-approved instruments. Data collection is not restricted to information gathered by bilingual diagnosticians (C); parents and other instructional personnel can provide valuable information for assessment. Assessment should promote self-monitoring (D) but should not emphasize weaknesses only. Instead, assessment should capitalize on the strengths that children bring to the learning process.

107. (C)

Rubric used in holistic scoring provide generic descriptors of the assessment components used for the writing sample. Traditionally, a numeric value is used to assess performance. Rubrics in holistic scoring are not designed exclusively to determine if students are using process writing (A), or if they are using the logic of the language (B); however, the use of both components in writing most likely can help in getting a good score in the test. Holistic scoring of writing samples takes into account discrete components like mechanics, capitalization and punctuation (D), but the assessment goes beyond those specific language components.

108. (B)

In the cloze technique, words are deleted from text at different intervals (every 8th word), creating a document similar to a fill-in-the-blank test. Based on their comprehension of the story, students are asked to supply the missing words in the document. Based on this explanation, options (A), (C), and (D) are incorrect.

109. (A)

Story retelling is used with pre-literate students. In this strategy, students are required to retell a story previously read to them to show listening comprehension. When they provide the summary, teachers can determine if children understood the story, and assess the speaking ability, sentence formation, and vocabulary development. Writing development (B) is not assessed, at this level of literacy development (pre-literate). Story retelling does not yield specific information about the writing style used in the story or the point of view of the author (D). The identification of these literacy components is probably too advanced for children at this level of development.

110. (D)

Informal assessment strategies like checklist and structured teacher observations are an efficient way to gather assessment data. The information can easily be used to support students who are having difficulties, and to expand the knowledge of students who have mastered the intended standards. Traditionally, these assessment strategies are not used for teaching (A and B), or to conduct formal assessment (C).

111. (B)

Running records is an informal assessment that allows the teacher opportunities to gather assessment data on ELLs. Since the information can be gathered on a daily basis, it can be used for re-teaching purposes. Running records is not designed to compare L1 and L2 (A), nor to measure how fast students are adjusting to the new culture (C). It could provide some insights on these two elements, but the technique was not designed to gather that kind of data. It could provide teachers with information on students (D), but this is a by-product of the technique, not its primary intent.

112. (D)

Authentic assessment, also known as alternative or performance assessment, is a form of evaluation in which students are required to perform a specific task. In this activity the pre-service teacher has to provide evidence that she possess the skills and abilities to deliver an effective lesson for ELLs. This type of assessment could be considered informal (A) and summative (B) in nature, but the real purpose of the assessment is to demonstrate mastery in teaching. Option (C) is incorrect because norm-referenced achievement tests (C) are used to compare the performance of students on a given examination. In the scenario, the pre-service teach-

er is being assessed based specific performance indicators.

113. (A)

Effective methods to teach a second language should evolve around the child and his/her communication needs. The statement, "student-centered and communication driven," describes an effective approach to teach a second language. (D) calls for the opposite, teacher-centered; thus, it can be ruled out. (B) and (C) call for the teaching of a second language following a grammatical syllabus. Research does not support a grammar-based approach to teach languages.

114. (D)

One of the key features of Sheltered English Instruction (SEI) is the delivery of comprehensible input through hands-on, discovery learning, and contextualized instruction. Speaking slowly (A), using non-verbal communication (B) to promote comprehension, and checking for understanding (C) are some of the features of SEI but individually they do not fully describe the concept of SEI.

115. (C)

As a result of the Lau ruling (1972), the Department of Health, Education and Welfare created the Lau Remedies in 1975 to force compliance of the ruling. One of the key components of the Lau Remedies was the diffusion of the criteria used to develop effective language programs to support ELLs. ESL became a component of bilingual education under the Lau Remedies, not a program in isolation (A). The Lau Remedies created an impact at the state level, but it did not impact legislation at the national level (B). As a result of the Lau ruling,

State legislatures began removing English-only legislation (D) and enacting laws to implement special language programs for ELLs.

116. (B)

The two-way dual language program was designed to serve language minority and language majority students. Consequently, children from mainstream groups can participate in the program and become bilingual. Despite this public support, the U.S. Department of Education has not officially endorsed the program (C). The program allows for the maintenance of L1 and L2 (A), and it is research based (D), but these features alone do not account for the popularity of this method.

117. (C)

The Individuals with Disabilities Education Act (IDEA) mandates the creation of the ARD only (B). The ARD makes placement decisions and determines the objectives of the individualized education plan (IEP) for each student. There is no federal bilingual education law (A); thus, decisions about placement are done at the state and local levels. States with special language legislation require the creation the Language Proficiency Assessment Committee (LPAC) or a similar body to make placement decisions in the program. Both committees have teachers, an administrator and at least a parent (D); however, the bilingual legislation require to have a single parent representative for all students, while in the special education, the parents of individual children are required to be part of the committee.

118. (C)

The one-way, also known as developmental bilingual education, serves language minority students (e.g., Chinese students), while the two-way serves both language minority and language majority students, (e.g., Chinese and English speakers). The language (A) and academic (B) goals of both programs are the same, to perform well academically and to maintain both languages. Both programs also follow a similar format for the distribution of L1 and L2 (D).

119. (B)

Marian possesses the basic interpersonal skills (BICS) in Spanish and English, but she lacks the academic language needed to do well in the English only classroom—(CALP). Based on this explanation, options (A), (C), and (D) are incorrect.

120. (C)

A shelter instruction is a content-based language program where students take their regular classes in English, but received additional support from teachers specialized in shelter English instruction. In this environment, she will get the support needed to develop the academic vocabulary to be successful in the traditional English-only classroom. The pull-out program (A) is the less effective option because the students are pull-out of their classes to receive language development classes. Grammar-based programs (B) or the newcomers approach are not commonly used to address the needs of students at this level of development; thus, both placement options are impractical for the student.

Practice Test 2

Praxis English to Speakers of Other Languages (0360)

ANSWER SHEET FOR PRACTICE TEST 2 (0360)

1. Ⓐ Ⓑ Ⓒ Ⓓ
2. Ⓐ Ⓑ Ⓒ Ⓓ
3. Ⓐ Ⓑ Ⓒ Ⓓ
4. Ⓐ Ⓑ Ⓒ Ⓓ
5. Ⓐ Ⓑ Ⓒ Ⓓ
6. Ⓐ Ⓑ Ⓒ Ⓓ
7. Ⓐ Ⓑ Ⓒ Ⓓ
8. Ⓐ Ⓑ Ⓒ Ⓓ
9. Ⓐ Ⓑ Ⓒ Ⓓ
10. Ⓐ Ⓑ Ⓒ Ⓓ
11. Ⓐ Ⓑ Ⓒ Ⓓ
12. Ⓐ Ⓑ Ⓒ Ⓓ
13. Ⓐ Ⓑ Ⓒ Ⓓ
14. Ⓐ Ⓑ Ⓒ Ⓓ
15. Ⓐ Ⓑ Ⓒ Ⓓ
16. Ⓐ Ⓑ Ⓒ Ⓓ
17. Ⓐ Ⓑ Ⓒ Ⓓ
18. Ⓐ Ⓑ Ⓒ Ⓓ
19. Ⓐ Ⓑ Ⓒ Ⓓ
20. Ⓐ Ⓑ Ⓒ Ⓓ
21. Ⓐ Ⓑ Ⓒ Ⓓ
22. Ⓐ Ⓑ Ⓒ Ⓓ
23. Ⓐ Ⓑ Ⓒ Ⓓ
24. Ⓐ Ⓑ Ⓒ Ⓓ
25. Ⓐ Ⓑ Ⓒ Ⓓ
26. Ⓐ Ⓑ Ⓒ Ⓓ
27. Ⓐ Ⓑ Ⓒ Ⓓ
28. Ⓐ Ⓑ Ⓒ Ⓓ
29. Ⓐ Ⓑ Ⓒ Ⓓ
30. Ⓐ Ⓑ Ⓒ Ⓓ

31. Ⓐ Ⓑ Ⓒ Ⓓ
32. Ⓐ Ⓑ Ⓒ Ⓓ
33. Ⓐ Ⓑ Ⓒ Ⓓ
34. Ⓐ Ⓑ Ⓒ Ⓓ
35. Ⓐ Ⓑ Ⓒ Ⓓ
36. Ⓐ Ⓑ Ⓒ Ⓓ
37. Ⓐ Ⓑ Ⓒ Ⓓ
38. Ⓐ Ⓑ Ⓒ Ⓓ
39. Ⓐ Ⓑ Ⓒ Ⓓ
40. Ⓐ Ⓑ Ⓒ Ⓓ
41. Ⓐ Ⓑ Ⓒ Ⓓ
42. Ⓐ Ⓑ Ⓒ Ⓓ
43. Ⓐ Ⓑ Ⓒ Ⓓ
44. Ⓐ Ⓑ Ⓒ Ⓓ
45. Ⓐ Ⓑ Ⓒ Ⓓ
46. Ⓐ Ⓑ Ⓒ Ⓓ
47. Ⓐ Ⓑ Ⓒ Ⓓ
48. Ⓐ Ⓑ Ⓒ Ⓓ
49. Ⓐ Ⓑ Ⓒ Ⓓ
50. Ⓐ Ⓑ Ⓒ Ⓓ
51. Ⓐ Ⓑ Ⓒ Ⓓ
52. Ⓐ Ⓑ Ⓒ Ⓓ
53. Ⓐ Ⓑ Ⓒ Ⓓ
54. Ⓐ Ⓑ Ⓒ Ⓓ
55. Ⓐ Ⓑ Ⓒ Ⓓ
56. Ⓐ Ⓑ Ⓒ Ⓓ
57. Ⓐ Ⓑ Ⓒ Ⓓ
58. Ⓐ Ⓑ Ⓒ Ⓓ
59. Ⓐ Ⓑ Ⓒ Ⓓ
60. Ⓐ Ⓑ Ⓒ Ⓓ

61. Ⓐ Ⓑ Ⓒ Ⓓ
62. Ⓐ Ⓑ Ⓒ Ⓓ
63. Ⓐ Ⓑ Ⓒ Ⓓ
64. Ⓐ Ⓑ Ⓒ Ⓓ
65. Ⓐ Ⓑ Ⓒ Ⓓ
66. Ⓐ Ⓑ Ⓒ Ⓓ
67. Ⓐ Ⓑ Ⓒ Ⓓ
68. Ⓐ Ⓑ Ⓒ Ⓓ
69. Ⓐ Ⓑ Ⓒ Ⓓ
70. Ⓐ Ⓑ Ⓒ Ⓓ
71. Ⓐ Ⓑ Ⓒ Ⓓ
72. Ⓐ Ⓑ Ⓒ Ⓓ
73. Ⓐ Ⓑ Ⓒ Ⓓ
74. Ⓐ Ⓑ Ⓒ Ⓓ
75. Ⓐ Ⓑ Ⓒ Ⓓ
76. Ⓐ Ⓑ Ⓒ Ⓓ
77. Ⓐ Ⓑ Ⓒ Ⓓ
78. Ⓐ Ⓑ Ⓒ Ⓓ
79. Ⓐ Ⓑ Ⓒ Ⓓ
80. Ⓐ Ⓑ Ⓒ Ⓓ
81. Ⓐ Ⓑ Ⓒ Ⓓ
82. Ⓐ Ⓑ Ⓒ Ⓓ
83. Ⓐ Ⓑ Ⓒ Ⓓ
84. Ⓐ Ⓑ Ⓒ Ⓓ
85. Ⓐ Ⓑ Ⓒ Ⓓ
86. Ⓐ Ⓑ Ⓒ Ⓓ
87. Ⓐ Ⓑ Ⓒ Ⓓ
88. Ⓐ Ⓑ Ⓒ Ⓓ
89. Ⓐ Ⓑ Ⓒ Ⓓ
90. Ⓐ Ⓑ Ⓒ Ⓓ

91. Ⓐ Ⓑ Ⓒ Ⓓ
92. Ⓐ Ⓑ Ⓒ Ⓓ
93. Ⓐ Ⓑ Ⓒ Ⓓ
94. Ⓐ Ⓑ Ⓒ Ⓓ
95. Ⓐ Ⓑ Ⓒ Ⓓ
96. Ⓐ Ⓑ Ⓒ Ⓓ
97. Ⓐ Ⓑ Ⓒ Ⓓ
98. Ⓐ Ⓑ Ⓒ Ⓓ
99. Ⓐ Ⓑ Ⓒ Ⓓ
100. Ⓐ Ⓑ Ⓒ Ⓓ
101. Ⓐ Ⓑ Ⓒ Ⓓ
102. Ⓐ Ⓑ Ⓒ Ⓓ
103. Ⓐ Ⓑ Ⓒ Ⓓ
104. Ⓐ Ⓑ Ⓒ Ⓓ
105. Ⓐ Ⓑ Ⓒ Ⓓ
106. Ⓐ Ⓑ Ⓒ Ⓓ
107. Ⓐ Ⓑ Ⓒ Ⓓ
108. Ⓐ Ⓑ Ⓒ Ⓓ
109. Ⓐ Ⓑ Ⓒ Ⓓ
110. Ⓐ Ⓑ Ⓒ Ⓓ
111. Ⓐ Ⓑ Ⓒ Ⓓ
112. Ⓐ Ⓑ Ⓒ Ⓓ
113. Ⓐ Ⓑ Ⓒ Ⓓ
114. Ⓐ Ⓑ Ⓒ Ⓓ
115. Ⓐ Ⓑ Ⓒ Ⓓ
116. Ⓐ Ⓑ Ⓒ Ⓓ
117. Ⓐ Ⓑ Ⓒ Ⓓ
118. Ⓐ Ⓑ Ⓒ Ⓓ
119. Ⓐ Ⓑ Ⓒ Ⓓ
120. Ⓐ Ⓑ Ⓒ Ⓓ

120 QUESTIONS
120 MINUTES

SECTION I. ANALYSIS OF STUDENT LANGUAGE PRODUCTION

Part A: Grammar and Vocabulary
Approximate time — 10 minutes

Directions: In this part of the test you are asked to read and answer questions regarding problems with the student's use of grammar or vocabulary reflected in their speech. We begin with a short recording of the English spoken by a non-native speaker. We encourage you to follow along with the transcript in your book to help you remember what you hear. After listening to the student's speech, please read and answer the questions about the student's grammar or vocabulary in the time allotted; mark them on your answer. sheet. We suggest that you make notes on the printed transcripts as you listen to the recordings.

Now let's listen to the first student talk about how to protect the earth. Once the student is done, I will give you time to mark your answer on the answer sheet.

So maybe we have to, uh, study or learn more about, uh, earth and recycling things.

1. This speech sample contains errors with the use of

    (A) articles
    (B) verbs
    (C) pronouns
    (D) adverbs

For Question 2, listen as a student talks about plans after school.

I go to do my homework. Then I borrow books from a library, so I have to read it, and I think I'll take a shower and I just want to sleep.

2. The speech sample contains an error in the use of

    (A) pronoun-antecedent agreement
    (B) prepositions
    (C) adjectives
    (D) irregular verbs

For Question 3, listen as a student talks about the advantages of studying abroad.

Advantages are I can learn more things, and maybe I can learn how to get along with other people instead of our families.

3. Which of the following is most likely to be true?

    (A) The student does not like her family members.
    (B) The student does not think it is important to get along with family members.
    (C) The student needs to learn more about how to get along with family members.
    (D) "Instead of" is not the student's intended meaning.

For Question 4, listen as a student talks about the Indians.

That was, um, difficult to me for in Korea there was no Indians or other, um, kind of people.

4. This speech sample contains NO errors in

    (A) prepositions.
    (B) plurals.
    (C) subject-verb agreement.

(D) adjectives.

For Question 5, listen as a student talks about a visit to a special place.

…and it was kind of interesting because I've never been to other country before, since that was the first time.

5.   Based on this speech sample, the student

(A) has knowledge of past perfect aspect.
(B) makes no errors with past tense.
(C) has mastered the use of perfect aspect.
(D) knows how to use "other" and "another."

For Question 6, listen as a student compares schooling between Korea and America.

Um, in <u>Korea school start at like 9:00</u>, *but is really hard that in America it's just we, I have to go like 7:00, so is really hard to go to school.*

6.   The underlined words indicate that the student hasn't mastered

(A) third person singular for irregular verbs.
(B) third person singular for regular verbs.
(C) proper nouns.
(D) placement of prepositions.

For Question 7, listen as a student answers what she plans to do after finishing high school.

Uh, exactly ideal is go to college.

7.   The student could make this sentence grammatical by

(A) addition of a preposition.
(B) addition of an article.
(C) omission of an article.
(D) addition of first person singular pronoun.

For Question 8, listen as a student talks about what she plans to do after getting home.

I'll take shower and, uh, draw a picture, um, do-ing homework and, uh, go to bed.

8.   The student's statement contains errors with

(A) modifiers.
(B) logic.
(C) parallelism.
(D) prepositions.

For Question 9, listen as a student talks about a way to save energy.

And don't turn the air current, air conditioner too hard.

9.   The choice of the word "hard" in the student's statement is most likely due to

(A) simplification.
(B) code-switching.
(C) imitation.
(D) interference.

For Question 10, listen as a student talks about how to protect the earth.

I will uh, do, um, pick up. I will do, um, clean the earth or help earth and governments.

10.   In this speech sample, the student fails to use "pick up" as

(A) an intransitive verb.
(B) a transitive verb.
(C) a prepositional phrase.
(D) an adverb.

This is the End of Part A.

Go on to Part B on the Next Page.

SECTION I. ANALYSIS OF STUDENT LANGUAGE PRODUCTION

Part B: Pronunciation
Approximate time — 10 minutes

Directions: In this part of the test you will listen to more speeches by English speakers of other languages. First, you will hear a short speech. To help you remember what you heard a transcript of the recording will be printed in your test book. Then, you will read the question about the student's problem with pronunciation. To help you answer each question, the recorded speech will be played a second time. Then you will be asked to answer the question and mark it on your answer sheet.

Again, it is strongly recommended that you make notes on the printed transcripts as you listen to the recordings.

For Question 11, listen as a student reads about Americans traveling abroad.

Sometimes when Americans travel <u>abroad</u>, they don't make an effort to speak the language of the nation visited.

11. In the speech sample, there is a problem with the pronunciation of the underlined word because

    (A) the final consonant is dropped.
    (B) the /r/ sound is dropped.
    (C) the vowel is incorrect.
    (D) the /r/ sound is replaced by /l/.

For Question 12, listen as another student reads the same passage.

Sometimes when Americans travel abroad, they don't make an effort to speak the language of the nation visited.

12. In which following way does the student pronounce the word "sometimes"?

    (A) [ˈsʌmˌtaɪmz]
    (B) [ˈsʌnˌtaɪmz]
    (C) [ˌsʌmˈtaɪmz]
    (D) [ˌsʌnˈtaɪmz]

For Question 13, listen as a student reads the following sentence.

Countries like Switzerland, Belgium and Finland are officially bilingual or multilingual nations.

13. The student's pronunciation of the word "Belgium" contains which of the following sounds?

    (A) [ʤ]
    (B) [g]
    (C) [k]
    (D) [ʒ]

For Question 14, listen as a student reads the following passage.

It is incredible that after eradicating the students' native language in elementary and middle schools, in high school they are required to learn a foreign language.

14. The student substitutes the /r/ sound in the word "eradicating" for which of the following sound?

    (A) [l]
    (B) [v]
    (C) [w]
    (D) [n]

For Question 15, listen as a student reads the following passage.

A lot of people think that the maintenance of foreign languages in the United States can lead to political <u>fragmentation</u>.

15. Which of the following shows how the student pronounces the underlined word?

(A) [ˌfrægəˈmɛnʃən]
(B) [ˌfrægmənˈteɪʃən]
(C) [ˈfrægmənˌteɪʃən]
(D) [ˌfrægmənˈtiʃən]

For Question 16, listen as a student reads from a passage about a language policy of the U.S.

Based on this inadequate linguistic policy, <u>these</u> *linguistic resources are lost forever.*

16. How does the student pronounce the underlined word?

(A) [ðiz]
(B) [ðɪs]
(C) [dɪz]
(D) [θɪs]

For Question 17, listen as a student reads the following passage.

These children replace their language with English and become <u>monolingual</u> *English speakers.*

17. Which one of the following occurs in the student's pronunciation of the underlined word?

(A) Substitutes an /r/ sound
(B) Deletes the stressed syllable
(C) Deletes a syllable
(D) Misplaces the stress

For Question 18, listen as a student reads the same passage.

These children replace their language with English and become monolingual English speakers.

18. In this speech sample, what occurs in the student's pronunciation of the last word?

(A) Pronounces the initial /s/ as /z/
(B) Adds a vowel at the initial /s/
(C) Pronounces /r/ as a trill
(D) Omits the final /s/ sound

For Question 19, listen as a student reads the following sentence.

This policy has not affected their political <u>integrity</u>.

19. The mispronunciation of the underlined word is NOT caused by

(A) inserting an [r] sound.
(B) substituting [g] for [dʒ].
(C) substituting [m] for [n].
(D) inserting a vowel.

For Question 20, listen as a student reads the following sentence.

We are losing valuable <u>linguistic</u> *and cultural resources.*

20. Which of the following sounds occurs when the student pronounces the underlined word?

(A) [g]
(B) [dʒ]
(C) [r]
(D) [tʃ]

STOP

This is the End of the Recorded Portion of the Test.

Go To Part C Below.

END OF RECORDING

SECTION I. ANALYSIS OF STUDENT LANGUAGE PRODUCTION

Part C: Writing
Approximate time — 7 minutes

Directions: The questions in this part refer to a number of excerpts from writings by ESOL students. Choose the best answer to each question and mark it on your answer sheet.

Question 21 is based on the following excerpt from a student's essay describing a family member.

My sister likes to clean. She wipes everything carefully, and everything looks neatly in the house. She also dresses nicely and looks beautifully. She is a good student. She studies hardly and she goes to bed lately.

21. The errors produced in this writing sample are due to

   (A) transfer
   (B) code-switching
   (C) overgeneralization
   (D) poor learning strategy

Question 22 is based on the following excerpt from an essay describing a student's best friend.

Jane is my best friend who is also my classmate. She's nice to everyone and will help anyone who asks for help. She's very smart and her English is the best in the class. Sometimes Mrs. Smith who is our English teacher asks

Jane to help other students. Next year she is going to move to New York which is 2,000 miles away. We'll all miss her.

22. The errors in the writing sample involve

   (A) superlatives
   (B) conditional clauses
   (C) nonrestrictive clauses
   (D) subject-verb agreement

Question 23 is based on the following excerpt from a student's note about a homework assignment.

Because my parents don't want me to spend too much time on the internet, so I don't have a computer. Although my teacher emailed to me the homework yesterday, but I didn't get it until this morning. My teacher says that it's okay to fax to her my homework tonight.

23. This writing sample contains errors in which of the two areas?

   I.   Correlative conjunctions
   II. Subordinating conjunctions
   III. Double-object construction

IV. Relative clauses

(A) I and II
(B) II and III
(C) II and IV
(D) I and III

Question 24 is based on the following excerpt from a student's essay about coming to America

I been here for two years. Before I came here, I studied English for three months. I didn't have the chance to listen to American music. But I been practicing listening through music since I got here. I like English and I watch many movies. I hope that I will become an English teacher in the future.

24. Based on the writing sample, the student has not yet mastered the use of

(A) past tense.
(B) present tense.
(C) perfect aspect.
(D) future tense.

Question 25-26 are based on the following excerpt from an essay describing a student's day.

I usually get up at 7 o'clock. I take the shower and brush the teeth. Then I eat the breakfast. I always have a milk with a bread. Then I take the bus to go to school.

25. This writing sample contains errors in the use of

(A) present tense.
(B) articles.
(C) plurals.
(D) prepositions.

26. The last sentence of the writing sample can be a result of

(A) imitation.
(B) code-switching.
(C) overgeneralization.
(D) simplification.

Question 27 is based on the following excerpt from a student's essay about a book.

My friend gots this book for me yesterday. It looks interesting. I like this book. Most childrens knows this story. This book wrote by an American.

27. Based on the writing sample, which of the following is true?

(A) The student has no concept that –s is required for the third person singular.
(B) The student does not have the concept of past tense.
(C) The student does not know how to form a sentence in present tense.
(D) The student does not know how to form a sentence with passive voice.

Question 28 is based on the following excerpt from a student's essay about Halloween.

There are more people doing trick-or-treating. I went with my sister together. We went very early because the earlier you go, you'll get more candy. We both wore hats. I think her hat was nicer than me. She got more candy than me. But I like candy more than her.

28. This writing sample contains NO errors of

(A) comparative forms.
(B) comparative structures.
(C) illogical comparison.
(D) ambiguous comparison.

Questions 29-30 are based on the following excerpt from a student's essay about annoying people.

I don't like people who use bad language. Some people curse when they are impatient. People seem to lose temper when they are driving. Walking down the crosswalk, some drivers try to rush the pedestrians.

29. The last sentence of the writing sample contains an error that is commonly described by which of the following terms?

   (A) Run-on sentence
   (B) Dangling modifier
   (C) Sentence fragment
   (D) Broken English

30. Which of the following can be the first step to help the student to correct the error?

   (A) Rewriting the sentence for the student
   (B) Asking a fellow student to read the essay to the class and identify the problem because embarrassing students can encourage learning.
   (C) Asking the student to read the essay and identify the problem.
   (D) No need to identify the error since it is a common problem among native speakers of English.

This is the End of Section I.

**Go On To Section II,
Read the Directions and
Begin Work On The
Questions In That Section.**

SECTION II: LANGUAGE THEORY AND TEACHING

Approximate Time: 60 minutes

31. Phonemic stress can alter the syntactic classification and the meaning of words. In which of the following sets of words does phonemic stress change the word from a noun to a verb? [The primary stress is identified with capital letters]

   (A) ATTribute-atTRIbute. OBject-obJECT; conDUCT-CONduct
   (B) PERmit-perMIT PROgress-proGRESS; DIgest-diGEST
   (C) proTEST-PROtest; CONtent-conTENT; PERvert-perVERT
   (D) REnegate-REnegate;REcord-reCORD; PROduce-proDUCE

32. Convergent research on the interdependence of first (L1) and second language (L2) shows that

   (A) cognitive and academic development in L1 is a prerequisite for the learning of concepts in the second language.
   (B) transferability of literacy skills from L1 to L2 applies to speakers of indo-European languages and those languages that evolved from Latin.
   (C) academic skills, literacy development, concept formation, learning strategies, and subject matter knowledge transfer from L1 to L2.
   (D) students exposed to L2 after puberty will not develop a native like pronunciation in L2.

33. In the area of second language acquisition, an interlanguage is a

   (A) transitional construction that individual ELLs go through in process of language mastery.

(B) traditional approach for the teaching of a second language.

(C) combination of fricative and stop sounds produced when the tip of the tongue is placed between the upper and lower teeth.

(D) combination of two languages within one sentence.

34. Graphophonemic differences in alphabetic languages can result in

(A) syntactic interference between L1 & L2.
(B) language interference at the phonological and spelling levels.
(C) lexical transfer across languages.
(D) semantic differences.

35. Which of the following statements BEST represents the concept of the pragmatic system of the language?

(A) Knowledge about the schema of the conversation and the intent of the speaker.
(B) Positive fit between the grapheme and the phoneme of L1 and L2.
(C) Knowledge about contrastive analysis theory between L1 and L2.
(D) Use of connotative and denotative word meaning.

36. The teaching of syllabication in English promotes phonological awareness and helps in the identification of words with

(A) morphemes like prefixes and suffixes.
(B) word with multiple meanings and cultural connotations.
(C) consonant diagraphs and idioms.
(D) phonic patterns and the alphabetic principle.

37. Which of the following statements BEST describe how a first language is acquired?

(A) Language acquisition appears to be the result of innate abilities, imitation of language, and environmental influences.
(B) Language is acquired through imitation of parents and caregivers.

(C) Language acquisition occurs naturally in contextualized situations with little support from parents or caregivers.
(D) Language is acquired when children receive explicit language instruction and apply the rules to mimic the linguistic behavior of native speakers.

38. Knowledge of the two words used to create compound words can help students in their interpretation. However, there are examples of compound words in which the meaning of the two components does not contribute to and often interfere with the interpretation of the new word. Which of the following sets of compound words fall under this category?

(A) doghouse, autograph, and boathouse
(B) greenhouse, fireplace, and the mouthwash
(C) butterfly, nightmare, and brainstorm
(D) hotdog, birdhouse, and underground

39. When teaching phonemic awareness in English to pre-kindergarten students using a phonics program, teachers ought to

(A) make the activity interesting to all students.
(B) compare the phonetic system of the students L1 and English.
(C) create an atmosphere of cooperation among students from diverse ethnic and linguistic backgrounds.
(D) control the inconsistency of the grapheme-phoneme correspondence of English by presenting consistent sounds first.

40. The words *beef, seeds, beach, meat, cool* and *food* represent examples of

(A) words with a single morpheme.
(B) consonant clusters.
(C) homophones.
(D) vowel diagraphs.

41. Identify the common feature among the following sounds: /m/ of matter, /ŋ/ in sing and /n/ of name.

(A) They are fricative and nasal.

(B) They are voiced and lateral sounds.

(C) They are voiced and nasal sounds.

(D) They are nasals and stop sounds.

42. Which syntactic structure BEST represents the following sentence?

The Democratic Party captured the presidency in 2008.

(A) Noun Phrase—Linking verb—Predicate adjective

(B) Noun Phrase—intransitive verb—predicate adjective

(C) Noun Phrase—transitive verb—indirect object

(D) Noun Phrase—transitive verb—direct object.

43. Identify the three bilabial sounds of English.

(A) /m/, /n/ and /ŋ/

(B) /v/, /f/ and /t/

(C) /p/, /b/ and /m/

(D) /p/, /t/, and /k/

44. What is the main difference between the final phonemes in the following contrasting pair of words: back-bag. and lack-tag?

(A) One sound is voiceless and the second is voiced.

(B) Both set of sounds are voiced.

(C) Both set of sounds are voiceless.

(D) One sound is fricative and the second sound is affricate.

45. Some native English speakers and English Language learners from various language groups substitute the voiceless, interdental fricative sound /θ/ in the words—think and thanks—for the /s/ or /t/ sounds. If we rule out the effect of language interference from L1, what might be the rationale for this sound substitution?

(A) The production of the /θ/ sound requires more considerable effort than the effort required for the production of the two substituting sounds—/s/ or /t/.

(B) All three sounds are produced in the same manner and with the same articulators; thus, it is difficult to establish a difference.

(C) These sounds in initial position sometimes are pronounced with the /s/ or /t/ sounds.

(D) The sound /θ/ does not exist in other language groups; thus, the sound is substituted for sounds available in L1.

46. Which set of words contains the two English affricate sounds—/ʤ/ and /ʧ/.

(A) Shower and George

(B) Jury-chop

(C) Sure—Chute

(D) Leisure—pleasure

47. Which statement BEST describes the initial sounds of the words *when* and *went*?

(A) The initial sound of *when* is voiceless, while the sound of *went* is voiced.

(B) Both sounds are fricative and voiceless.

(C) Both sound are velar and stop.

(D) The sound of *when* is fricative, while the sound of *went* is affricate.

48. What are the descriptors used to identify English vowel sounds?

(A) stop, fricative, and affricates

(B) round-unround, high-low, and front, central, back

(C) voiced and voiceless

(D) high-low, hard-soft and closed-open

49. Marcos is a five-year-old student in the process of first language acquisition. He often produces statements like: "I wented to school yesterday." Based on this speech sample this child is

(A) applying language rules.

(B) experiencing language interference.

(C) applying the concepts from L1 to L2.

(D) imitating the speech sample of cartoons on television.

50. When two similar phonemes occur in complementary distribution, we identify these sounds as

(A) phonemes.

(B) allophones.

(C) morphemes.

(D) phones.

51. What makes the sounds of the letter P in the words *spring* and *prank* two different phonemes?

(A) the meaning of the words

(B) the morpheme that they represent

(C) one of fricative and the other is a stop sound

(D) one sound is aspirated and the other is not

52. How many phonemes are in the word *thoughtful?*

(A) nine phonemes

(B) six phonemes

(C) three phonemes

(D) five phonemes

53. How many morphemes are in the word *subconsciously*?

(A) three morphemes

(B) six morphemes

(C) four morphemes

(D) thirteen morphemes

54. Identify the choice that BEST describe the number and types of morphemes present in the word *preconceived.*

(A) Two derivational morphemes and a root word.

(B) Three inflectional morphemes and the root of the word.

(C) A free morpheme and two inflectional morphemes.

(D) One derivational morpheme, one inflectional morpheme, and a root word.

55. The third person singular, possessive and the short and long plurals are examples of

(A) derivational morphemes.

(B) function words.

(C) inflectional morphemes.

(D) free morphemes.

56. What are the two key features of inflectional morphemes?

(A) They come from the Latin and the Greek, and they do not change the syntactic classification of the word.

(B) They are native of English and they can change the syntactic classification of the words.

(C) They are native of English and they always occur at the end of the word.

(D) They can precede or follow a derivational morphemes, and they come from the Greek and the Latin languages.

57. Identify the sentence structure that BEST represents the following sentence:

Joe Biden is the new vice-president of the United States.

(A) Noun Phrase + Intransitive Verb + Predicate Adjective

(B) Noun Phrase + Transitive Verb + Predicate nominative

(C) Noun Phrase + Intransitive Verb + Predicate Nominative

(D) Noun Phrase +Transitive Verb + Direct Object

Read the following scenario and use the chart below to answer Questions 58 and 59.

Mr. John Smith is an ESL teacher in the school district of New Town. As part of his morning routine, he introduces pronunciation and vocabulary concepts through a chart. The chart is color–coded to guide students in the pronunciation of phonemes, i.e., he uses yellow for the /ʃ/, brown for /tʃ/, green for /k/. Every week he adds new words to the chart to help students with the grapheme–phoneme correspondence of these three sounds. The chart for this week is shown below.

58. English language learners in general have problems establishing the grapheme-phoneme correspondence of word with the sounds /ʃ/ /tʃ/. Based on the graph above, what might be rationale for this problem?

(A) They cannot distinguish the difference between the two phonemes.
(B) They cannot distinguish between the two sounds.
(C) The phonemes have different pronunciation.
(D) The graphemes representing the sounds are inconsistent.

59. What is the advantage of using the chart above to teach pronunciation?

(A) The chart provides examples of the graphophonemic consistency of English.
(B) The chart can be used to represent grapheme phoneme correspondence to guide for pronunciation.
(C) The students become aware of the words that follow one-to-one grapheme-phoneme correspondence in two languages.
(D) Children get exposed to vocabulary words and develop graphophonemic awareness

60. Kwame is a high school student having difficulties with American idioms. He often gets confused with statements like "keep an eye on the baby" and "keep your nose clean." Kwame is having problems dealing with

(A) academic English.
(B) denotative language.
(C) connotative language.
(D) metaphor and simile.

61. First language acquisition and especially oral language development appear to be the result of

(A) imitation and stimulus from the environment and practice.
(B) innate abilities, imitation and memorization.
(C) environmental influences, practice and memorization.
(D) innate mechanism, imitation and environmental influences.

62. Alex is a three-year-old child who makes statements like "go away," "open door," and "no more vacuum." Through which stage of first language acquisition is this child passing?

(A) Holophrastic Stage
(B) Babbling Stage
(C) Telegraphic Stage
(D) Egocentric Stage

63. Children experiencing language disorders caused by aphasia are most likely having

(A) articulation problems.
(B) language processing disorder.
(C) fluency disorders.
(D) hoarseness.

Chart for Questions 58 and 59 above.

SH – /ʃ/	CH – /tʃ/	CH – /k/	CH – /ʃ/	S – /ʃ/	T – /ʃ/
Shower	Church	Christopher	Chef	Sure	Caution
Short	Chart	Chemistry	Chevron	Sugar	Contribution
Shell	Choice	Chrome	Chevrolet	Mission	Communication

64. Mr. Rovira guides five year-old children in the recitation of the following utterance "Sally sells sea shells by the sea shore." Children have fun with the activity and try to say it without errors. What literary technique is he using?

(A) alliteration
(B) tongue twister
(C) nursery rhyme
(D) memorization drills

Read the following scenario and answer Question 65.

Ms. Thomas introduces new vocabulary words within the context of a sentence and through the use of visuals. Once children understand the concept linked to the word, she repeats individual words pausing after each syllable. Once children are able to separate the words into syllables, she asks them to separate syllables into individual phonemes.

65. What skill is Ms. Thomas introducing with the latter activity?

(A) the intonation pattern of the language
(B) phonological awareness
(C) vocabulary development
(D) pronunciation drills

66. The key feature of a balanced reading program is that it uses

(A) a balance between the receptive and productive skills of the language.
(B) a balance between theory and application of reading concepts.
(C) phonics instruction as the primary method to teach English reading.
(D) best practices from skill-based and meaning-based approaches.

67. Kindergarten students need to have a strong background in syllabication in English because syllabication is the foundation for

(A) oral communication and reading.
(B) reading comprehension.
(C) writing compositions.
(D) the transferring of reading skills to the second language.

68. Ms. Jefferson has guided first grade students to read polysyllabic words until they can read them fluently; later, students are asked to separate the words into syllables. Finally, she guided students to identify the main stress in each word. What skill is Ms. Jefferson emphasizing?

(A) Alphabetic awareness
(B) Reading fluency
(C) Phonological awareness
(D) Syllabication

69. When teaching the grapheme-phoneme correspondence of English, teachers must

(A) make the activity interesting to all students.
(B) monitor the children so they do not pronounce the letters with a foreign accent.
(C) create an atmosphere of cooperation among students from diverse ethnic and linguistic backgrounds.
(D) control the inconsistency of the grapheme-phoneme correspondence of English by presenting consistent sounds first.

70. Ms. Jefferson also uses monosyllabic words to present the concept of onset and rimes. Identify the pair of words that BEST represent this concept.

(A) want-ed—walk-ed
(B) very—berry
(C) think-ing—eat-ing
(D) s-ank—b-ank

71. What is the rationale for the popularity of onset and rimes to teach spelling skills in English?

(A) It is used to compensate for the grapheme-phoneme inconsistency in English.

(B) It is used to teach words as sight words.

(C) It is the best approach to teach words with multiple syllables.

(D) It is the best approach to teach the spelling pattern for prefixes and suffixes

72. What is the main reason for introducing the letter-sound correspondence of the *m, b, t, p,* and *s* prior to the letters like the *x* or *q*?

(A) Children might have more interest in the first set of sounds.

(B) The first set of graphemes occurs more frequently in reading.

(C) Children have muscular control and can pronounce nasal sounds

(D) The last set of graphemes can create language interference.

73. The use of phonics instruction in conjunction with components from the whole language approach is typical for programs emphasizing a

(A) skill-based approach.

(B) balanced-reading approach.

(C) meaning-based approach.

(D) humanistic approach.

74. Identify the statement that BEST describes the advantages of using the Language Experience Approach to teach reading to language minority students.

(A) LEA provides the schema or experiential background to facilitate the comprehension of the story.

(B) LEA uses the vocabulary and the experience common to both language minority and mainstream students.

(C) LEA minimizes the possibility of errors due to idiomatic expressions from both L1 and L2.

(D) LEA facilitates reading by ensuring a positive match between L1 and L2.

75. Identify the main benefit of the shared book experience.

(A) Stories are shared in a supportive environment.

(B) The whole class can read with the teacher.

(C) Children like big books.

(D) It contains attractive pictures and big letters.

76. During the pre-reading stage of the shared book experience, teachers can increase interest in the story by

(A) encouraging them to make predictions based on the title and the pictures.

(B) encouraging drawing a picture representing the main idea of the story.

(C) encouraging students to draw pictures representing the characters of the story.

(D) introducing the biography and other books of the author.

77. During the first reading of the shared book experience, the teacher reads the whole story in an enthusiastic and dramatic manner. The main purpose of this activity is to

(A) make the content understood to children so they can enjoy it and corroborate earlier predictions.

(B) introduce decoding skills and main idea.

(C) introduce vocabulary unknown to the children and decoding skills.

(D) review the parts of the book, check for comprehension and practice the use of contextual clues.

78. Identify activities that can promote emergent literacy in an indirect or subconscious manner.

(A) Guide children to follow and read the subtitles used in movies and television programs.

(B) Play board games where students have to read rules and information to be successful.

(C) Guide children to translate English stories in their native language.

(D) Share stories (storytelling) and write them down. Allow the child to see how the story looks in print.

79. Vocabulary development is a key predictor of success in reading. Identify strategies that parents can use with preschool children to promote vocabulary development in a fun and relaxed environment.

(A) Use flash cards with pictures and concrete objects to introduce vocabulary words.

(B) Play a game where the parents and the child teach each other the spelling of a dictionary word.

(C) Play games where children have to name homographs and homophones.

(D) Ask children to memorize a list of vocabulary words every day.

80. A teacher that uses words and sentences to analyze language and to teach reading skills uses a

(A) skill-based approach.

(B) meaning-based approach.

(C) bottom-up approach.

(D) literature-based approach.

81. Second language learners often experience problems with schema and the cultural framework required to understand English. What language component is more likely affected by this lack of background?

(A) the use and understanding of figurative language or idioms

(B) the application of phonological analysis

(C) the use of syntactic and phonological components

(D) the application of the lexical and structural components

82. Why might the sentence, "We have to make more headway," be a problem for an ESL student?

(A) Because the student is not used to making headway.

(B) Because "make headway" is an idiom.

(C) Because making headway is frowned upon in some cultures.

(D) Because inserting "more between "make" and "headway" is confusing.

83. Which of the following pairs demonstrates an example of a minimal pair?

(A) Big/Large

(B) Two/Too

(C) Bad/Bat

(D) Hot/Cold

Read the following scenario and answer Questions 84 and 85.

Mary Stewart is a former elementary school teacher that recently moved to teach at the high school level. She believes that her elementary background can support her teaching at the high school level. To implement this belief, she developed a word wall representing the different sounds of the grapheme S.

Has	tanks
Was	caps
Calls	walks
Runs	cats
Cars	parts

She presented these and other words without analyzing the rationale for their pronunciation. Later she asked students to identify the rationale for the difference in pronunciation.

84. Identify the method or strategy used to present the different phonemes used to pronounce the grapheme S.

(A) phonics instruction

(B) inductive teaching

(C) deductive teaching

(D) whole language instruction

85. What linguistic rules was Ms. Steward trying to present with these examples?

(A) The grapheme S has a very consistent grapheme-phoneme correspondence.

(B) After vowel sounds, the sound of the S becomes voiced.

(C) After voiced sounds, the grapheme S is pronounced as /z/.

(D) After voiceless sounds and vowels the grapheme S is pronounced as /z/.

86. On a different section of the wall, Ms. Steward has the following sets of words.

Column A	Column B
Cages	balls
Boxes	boys
Washes	girls
Churches	motors
Cases	windows

What grammatical component is she presenting?

(A) the distinction between voiced and voiceless sounds

(B) the rules for long and short plurals in English

(C) syllabication phoneme segmentation in English

(D) the stress pattern and intonation pattern in English words

87. Ms. Stewart encourages students to search for additional words for the word walls. This morning, Marguerite and Jonathan suggested two new words for long plural section (column B) of the word wall—*wires* and *tires*. What should the teacher do with these new words?

(A) Place them in both columns A and B, and discuss the rationale for the decision

(B) Place them in column A, and discuss the rationale for the decision.

(C) Place them in column B only, and discuss the rationale for the decision.

(D) Avoid placing them in either column to avoid confusion.

88. After a few weeks of using this approach, several students became apprehensive about her teaching style, and started complaining about it. What can Ms. Stewart do to support these ESL students?

(A) Continue teaching inductively, since she knows what is best for the students.

(B) Modify her teaching approach by including more deductive teaching strategies.

(C) Avoid teaching ESL using the inductive approach.

(D) Modify her teaching style to include rote memorization and repetition drills.

Study the content and the organization of ideas in this essay written by Almahdi, a middle school ELL student; then answer Question 89.

My Family

My family is composed of three children and my parents. We are from Dubai, the most populated city of the United Arab Emirates. Dubai is one small but prosperous city. Our main source of income is tourism. We are Arabs. Arabs are good people. We are very religious and very respectful of human rights. There are different kinds of Arabs Iranians are not Arabs, they are Persians. They don't speak Arabic; they speak a language called Farsi. Some of my friends are from Iran, Iraq and Israel. All my friends are nice and very religious.

My family is lives in a middle class neighborhood in the northern part of the city. We enjoy fishing and water sports...

89. How do you characterize the rhetorical patterns used in this portion of the composition?

(A) It is well written but it lacks supporting details.

(B) It uses sophisticated vocabulary, and follows a linear progression.

(C) It uses very good English vocabulary but it does not provide sufficient information to make it interesting.

(D) It uses sophisticated vocabulary, and presents the ideas in a curvilinear fashion.

Read the following scenario and answer Questions 90.

Mike and Carla are fifth grade bilingual students who were exited from the program a year ago. Both spent three years in the ESL program, and performed well socially and academically while in the program. After a year in the regular program, Mike is performing well as evidenced by his passing score on the most recent mid semester examination. On the other hand, Carla is doing fine socially, but not that well academically. She has difficulties handling the academic requirements in the regular English classroom. She feels depressed and wants to go back to the security of the ESL program.

90. Identify the statements that might explain the reasons for the difficulties that Carla is experiencing in the English classroom.

(A) She mastered the basic interpersonal skills (BICS) but not the cognitive academic language proficiency (CALP) of the language.

(B) She needs to go back to the bilingual classroom.

(C) She does not have the verbal intelligence needed to do well in the regular program.

(D) She mastered the CALP but still needs additional training to master BICS.

Read the following scenario and answer Question 91.

Ms. Fuentes is a bilingual third grade teacher in El Monte School District. In her class, she has students of different English and Spanish speaking proficiencies. Every morning she reads stories from a Spanish reader that contains stories about the different ethnic and linguistic groups represented in the school community. Students are instructed to close their eyes and listen to the story. She uses dramatic reading and different tones of voice to highlight important parts of the story, and to make the story more interesting. After this activity she asks questions about the story. Later, she allows students opportunities to read the story silently on their own to get more information about the story.

91. What language skill(s) is Ms. Fuentes emphasizing through dramatic reading?

(A) listening and reading comprehension

(B) reading comprehension

(C) listening, speaking, reading and writing

(D) listening comprehension

92. Mr. Lawrence reads stories to his kindergarten students in a very pleasant and natural tone of voice. Later, he uses a series of connected pictures representing events in the story. In addition to helping children understand the story, what other element is he teaching?

(A) The teacher is introducing the sound-symbol correspondence of the story.

(B) The teacher is filling the experiential gaps to be sure students can understand the story.

(C) The teacher is introducing sequencing and the story structure.

(D) The teacher is using developmentally appropriate practices since children at this stage cannot read on their own.

93. Minimal pairs are used to teach

(A) phonics skill.

(B) phonemic awareness.

(C) structural analysis.

(D) cognates and false cognates.

94. Identify the most appropriate evaluation techniques that can promote self-directed learning for ESL students.

(A) In the writing samples of beginner English language learners (ELLs), discuss the source of the problem and allow students time to figure out the type of correction(s) needed.

(B) In activities designed to polish the English pronunciation of advanced students, record their speech electronically and allow sufficient time for them to listen and evaluate their own performance.

(C) In communication activities, provide immediate specific corrective feedback emphasizing the areas in where improvement is needed.

(D) In communication activities, provide direct feedback and guide students to produce standard English.

Read the following scenario and answer Question 95.

Husna is an ELL from Pakistan attending Washington Heights Elementary. She is fluent and literate in her native language, Urdu. She is experiencing academic problems in school and was referred for testing. A certified bilingual (Urdu–English) diagnostician administered the test, and provided the appropriate linguistic accommodations. The diagnostician used a state-approved standardized achievement test to evaluate the child. Husna scored 25% in the test. Based on this score, she was re-tested two weeks later and scored at 69%. The diagnostician was very puzzled by the results and re-tested her the following week. This time she scored at 15%.

95. Based on Husna's performance in the test, what are the key components of the testing process that must be evaluated before placement decisions are made?

(A) the reliability of the test
(B) the credentials of the diagnostician
(C) the accuracy of the testing instrument
(D) the content of the testing instrument

96. The Language Proficiency Assessment Committee (LPAC), or an equivalent body, is in charge of studying the data on ELLs and making placement decisions. In addition to the results of the state-mandated instruments, what else should the LPAC committee consider before making placement decisions?

(A) Results of the language proficiency tests in L1
(B) Evaluation and input from peers.
(C) Formal evaluations conducted by parents.
(D) Medical history of the child and input from parents

97. When analyzing and interpreting assessment data from culturally and linguistically diverse students (CLD), assessors must take into account that

(A) the main objective of assessment is to make students feel valued and wanted in school.
(B) students go through different stages of development and these stages should not affect the way that children are assessed.
(C) students might express their potential differently due to linguistic and cultural influences.
(D) students may have culture and language deficits, which can preclude them from effective participation in the testing process.

98. One of the key problems associated with the use of standardized tests to measure the intelligence of culturally and linguistically diverse students (CLD) in grades three and up is that these tests

(A) are designed to measure achievement as opposed to intelligence and potential.
(B) are designed to measure content that has not been covered in class.
(C) overemphasize logic and mathematical skills at the expense of other indicators of intelligence.
(D) require a specific cultural framework and knowledge of academic language to be successful.

99. Modern assessment approaches for culturally and linguistically diverse (CLD) students use multiple assessment measures and contain the following key characteristics.

    (A) History of the physical development of the child and evidence of the legal status of parent in the country.
    (B) Instruments are administered using Spanish.
    (C) Instruments are validated for the population in question.
    (D) A multidisciplinary team of professional evaluates the data.

100. Which of the following statements BEST describes the value of portfolio assessment?

    (A) It allows the collection of student's work throughout their schooling in the United States.
    (B) It provides the opportunity to compete with other students.
    (C) It provides teachers with an opportunity to collect confidential information about students.
    (D) It provides students with a sense of ownership and participation in the assessment process.

101. Effective assessment practices generally share the following guiding principle.

    (A) It is child-centered, ongoing and collected as part of daily instruction.
    (B) It is summative in nature and collected through instruments approved by the state.
    (C) It is restricted to data gathered by competent bilingual diagnosticians.
    (D) It emphasizes student weaknesses and should promote self-monitoring.

102. English language learners might have problems understanding the statement, "All the gold in Fort Knox cannot make me change my opinion." What type of knowledge should ELLs have to understand this statement?

    (A) The concept of metaphor and allusion.
    (B) The concept of a simile.
    (C) The concept of an allusion.
    (D) The concept of a hyperbole.

103. Identify the informal activities/instruments used to assess oral communication skills in Pre-K students.

    (A) Teacher observation checklists, retelling stories, and anecdotal records.
    (B) Multiple-choice tests, cloze tests and an informal reading inventory.
    (C) Audio-taped conversations, written cloze tests, and standardized achievement test.
    (D) Repetition drills, choral reading, and chants.

104. One of the main functions of portfolio assessment for ELLs is to

    (A) document the social development and the interaction with native English speakers.
    (B) document progress toward language and content mastery.
    (C) collect all assignments and daily activities completed during the day.
    (D) collect all sample art work and artistic manifestations of children.

105. Which of the following statements BEST describes the advantages of students who arrive at the threshold level of L1?

    (A) They have developed the positive self-esteem needed to acquire a second language.
    (B) They have a deep understanding of culture and its implications for the acquisition of L2.
    (C) They possess the linguistic knowledge-base in L1 needed to transfer to L2.
    (D) They can apply contrastive analysis theory to the acquisition of L2.

106. Identify the statement that correctly describes Normal Curve Equivalent (NCE) scores and National Percentiles (NPRs).

    (A) NCEs are based on actual raw scores and NPRs are not.

(B) NPRs are based on the scores of a national norm and NCE are based on scores from a local norm.

(C) Both NCEs and NPRs are derived from raw data.

(D) NPRs are based on raw scores and NCEs are based on derived scores.

107. Identify the statements that BEST describe portfolio assessment and/or its advantages.

(A) Portfolio provides information about academic progress in the content areas.

(B) Portfolio assessment is a collection of the student's work that helps in tracking student progress.

(C) Data from portfolio is confidential and should used for official purposes only.

(D) Portfolio assessment provides students with opportunities to understand the assessment process used in the United States.

108. Ms. Kelly Rojo developed a test for kindergarten students. The test had illustrations to improve students' comprehension. For beginner ESL children, she read the questions to be sure that language did not interfere in the process. These testing modifications are an example of

(A) linguistic accommodation.

(B) summative evaluation.

(C) content validity.

(D) formative evaluation.

109. At the campus and classroom levels, the purpose of formative evaluation is

(A) to compare students with a national norm.

(B) to assess the performance of students in special education.

(C) to improve instruction and to monitor progress.

(D) to determine mastery and to comply with the NCLB legislation.

110. Teacher-made tests are examples of

(A) criterion-referenced tests.

(B) norm-referenced tests.

(C) informal assessment.

(D) standardized achievement tests.

111. Which field of study is concerned with the productivity of word formation to build vocabulary?

(A) Syntax

(B) Semantics

(C) Morphology

(D) Psycholinguistics

112. The main purpose of rubrics is to

(A) guide students to comply with the objectives of the lesson.

(B) provide students with guidelines for the development of effective instruction for English language learners.

(C) Guide students to use high order thinking skills.

(D) Provide students with information on the content and the level of mastery required for an assessment activity.

113. One of the key provisions of the No Child Left Behind (NCLB) Act in regard to the education of English language learners is to

(A) allow local autonomy in the implementation of services.

(B) empower parents and children.

(C) allow control of the federal government over the education process.

(D) promote bilingualism in the United States.

114. In the Transitional Bilingual Education (TBE) model, ESL is used as

(A) a component of the program.

(B) the program of choice to teach the content areas.

(C) a pull-out system to promote English development.

(D) a way to avoid the use of L1 to teach the content areas.

115. The key disadvantage of the pull-out approach to teach English to ELLs is

(A) children might feel embarrassed for being placed in the ESL program.

(B) children might feel uncomfortable spending most of the time in mainstream classrooms.

(C) children can fall behind academically when they are pulled out for ESL instruction.

(D) children will not be able to learn English using this approach.

116. Convergent research shows that Sheltered English Instruction is more appropriate for students who are

(A) field independent and have strong foundation in L1.

(B) at the intermediate or advanced proficiency level in English.

(C) native speakers of a language other than Spanish.

(D) already literate in their native language.

117. Traditionally, newcomer programs are designed to address the language and cultural needs of students

(A) from low socio-economic backgrounds.

(B) from non-traditional backgrounds without prior schooling.

(C) who are from non-Spanish speaking backgrounds.

(D) who are at the intermediate or advanced level of English proficiency.

118. Identify the main contribution of the landmark case of *Lau v. Nichols*.

(A) It mandated the creation of a bilingual education program in San Francisco.

(B) It empowered the Office of Civil Rights (OCR) to force school districts to provide

better education to linguistic minority students.

(C) It guided other courts to find in favor of bilingual education.

(D) It resulted in the signing of a federal law mandating bilingual education in the United States.

119. As a result of the AIR Study, sponsored by the American Institute of Research in 1981,

(A) bilingual education was eliminated in California.

(B) the structured immersion program was introduced as a program option for ELLs.

(C) the Bilingual Education Act mandated dual language immersion for school districts in the nation.

(D) the Bilingual Education Act prohibited the use of federal funding to create transitional bilingual education programs.

120. In the last few years, Dual Language Programs have received support from mainstream groups. The main reason for this popularity is because the program

(A) allows for the maintenance of L1 and L2.

(B) allows the inclusion of children from mainstream groups in the program.

(C) is supported by the U.S. Department of Education.

(D) is grounded in solid scientific research.

Detailed Explanations of Answers for Practice Test 2

Praxis English to Speakers of Other Languages

ANSWER KEY AND COMPETENCIES

Question Number	Correct Answer	Content Category
1	A	Analysis of Student Language Production; Linguistic Theory: Syntax
2	A	Analysis of Student Language Production; Linguistic Theory: Syntax
3	D	Analysis of Student Language Production; Linguistic Theory: Syntax
4	D	Analysis of Student Language Production; Linguistic Theory: Syntax
5	B	Analysis of Student Language Production; Linguistic Theory: Syntax
6	B	Analysis of Student Language Production; Linguistic Theory: Syntax
7	A	Analysis of Student Language Production; Linguistic Theory: Syntax
8	C	Analysis of Student Language Production; Linguistic Theory: Syntax
9	D	Analysis of Student Language Production; Linguistic Theory: Psycholinguistics
10	B	Analysis of Student Language Production; Linguistic Theory: Syntax
11	C	Analysis of Student Language Production; Linguistic Theory: Phonology
12	B	Analysis of Student Language Production; Linguistic Theory: Phonology
13	B	Analysis of Student Language Production; Linguistic Theory: Phonology
14	B	Analysis of Student Language Production; Linguistic Theory: Phonology
15	A	Analysis of Student Language Production; Linguistic Theory: Phonology
16	B	Analysis of Student Language Production; Linguistic Theory: Phonology
17	A	Analysis of Student Language Production; Linguistic Theory: Phonology
18	D	Analysis of Student Language Production; Linguistic Theory: Phonology
19	C	Analysis of Student Language Production; Linguistic Theory: Phonology
20	B	Analysis of Student Language Production; Linguistic Theory: Phonology
21	C	Analysis of Student Language Production; Linguistic Theory: Psycholinguistics
22	C	Analysis of Student Language Production; Linguistic Theory: Syntax
23	B	Analysis of Student Language Production; Linguistic Theory: Syntax
24	C	Analysis of Student Language Production; Linguistic Theory: Syntax
25	B	Analysis of Student Language Production; Linguistic Theory: Syntax
26	A	Analysis of Student Language Production; Linguistic Theory: Psycholinguistics
27	D	Analysis of Student Language Production; Linguistic Theory: Psycholinguistics
28	A	Analysis of Student Language Production; Linguistic Theory: Syntax
29	B	Analysis of Student Language Production; Linguistic Theory: Syntax
30	C	Analysis of Student Language Production; Teaching Methods and Techniques
31	B	Linguistic Theory: Phonology
32	C	Teaching Methods and Techniques
33	A	Linguistic Theory: Psycholinguistic
34	B	Linguistic Theory: Psycholinguistic
35	A	Linguistic Theory: Sociolinguistics
36	A	Teaching Methods and Techniques
37	A	Linguistic Theory
38	C	Linguistic Theory: Morphology

Question Number	Correct Answer	Content Category
39	D	Teaching Methods and Techniques
40	D	Linguistic Theory: Phonology
41	C	Linguistic Theory: Phonology
42	D	Linguistic Theory: Syntax
43	C	Linguistic Theory: Phonology
44	A	Linguistic Theory: Phonology
45	A	Linguistic Theory: Phonology
46	B	Linguistic Theory: Phonology
47	A	Linguistic Theory: Phonology
48	B	Linguistic Theory: Phonology
49	A	Linguistic Theory: Syntax
50	B	Linguistic Theory: Phonology
51	D	Linguistic Theory: Phonology
52	B	Linguistic Theory: Phonology
53	C	Linguistic Theory: Morphology
54	D	Linguistic Theory: Morphology
55	C	Linguistic Theory: Morphology
56	C	Linguistic Theory: Morphology
57	C	Linguistic Theory: Syntax
58	D	Linguistic Theory: Phonology
59	D	Linguistic Theory: Phonology
60	C	Linguistic Theory: Syntax
61	D	Linguistic Theory: Psycholinguistic
62	C	Linguistic Theory: Syntax
63	B	Linguistic Theory: Psycholinguistic
64	A	Teaching Methods and Techniques
65	B	Teaching Methods and Techniques
66	D	Teaching Methods and Techniques
67	A	Teaching Methods and Techniques
68	C	Teaching Methods and Techniques
69	D	Teaching Methods and Techniques
70	D	Teaching Methods and Techniques
71	A	Teaching Methods and Techniques
72	B	Teaching Methods and Techniques
73	B	Teaching Methods and Techniques
74	A	Teaching Methods and Techniques
75	A	Teaching Methods and Techniques
76	A	Teaching Methods and Techniques
77	A	Teaching Methods and Techniques

ANSWER KEY AND COMPETENCIES

Question Number	Correct Answer	Content Category
78	D	Teaching Methods and Techniques
79	A	Teaching Methods and Techniques
80	B	Teaching Methods and Techniques
81	A	Linguistic Theory: Syntax
82	B	Linguistic Theory: Syntax
83	C	Linguistic Theory: Phonology
84	B	Teaching Methods and Techniques
85	C	Teaching Methods and Techniques
86	B	Teaching Methods and Techniques
87	C	Teaching Methods and Techniques
88	B	Teaching Methods and Techniques
89	D	Assessment Techniques and Cultural Issues: Evaluation and Assessment
90	A	Assessment Techniques and Cultural Issues: Evaluation and Assessment
91	D	Teaching Methods and Techniques
92	C	Teaching Methods and Techniques
93	B	Teaching Methods and Techniques
94	B	Teaching Methods and Techniques
95	A	Assessment Techniques and Cultural Issues: Evaluation and Assessment
96	D	Assessment Techniques and Cultural Issues: Evaluation and Assessment
97	C	Assessment Techniques and Cultural Issues
98	D	Assessment Techniques and Cultural Issues
99	D	Assessment Techniques and Cultural Issues: Cultural Issues
100	D	Assessment Techniques and Cultural Issues: Evaluation and Assessment
101	A	Assessment Techniques and Cultural Issues: Evaluation and Assessment
102	C	Assessment Techniques and Cultural Issues: Evaluation and Assessment
103	A	Assessment Techniques and Cultural Issues: Evaluation and Assessment
104	B	Assessment Techniques and Cultural Issues: Evaluation and Assessment
105	C	Assessment Techniques and Cultural Issues: Evaluation and Assessment
106	A	Assessment Techniques and Cultural Issues: Evaluation and Assessment
107	B	Assessment Techniques and Cultural Issues: Evaluation and Assessment
108	A	Assessment Techniques and Cultural Issues: Evaluation and Assessment
109	C	Assessment Techniques and Cultural Issues: Evaluation and Assessment
110	A	Assessment Techniques and Cultural Issues: Evaluation and Assessment
111	C	Linguistic Theory: Morphology
112	D	Assessment Techniques and Cultural Issues: Evaluation and Assessment
113	A	Professional Issues: Legal Foundations
114	A	Professional Issues: Programs and Models
115	C	Professional Issues: Programs and Models

Question Number	Correct Answer	Content Category
116	B	Professional Issues: Programs and Models
117	B	Professional Issues: Programs and Models
118	B	Professional Issues: Legal Foundations
119	B	Professional Issues: Programs and Models
120	B	Professional Issues: Programs and Models

PRACTICE TEST 2 (0360): DETAILED EXPLANATIONS OF ANSWERS

Section I: Part A–Oral Grammar and Vocabulary

1.   (A)

This question tests your ability to identify some common grammatical errors in a student's speech. In this speech sample, the student fails to place a definite article before the word "earth." Therefore, the correct answer is (A).

2.   (A)

This question tests your ability to recognize grammatical errors in a student's speech. In this speech sample, the student uses the third person singular pronoun, "it," to refer to the plural antecedent, "books." Therefore, the correct answer is (A).

3.   (D)

This question tests your ability to understand the reason for a student's mistake. In the context of the speech sample, it is most likely that the student incorrectly substitutes "instead of" for the preposition "besides." Therefore, the correct answer is (D).

4.   (D)

This question tests your ability to identify some common grammatical errors in a student's speech. The student incorrectly uses the preposition "to" to follow "difficult." Further, the word "kind" should be in the plural form because it follows "other." Finally, in the there is/are structure, the main subject follows the verb. Since the word "Indians" is in the plural form, the verb should be "were." Therefore, the correct answer is (D)

5.   (B)

This question tests your ability to identify grammatical errors in a student's speech. Option

(A) is incorrect because the present perfect aspect (i.e., "I've never been") is used where the past perfect aspect (i.e., "I had never been") is required. This error also indicates that the student hasn't mastered the use of the perfect aspect. So, option (C) is also incorrect. Further, option (D) is incorrect because the student fails to use "another" to precede the singular noun, "country." There are no errors in the use of past tenses in this speech sample. Therefore, the correct answer is (B).

6.   (B)

This question tests your ability to identify grammatical errors in a student's speech. In this part of the speech sample, the word "school," a singular noun, serves as subject, but the student fails to use a third person singular form "-s" for the verb "start." Therefore, the correct answer is (B).

7.   (A)

This question tests your ability to determine a grammatical error in a student's speech. In this speech sample, the verb "go" is in the infinitive form. However, the preposition "to" is needed to function as an infinitive maker. The student fails to place the preposition "to" before the verb "go." Therefore, the correct answer is (A).

8.   (C)

This question tests your ability to identify some common errors in a student's speech. In this speech sample, the student describes a series of activities in one sentence. The four verbs should be parallel. That is, these four verbs should be in the same form. However, the third verb is in the –ing form. Therefore, the correct answer is (C).

9. (D)

This question tests your knowledge of theories in second language acquisition. The choice of the word "hard" shows no indication of simplification. So, option (A) is incorrect. Further, "hard" is an English word, not an instance of mixing up with the student's native language. So, option (B) is incorrect. Since "hard" is an error, option (C) is incorrect because imitation refers to positive production. The correct word to use is "high," which in this context is equivalent to "hard, strong, much, and big" in some other languages. As a result, a student might choose a similar yet incorrect word due to interference from the mother tongue. Therefore, the correct answer is (D).

10. (B)

This question tests your ability to recognize grammatical errors in a student's speech. In this context, "pick up" should be used as a transitive verb. However, the student fails to let an object follow the verb. Therefore, the correct answer is (B).

Section I: Part B–Pronunciation

11. (C)

This question tests your ability to identify errors in pronunciation. In this speech sample, the student incorrectly produces the vowel in the same way as the vowel in the word "road." Therefore, the correct answer is (C).

12. (B)

This question tests your ability to detect phonetic errors in a student's speech and your knowledge of phonetic transcriptions. Option (A) is how the word should sound, but the student incorrectly substitutes the /n/ sound for the /m/ sound in the first syllable. Therefore, the correct answer is (B).

13. (B)

This question tests your ability to identify sounds in speech and your knowledge of phonetic transcriptions. In this speech sample, the student incorrectly substitutes the /g/ sound for /dʒ/. Therefore, the correct answer is (B).

14. (B)

This question tests your ability to detect pronunciation errors in a student's speech. Speakers with a certain language background have a tendency to substitute /l/ for /r/. However, in this speech sample, the student pronounces the /r/ sound as /v/. Therefore, the correct answer is (B).

15. (A)

This question tests your ability to analyze speech sounds and recognize their phonetic transcriptions. The correct pronunciation of the underlined word is as option (B) indicates. In this speech sample, the student shifts the stress from "ta" to "men" and deletes "ta." In addition, the student inserts a schwa after "g." Therefore, the correct answer is (A).

16. (B)

This question tests your ability to identify speech sounds and their phonetic transcriptions. The correct pronunciation of the word "these" is as option (A) indicates. In the speech sample, the student devoices the final sound and pronounces the word as option (B) indicates. Therefore, the correct answer is (B).

17. (A)

This question tests your ability to detect and describe speech errors. In this speech sample, the student substitutes the stressed /l/ sound for /r/. Therefore, the correct answer is (A).

18. (D)

This question tests your ability to detect and describe speech errors. In the speech sample, the student incorrectly omits the final /s/ sound of the word "speakers." Therefore, the correct answer is (D).

19. (C)

This question tests your ability to detect and describe speech errors. In the pronunciation of the word "integrity," the student adds /r/ at the second syllable. In addition, the student substitutes the /dʒ/ sound for /g/ and then adds a schwa after it. Therefore, the correct answer is (C).

20. (B)

This question tests your ability to identify speech errors and your knowledge of phonetic transcriptions. In this speech sample, the student incorrectly substitutes /dʒ/ for /g/. Therefore, the correct answer is (B).

Section I: Part C–Writing

21. (C)

This question tests your ability to identify production problems associated with second language acquisition. The student shows an awareness of the general rules of adverbs: adverbs are to modify verbs and have the suffix –ly. However, the student over generalizes the rule and uses the form, –ly, where it is not appropriate. Therefore, the correct answer is (C).

22. (C)

This question tests your ability to recognize the requirement of commas for nonrestrictive clauses. The writing sample contains no errors in the superlatives and no problems with subject-verb agreement. The second sentence shows that the student correctly uses the restrictive clause. In the first, fourth and fifth sentences, the failure to use commas makes nonrestrictive clause restrictive. Therefore, the correct answer is (C).

23. (B)

This question tests your knowledge of some grammatical terms and their applications. Subordinating conjunctions (such as *because, although*) are used to introduce a subordinate clause/dependent clause. In the first sentence of this writing sample, the sub-

ordinating clause is supposed to join a main clause; the student, however, incorrectly uses a coordinating conjunction. By the same token, the coordinating conjunction, "but," should be removed. Further, there are two instances of using double object construction, in which a verb (such as give) takes two objects and can appear in two basic patterns: (1) verb + indirect object + direct object (2) verb + direct object + preposition + indirection object. Since the student uses the first pattern, the insertion of a preposition is incorrect. The writing sample does not include uses of correlative conjunctions or restrictive clauses. Therefore, the correct answer is (B).

24. (C)

This question tests your ability to detect grammatical errors with tenses. This writing sample shows that the student correctly uses past tense, present tense and future tense. There are three errors in the writing sample: (1) the first sentence should be in present perfect aspect (*Have + en*), (2) the main clause of the second sentence should be in the past perfect aspect, and (3) the fourth sentence should be in present perfect progressive for the fourth sentence. What makes all three sentences perfect is the necessary component of *have*, which is missing from the writing. Therefore, the correct answer is (C).

25. (B)

This question tests your ability to identify some common errors with articles. The student consistently places articles before nouns except in one place. The writing sample shows that the student is aware that articles are required for most nouns, but has not mastered when to use a definite article, indefinite article, or no article. The sample contains no errors in present tense, plurals or prepositions. Therefore, the correct answer is (B).

26. (A)

This question tests your knowledge of terms associated with second language acquisition. This writing sample indicates that the student is confused with the uses of definite/indefinite articles. The student has a tendency to place an article before every noun. The correct forms used in the last sentence can be due to imitation of set phrases: the student might have memorized "go to school" as a chunk. As a result, there is no insertion of an article. All three other options refer to errors in production. Therefore, the correct answer is (A).

27. (D)

This question tests your ability to identify the student's learning progress. Although the student incorrectly adds –s to the past tense in the first sentence, it indicates that the student is aware that –s is required for the third person singular, which is also demonstrated in the second sentence. So, option (A) is incorrect. "Knows" in the fourth sentence shows that the student probably overgeneralizes the rule and use –s for third person plurals. The use of "wrote" indicates that the student has the concept of past tense. So, option (B) is incorrect. The second sentence and the third sentence show that the student knows how to form a sentence in present tense. So, option (C) is incorrect. Finally, the error in formation of passive voice indicates that the student does not know how to form a passive voice. Therefore, the correct answer is (D).

28. (A)

This question asks you to identify some common problems with expressing a comparison. The student correctly uses comparative forms by adding –er or more. However, the writing sample displays other problems. The first sentence is an instance of an incomplete comparison. It is not stated on what basis the comparison is made. The third sentence also shows a problem with the structure because the student writes an independent clause, "you'll get more candy," instead of the form, "the more candy you will get." Further, although the reader can guess that the student means to compare, the comparison between a hat and a person is illogical. Finally, the last two sentences are examples that produce ambiguous readings. Therefore, the correct answer is (A).

29. (B)

In the initial clause of the last sentence, the subject of the verb "walking" has been deleted, but cannot be linked to the subject of the main clause, "some

drivers." As a result, the particle is left dangling. The correct answer is, therefore, (B).

30. (C)

This question asks for your judgment on an appropriate step to help correct a student's errors. Based on the writing sample, the student probably has the ability to self-correct the error if given the opportunity. So, option (A) would be a possible step after the student fails to self-correct. Making a student feel embarrassed can have an ill-effect, rather than promoting learning. So, option (B) is not appropriate. Errors of dangling modifiers occur commonly among native English speakers, which, however, does not mean a teacher should ignore the problem. Instances of dangling modifier often create some ridiculous verbal pictures, which can make it easier for writers to spot the error on a second reading of their own writing. Therefore, the correct answer is (C).

31. (B)

The first word in each pair is a noun, while the second sound represents an adjective. (A) and (C) are incorrect because they contain at least one example, where the pair of words does not follow the required noun to verb sequence. (D) are incorrect because it contains one example where the stress did not change the meaning of the word.

32. (C)

Students with a strong background in the native language, who have arrived at the threshold in L1, can generally transfer a lot of these skills to the second language. However, those students who are illiterate or have minimum skills in their native language, do not have skills to transfer to the new language. (A) is in correct in certain way because the development of strong foundations in L1 can help in the acquisition of L2; however, cognitive and academic development in L1 is not a prerequisite for L2 development. (B) is incorrect because the transferability of skills from L1 to L2 is not restricted to speakers of Indo-European languages. (D) is incorrect because young adults might experience some degree of language interference at the phonological level, but it will not necessarily preclude them from developing a native-like pronunciation.

33. (A)

An interlanguage describes a process where ELLs develop provisional structures in the second language through a combination of elements from L1 and L2. These structures are unique to the individual learners, and will disappear once the students master the second language. (B) is an incorrect statement based on the definition of an Interlanguage. (C) is incorrect because it describes the production of a specific English sound. (D) is incorrect because it describes the term, "intransentential codeswitching," the use of two languages in one utterance.

34. (B)

The term *graphophonemic* refers to the connection between letters (grapheme) and sounds (phonemes). In alphabetic languages, individual graphemes and groups of graphemes on a given sequence are used to represent the sounds of the language. When the connection between letters and sounds is not consistent, it can affect students' ability to decode and spell written language. (A) is incorrect, because graphophonemic differences do not necessarily affect the syntax (word order) of the language. (C) is incorrect because the connection between letters and sounds does not necessarily affect the vocabulary (lexicon) transfer. (D) is incorrect because there is no evidence to suggest that graphophonemic inconsistency can necessarily affect the meaning system (semantics) of the language.

35. (A)

The pragmatic system describes the nonverbal component of the language, including the context of the interaction, which includes the maxims for interaction in the culture. (B) is incorrect because the pragmatics of the language does not describe the phonological component of the language or the grapheme-phoneme connection of the language. (C) is incorrect because contrasting language will not help in determining the background knowledge needed to understand communication. (D) is incorrect because the literal (denotative) and implied (connotative) meaning of the language is not directly related to the pragmatics of the language.

36. (A)

English contains several monosyllabic (one-syllable) prefixes and suffixes. When students learn to identify syllables in words, they can isolate prefixes and suffixes. Identification of these language components can help in decoding words and getting meaning from print. (B) is incorrect because syllabication will not help in the identification of cultural connotations or words with multiple meanings. (C) is incorrect because syllabication will not help necessarily in the identification of two graphemes that represent a single sound (diagraphs), not it will help in understanding the meaning of idiomatic expressions. (D) is incorrect because there is no one-to-one correspondence between the ability to understand that letters represents sound (alphabetic principle) and the ability to separate words in syllable.

37. (A)

Children are born with innate mechanism for language development. They begin imitating language, but later they become rule-makers and able to invent strategies to assist them in figuring out how language operates. (B) is incorrect because imitation appears to be a learning strategy young children frequently use through age two, but it decreases in effectiveness as language learning becomes more complex. (C) is incorrect because language development requires some level of input from speakers of the language. For example, children initially acquire the first language components through imitation of parents and care givers. Context definitely helps in the acquisition of languages, but by itself context cannot fully describe how a language is learned. (D) is incorrect because initially children do not have to receive explicit instruction to develop language.

38. (C)

When the learner combines the two words to create the compound word—*butterfly, nightmare,* and *brainstorm*—these can create confusion since they do not provide reliable semantic clues for the new word. The words that created the compound words in (A), (B), and (D) provide reliable and consistent clues that help in determining the meaning of the new word.

39. (D)

Typically, phonic programs introduce consistent sounds first to make the grapheme-phoneme connection easier to follow. Once students see the connection, they are introduced to more challenging sounds. (A) and (C) are incorrect because making an activity interesting and guiding students to cooperate can contribute to learning but they do not guarantee that students will understand phonemic awareness. (B) is incorrect because comparing the phonology of the two languages is not a prerequisite for mastering phonemic awareness is the target language.

40. (D)

All examples presented contain vowel diagraphs. A vowel diagram describes the union of two vowels together representing a single sound. (A) is incorrect because one of the examples (seeds) contain two units of meaning (morphemes). (C) is incorrect because the words are not pronounced in the same way (homophones). (D) is incorrect because there are only a few consonant clusters in the samples presented.

41. (C)

All nasal sounds are voiced, and English has three nasal sounds, represented by the graphemes, ng, n, and m. (A), (B), and (C) are incorrect because they used terms fricative, lateral, and stop which are used to describe oral sounds only.

42. (D)

The verb capture is a transitive verb, and transitive verbs can take objects. In this case the object of the verb is the *presidency*. (A) and (B) are incorrect because linking verbs are intransitive verbs, and these verbs cannot take objects. They can take only a predicate adjective or a predicate nominative (noun). (C) is incorrect because the sentence does not have an indirect object.

43. (C)

English has three bilabial sounds. These sounds are produced when both lips come together to pro-duce the sound of the /p/, /b/, and /m/. (A) is incorrect because it contains the three nasal sounds of English, but only one is a bilabial, /m/. (B) contains two labio dental sounds, /v/ and /f/, and one alveolar sound, /t/. (D) is incorrect because it contains an alveolar (/t/) and velar (/k/) sound.

44. (A)

The two pair of words have two final contrasting sounds, the /k/ and /g/. In the first sounds /k/, the vocal cords are not engaged (voiceless), and in the second example, the vocal cords are activated creating a voiced sound. Based on this analysis, (B) and (C) are incorrect. (D) is incorrect because both of these sounds (/k/ and /g/) are identified as stop sounds, not fricative or affricate.

45. (A)

The complexity of interdental sounds might guide speakers to substitute these sounds with more common English sounds—alveolar sounds /s/ or /t/. (B) is incorrect because the /t/ and /s/ sounds are alveolar sounds, while the /θ/ an interdental sound. The manner of articulation is also different; the /t/ is a stop sound, while the /s/ and /θ/ are fricative sounds. (C) is incorrect because in standard English the grapheme TH has two sounds only the /θ/ or the voice counterpart /ð/, like in the word, them. (D) is incorrect because the question ruled out language interference as an option.

46. (B)

The initial sound of the words *jury* and *chop* contains the two English affricates—ʤ/ /tʃ/. (A) and (C) are incorrect because they contain only one affricate sound in the words, *George* and *chute*. (D) is incorrect because it does not contain affricate sounds; it has two palatal sounds.

47. (A)

Both sounds are velar, but the initial sound of the word when is voiceless, while the sound of went is voiced. Based on the previous explanation the rest of the choices (B, C, and D) are incorrect.

48. (B)

English vowels are described based on the shape of the lips used to produce the sounds—round-unrounded—how high the tongue in the mouth—high, mid, low—and the part of the tongue used to produce the sounds—front, central and back. (A) and (C) are incorrect because these options presents descriptors used for consonants. (D) is incorrect because it contains terms that are not used to describe English vowel sounds.

49. (A)

When children overgeneralize like in the example—*wented*—they are in reality applying grammar rules. This data suggest that they have passed the stage of mere repetition, and they are beginning to decipher the grammar of the language. It also shows that children are beginning to conceptualize that the inflectional morpheme ed can be used to create the past tense. It also shows that they have problems identifying irregular verbs, like the verb *to go*. This overgeneralization is typical of English native speakers acquiring a language, and does not show any kind of interference from a language. Based on this explanation, options (B), (C), and (D) are incorrect.

50. (B)

Allophones describe an alternating way to pronounce a phoneme, like the nasal–oral contrasting sounds in the words—nõ and on. In the first example, the nasal sound of the /n/ moves to the vowel, creating a nasal vowel sound. In the second example, the vowel sound remains oral since the nasal sound occur at the end of the word. (A) and (D) are incorrect because the term phone is used to describe sounds in general, and phonemes are used to describe linguistic sounds. (C) is incorrect because the term morpheme (basic units of meaning) is not used to describe phonemes.

51. (D)

The English sounds /p/, /t/ and /k/ have an alternating sound, depending on when they occur in the word. When these sounds happen at the beginning of a syllable, the aspirated sound is produce, like in the word prank; when the sound occur in other conditions, like in the word *spring*, the unaspirated sounds occur. (A) and (B) are incorrect because the questions calls for more than the obvious, that the words represent two different units of meaning (morpheme) leading to the creation of two different words. (C) is incorrect because both sounds of the grapheme *p* are stop sounds.

52. (B)

The word contains six phonemes. The digraphs *th* and *ou* represent one sound each—two phonemes. In the string *ght*, only the *t* is pronounced—the third phoneme. Finally in the suffix, *ful*, each of the three sounds are produced for a total of six sounds. Based on this explanation, options (A), (C) and (D) are incorrect.

53. (C)

The word contains four morphemes—the prefix (sub), the root word (consci), the adjective morpheme (ous), and the adverb morpheme (ly). Based on this explanation options (A), (B), and (D) are incorrect.

54. (D)

The word *preconceived* has three morphemes—the prefix (pre) which is a derivational morpheme, the root word (conceiv), and the inflectional ending (ed). Based on this explanation, options (A), (B), and (C) are incorrect.

55. (C)

The question identifies three of the eight inflectional morphemes of the English language. The remaining morphemes are the present progressive (ing), the comparative (er or better) superlative (est or best), past tense (ed), and the participle (en). Given the explanation, options (A), (B), and (D) are incorrect.

56. (C)

Inflectional morphemes are also called inflectional endings because they occur the end of the word. (A) and (B) are incorrect because inflectional morphemes are native to English, and they do not change the syntactic classification to the word attached. (D) is incorrect because inflectional morphemes always follow derivational morphemes.

57. (C)

All forms of the verb *to be* (*is*) are intransitive verbs, and intransitive verbs cannot take objects. Based on this grammar rule, only options containing intransitive verbs—(A) and (C)—can be considered as possible answers. The sentence reinstates who Joe Biden is—the new vice-president. (A) is incorrect because the sentence does not describe, but indentifies him as the new vice-president.

58. (D)

A visual analysis of the last three columns shows that the phoneme / š / can be represented by at least four different graphemes—*ch, s, ss*, and *t*—in words like *chef, sure, mission*, and *caution*. The grapheme *ch* is also inconsistent. Column 3 shows that the grapheme ch represents the sound /k/ or /tʃ/. This inconsistency affects the ability of ELLs to separate the two phonemes. (A), (B), and (C) are incorrect because the scenario does not provide evidence to suggest that ELLs cannot establish a difference or pronounce the two phonemes, or that they might not be interested in learning the difference between the two.

59. (B)

The chart provides examples of words that follow grapheme-phoneme correspondence. It also provides examples of words that use different graphemes to represent the sounds. This chart provides students with tangible information to help them deal with graphophonemic inconsistencies. (A) is incorrect because this particular chart places more emphasis on graphophonemic inconsistencies than consistencies. (C) is incorrect because the chart presents words in isolation; thus it cannot present information about the intonation pattern used in sentences or larger units. (D) is a plausible answer, but it does not capture the true intent of the activity. The chart is designed to deal with specific inconsistent sounds only.

60. (C)

Idiomatic expressions rely on culture referents and connotative or implied meaning. That is why ELLs experience difficulties understanding them. (A) is incorrect because idioms are part of social language, as opposed to academic English. (B) is incorrect because denotative language refers to the literal meaning of the words and obviously idioms have implied meaning. (D) is incorrect because idioms do not necessarily have direct (metaphor) or indirect comparisons (simile).

61. (D)

Current research suggests that language development is the result of innate abilities, imitation of parents and caregivers, and stimulus from the linguistic community. (A) is incorrect because it does not mention the most important component of the process, the role of nature. (B) is incorrect because memorization does not play an important role in the process of first language acquisition. (C) is incorrect because practice and memorization do not play an important role in the process.

62. (C)

In the telegraphic stage of first language acquisition, children produce two and three-word statements. (A) is incorrect because the child is going beyond the one-word stage—holophrastic stage. (B) is incorrect because children at the babbling stage, children do not produce specific words. (D) is incorrect because it does not describe a specific stage of language development. It describes a stage of social development.

63. (B)

Aphasia is a brain-based disturbance that causes receptive and productive language disorders. (A) is incorrect because voice disorders are caused mostly by a distortion of the sounds as they are produced in the vocal tract. (C) is incorrect because fluency problems are usually caused by external factors like nervousness or language interference. (D) is incorrect because hoarseness is a type of articulation disorder caused by abnormality in the vibration of the vocal fold.

64. (A)

Alliteration is a technique to emphasize the connection between the consonant and the sound that it represents. In this particular case, the tongue twister is used to emphasize the sound of the /s/ and /Š/. (B) is incorrect because the technique goes beyond the use of a tongue twister. Tongue twisters are examples of alliteration and they emphasize pronunciation and fluency. (C) is incorrect because the utterance does not represent an example of traditional nursery rhymes. Nursery rhymes are short poems, stories or songs written to entertain children. The most famous nursery rhyme is the Mother Goose collection from England.

65. (B)

The answer calls for syllabication and phoneme segmentation. Both concepts are part of phonological awareness. (A) is incorrect because sentence analysis was not the primary concern in the scenario. The intonation pattern describes the rhythm and pitch used in phrases and sentences. (C) is incorrect because in the latter activity, the issue is the phonological analysis of words. Vocabulary development was emphasized in the first part of the scenario only. (D) is incorrect because the scenario does not address pronunciation at all.

66. (D)

A balanced reading program combines phonics instruction, a skill-based approach, to teach decoding skills, and features from the whole language, a meaning-based approach, to teach reading. (A) is incorrect because the main thrust of a balanced reading program is not directly related to the listening and reading (receptive) and the speaking and writing (productive) components of language. (B) It makes sense to establish a balance between theory and application, but there is no direct connection with the concept of balanced reading program. (C) is incorrect because a balanced approach uses not only phonics skills but also whole language strategies.

67. (A)

The ability to separate words into syllables constitutes the main foundation for developing phono-logical awareness which can be linked to success in oral communication and decoding written language. (B) is incorrect because there is no direct connection between syllabication and developing reading comprehension. (C) is incorrect because syllabication does not play a vital role in writing compositions. It might only help in spelling. (D) is incorrect because transferring reading skills from L1 to L2 definitely goes beyond the ability to separate words into syllables.

68. (C)

Syllabication and word stress are part of the concept called phonological awareness. (A) is incorrect because the activity goes beyond establishing the connection between letters and sounds typical of the alphabetic principle. (B) is incorrect because the development of fluency goes beyond the analysis of individual words. The development of phonological awareness is a prerequisite for the development of fluency. (D) is incorrect because the concept of syllabication is only one of two elements presented in the scenario—syllabication and word stress.

69. (D)

Teachers have to present the consistent sounds of English first to develop self-confidence among children. Once they master those initial grapheme-phoneme correspondences, then they can venture with more challenging components. (A) is incorrect because it deals with a generic well-accepted practice, but it does not address the question. (B) is incorrect because the alphabetic principle does not specifically deal with the issue of the development of foreign accents. (C) is incorrect because it failed to address the question. It is always important to create an atmosphere of collaboration among students, but this statement does not address the linguistic nature of the questions.

70. (D)

Onsets represent the first phoneme of a syllable or a monosyllabic word like the words presented in (D). Rimes follow onsets, and these are linked to the concept of word families. The rime *ank* can be used to create multiple words, like *blank, tank, rank* and *flank.* (A) and (C) are generally used to represent verb tenses and cannot be considered part of a word family. (B) is incorrect because the two words do not represent onset and rimes, because both the onsets and the rimes are different in both words.

71. (A)

The use of onset and rimes are used to compensate for the phoneme-grapheme inconsistency of the English language. Through the use of rimes, children can learn to recognize and spell multiple words. (B) is incorrect because the use of onset and rimes can contribute to the ability to recognize words, but it does not constitute the main reason for their use. (C) is incorrect because traditionally, onsets and rime are not used to deal with polysyllabic words. (D) is incorrect because prefixes generally represent morphemes while the onsets generally do not. Prefixes and suffixes are generally introduced using structural analysis.

72. (B)

Teachers generally introduce letters that can help the most in decoding written language. The first set of letters occurs more frequently in written text than the second set of words. (A) is incorrect because there is no evidence to suggest that children might be more inclined to prefer one set of letters over the other. (C) is incorrect because only the phoneme /m/ is a nasal sound. (D) is incorrect because there is no evidence to suggest that the sounds of the graphemes x and q can create language interference.

73. (B)

A balanced-reading approach uses best practices from both phonics and whole language. It also places emphasis in the use of authentic literature and the use of a literature-based approach to construct meaning. (A) is incorrect because the skill-based approach emphasizes mostly phonics instruction. (C) is incorrect because the meaning-based approach emphasizes mostly the Whole Language Approach. (D) is incorrect because there is no connection between Humanistic Psychology and the question asked.

74. (A)

The main reason for the creation of the Language Experience Approach was to eliminate the discrepancy between the background knowledge that the child brings to the reading process and the experiential background required to understand the story, i.e., the schema of the author. (B) is incorrect because it eliminates the need to discuss schema of the story by exposing children to a common experience and guiding them to dictate a story using the experience. (C) is incorrect because students will use their own vocabulary in the story; if they use idioms, these are probably known to children in the group. (D) is incorrect because the main purpose of the LEA is not contrast L1 and L2.

75. (A)

The overall purpose of the shared book experience is to guide children to be successful in reading and to develop interest in learning to read. The story is read to the students in a very supportive environment using visuals to enhance comprehension. The main goal is to make reading an enjoyable activity and to motivate children to read on their own. (B) is incorrect because reading with the whole class is a byproduct of shared book experience, but it is not the main goal. (C) and (D) are true statements, but these features are not the main reason for conducting shared reading.

76. (A)

By guiding children to notice the title, major headings, and pictorial clues they can make predictions about the story. Predictions can increase interest in the story because children want to corroborate their predictions. (B), (C) and (D) are incorrect because they describe activities typical of the post-reading stage, not pre-reading.

77. (A)

The first reading is designed to communicate the content of the story and by doing so, children will determine if their predictions were accurate. (B) is incorrect because decoding strategies and main idea are usually addressed after the initial activity. (C) and

(D) are incorrect because the parts of the book and the vocabulary of the story are usually introduced prior to reading the story.

78. (D)

Storytelling and reading to children can guide them to notice the correlation between the letters and the sounds they produce. This phonemic awareness is a foundation for learning to read—emergent reading. (A) is incorrect because traditionally, children at the emergent reading stage are not able to read or comprehend the subtitles of movies and television shows. (B) is also incorrect because children at the emergent stage cannot read instructions from board games. (C) is incorrect because translating stories by itself does not guarantee that children will develop the reading readiness skills to begin reading.

79. (A)

The use of flash cards, pictures or concrete objects can promote vocabulary development and at the same time expose children to sight words. (B) is incorrect because the child might not have sufficient vocabulary to participate in a game where parents and children teach each other words taken from a dictionary. (C) is incorrect because preschool children might not be ready to understand the complexity of the homographs and homophones. (D) is incorrect because rote memorization is not the best way to promote vocabulary development in preschoolers.

80. (B)

The meaning-based or the top-down approach use whole units like words and sentences to teach reading. From the sentence, it goes to the word. From the words, it proceeds to smaller units like syllables, graphemes and phonemes. (A) and (C) are incorrect because the skill-based and the bottom-up approaches proceed from the parts to the whole, i.e., phonemes, letters, syllables, words, and sentences. (D) is incorrect because literature-based does not describe how the language is analyzed to teach reading. A literature-based approach is part of a balanced reading approach.

81. (A)

Understanding the use of figurative language in English requires learners to have an understanding of the American culture, and how language is used in daily speech. Traditionally, ELLs fail to capture the implied meaning in these idioms, creating communication problems. (B), (C), and (D) are incorrect because phonology and syntax (structure) do not rely heavily on culture to convey meaning.

82. (B)

Answer choice (B) is correct because with idioms it is often difficult to guess the meaning. (A) is not correct; speakers can talk about things that they have not done. (C) is not correct, although not all cultures might view the words in an idiom in the same way. For example, dogs have a negative connotation in some cultures that they do not have in America. This might be significant in an idiom like "every dog has his day." (D) Having an adverb between a verb and an object should not be confusing for most students of English.

83. (C)

The minimal pair is a test to determine if a sound contrast is meaningful in a language. Each member of the pair is identical except for one sound. If the difference in sound causes a difference in meaning, then we say we have a minimal pair. *Bad* and *bat* are a minimal pair. Choice (A) is not correct because it applies to semantics and (B) applies to spelling, not sound. (D) refers to antonyms, which are in the realm of meaning, not sound.

84. (B)

The teacher presented the lesson inductively. That is, students were guided to discover the rule behind the two different ways to pronounce the grapheme S. (A) and (D) are incorrect there is no evidence to suggest that phonics or whole language formats were used to introduce the sounds. (C) is incorrect based on the definition of inductive teaching presented.

85. (C)

The grapheme S is usually pronounced as a voiceless sound /s/; however, when a voiced sound precedes the grapheme, the sound is pronounced as its voiced counterpart, /z/. (A) is incorrect because the evidence shows that the grapheme—phoneme correspondence for the letter S is inconsistent. (B) is partially correct because vowels are voiced and the rule applies; however, it fails to explain that the rule also applies to voice consonants. (D) is incorrect because it contradicts the rule presented in the correct answer, option (C).

86. (B)

The data shows that after the graphemes g, x, sh, ch, and s, the long plural form is required. In any other conditions, the short version is used. Based on the explanation presented, options (A), (C), and (D) are incorrect.

87. (C)

The words *wires* and *tires* do not belong to the long plural section. Instead, they represent examples of short plural forms. The teacher needs to be sure that students do not get confused with words these kinds of words. Based on the explanation provided, options (A), (B), and (D) are incorrect.

88. (B)

Inductive learning is an effective strategy for language development in general. However, older students also need to be exposed to deductive teaching because they have the cognitive development required to understand abstract language rules. Young children, on the other hand, might not have the cognitive maturity to understand rules; thus, inductive teaching might be more appropriate for them. It seems Ms. Stewart should modify her teaching style to include more deductive teaching to make students feel more confident with the language. (A) is incorrect because obviously inductive teaching alone is not working for all the students. (C) is incorrect because avoiding inductive teaching completely might be counterproductive. (D) is incorrect because the use of rote memorization and repetition drills alone have proven to be ineffective to teach ESL.

89. (D)

The student began describing his family and quickly went on to describe the City of Dubai and his friend. In the second paragraph, he went back to the main topic of the essay, family. This type of communication is identified as curvilinear or associational. (A) and (C) present statements that might be correct, but these do not address the core of the problem, the organization and delivery of information. (B) is incorrect because the writer does not follow the linear progression; instead, he deviated from the topic in the first chapter, and then went back to it in the second paragraph.

90. (A)

The BICS describes the social language that ELLs acquire after 2 to 4 years of exposure to the language. This type of proficiency is used in face-to-face communications and in highly contextualized situations. The CALP, on the other hand, describes the academic language required to do well in the content areas. It takes from 5 to 7 years of meaningful exposure to the language to achieve this level of proficiency. Students who are exited from the bilingual program without developing CALP can experience academic problems in school. (B) and (C) contain opinions not directly supported in the scenario. (D) is incorrect because Carla is lacking academic language not the social language component.

91. (D)

Teachers use dramatic reading to make the story more interesting and to improve listening comprehension. Often teachers ask students to close their eyes to guide students to concentrate and listen for comprehension. Since students were instructed to close their eyes, reading comprehension is not the main purpose of the activity, thus options A and B are incorrect. Dramatic reading does not impact directly the speaking or writing skills, thus option C is also out.

92. (C)

The use of pictures to represent events in the story can be used to represent the sequencing of events in the story. It can also be used to introduce visually the parts of the story, i.e., characters, setting, plot, climax, and resolution. (A) is incorrect because the teacher is not connecting the pictures with the written text. Teachers can fill-in the background knowledge of the students through visuals (A); however, this activity is usually done as a pre-reading activity. Since the visuals were used as a post-reading activity, we can believe that filling the gaps was not the primary purpose of the activity. The teacher is definitely using developmentally appropriate practices (D), but the real intent of the activity goes beyond that.

93. (B)

Phonemic awareness describes one of the basic skills to learn to read. It requires the ability to manipulate the sounds of the language, including identifying sounds in words. Minimal pair is an assessment activity designed to determine if students can identify differences between phonemes (sounds). For example, to test if the child is able to identify similar sound, students are given a set of words that differ in only one phoneme, e.g., *fine-vine*. The term *phonic skill* is a generic term that fails to capture the real purpose for using minimal pair, thus option (A) is incorrect. Choice (C) is incorrect because structural analysis describes the ability to analyze structure of words and sentences, and minimal pair does not deal with this component. (D) is incorrect because cognates and false cognates refer to similar words across two languages, instead of the phonology.

94. (B)

The question calls for activities that promote self-directed learning. Advanced students generally have sufficient knowledge about the language to analyze the source of the errors and make their own corrections. Students at the beginning stage of second language acquisition might not have the knowledge to make their own corrections, thus option (A) incorrect. In communication activities (C), ESL teachers do not provide direct corrective feedback; instead, they are encouraged to provide indirect feedback by modeling the structures in question. The same principle applies to (D), direct corrections are not the best tool during communication activities. However, teachers can take notes of the grammatical problems and design a grammar lesson to teach the concepts.

95. (A)

Results of the test change in each administration, thus, reliability of the instrument becomes the key issue in this question. Reliability is defined as the ability of the test to produce consistent results, which obviously does not happen in the scenario. The credentials of the diagnostician (D) should not be part of the problem since he/she is bilingual and fully certified. The scenario does not provide negative information about the accuracy of the test and it just indicated the instrument was approved by the state. Based on lack of information of the accuracy of the instrument, we can rule it out (C). (B) is incorrect because the scenario does not provide information about the content of the test.

96. (D)

Modern assessment practices call for the use of multiple assessment instruments to make instructional decisions. The medical history of the child and input from parents can yield vital information to develop a better picture of the child. (A) is out because the question calls for elements "beyond state-mandated tests" and the language proficiency tests are part of the state-mandated instrument. Evaluation and input from peers (B) are not generally taken into account to make placement decisions. The input from parents is important but generally they do not perform formal evaluations (C) on their children.

97. (C)

Culture shapes the way that children behave and perform in school. Linguistic limitations can also affect the ability of children to demonstrate capabilities and potential. The option of making students feel valued and wanted (A) is a noble cause, but it should not be the main concern when assessing CLD learners. (B) presents a true statement when indicated that students go through different stages of development, but invalidated the answer by saying that these should not affect the way in which they are assessed. The term *cultural deficit* used in (D) invalidates the answer because CLD learners cannot be considered culturally deficient since they already bring with them their language and culture.

98. (D)

Traditionally, standardized test used to measure intelligence and achievement contain middle class values and experiences that might be foreign to CLD students. This mismatch can affect students' performance in these tests. (A) presents an opinion difficult to support and probably inaccurate. Written tests of intelligence are generally norm-reference tests designed to show general ability and potential. They are not designed to measure content covered in class (B); thus, the fact that they do address class content should not be construed as a flaw. Intelligence tests often overemphasize logic and mathematics at the expense of other indicators of intelligence (C), and this will create problems for all children. However, for CLD learners the way that the test is organized and the values represent in the test constitute an additional and more important hurdle.

99. (D)

Culture and language can affect the interpretation of assessment results of CLD student populations. For that reason, it is important to assess students using multiple instruments and assemble a team with multiple areas of specialization (multidisciplinary) to be sure those results are interpreted accurately. The physical development of the child is important but the legal status of the child is irrelevant (A). Depending on the purpose of the assessment, some instruments should be administered in the students' native language but not necessarily in Spanish only (B). The instrument should be validated for the intended population (C); however, perhaps more important than that is how the results are finally interpreted.

100. (D)

Portfolio assessment contains a sample collection of the students' work. Students are active participant in the gathering and organization of the portfolio, which provides a sense of ownership in the assessment process. (A) provides a generic definition of portfolio assessment, but it failed to present its real value. (B) presents a false statement since the main purpose of portfolio assessment is not to complete with other students. Portfolio is used to document progress through a specific time frame and its content is commonly shared with parents, thus its

content is not confidential as suggested in (C).

101. (A)

Effective assessment practices are generally part of instruction, ongoing, and interpreted based on the developmental and cultural characteristics of the child (student-centered). It can be formative as well as summative (end product) (B), but its data collection cannot be restricted to documentation collected using state-approved instruments. Data collection is not restricted to information gathered by diagnosticians (C); parents and other personnel can provide valuable information for assessment. Assessment should promote self-monitoring (D) but should not emphasize weaknesses only. Instead, assessment should capitalize on the strengths that children bring to the learning process.

102. (C)

The idiomatic expression is alluding or making reference to Fort Knox, one of the main depositories of gold reserves in the United States. Listeners need to make a connection between the large amounts of gold in Fort Knox and the implications of the statement. (A) contains part of the answer, allusion, but includes the concept of a metaphor which is not present in the statement. A metaphor is a figure of speech that makes a direct comparison of two ideas as in the statement, "You are my Venus." In this case the speaker is comparing someone to Venus, the goddess of love in the Roman mythology. The concept of simile (B) is not present in the statement. A simile is similar to a metaphor but makes an indirect comparison by using the word, like or as—"You are like Venus." A hyperbole (D) is an exaggeration like in the statement, "I am so hungry that I can eat a horse." There is some degree of exaggeration in the statement but not strong enough to be considered a hyperbole.

103. (A)

Checklists, retelling stories and the use of anecdotal records are examples of informal assessment measure commonly used to assess the development of communication skills among ELLs. The informal nature of these assessment strategies eliminates the stress associated with formal assessment procedures.

Multiple choice, cloze tests, and informal reading inventory (B) are not generally used to assess oral communication skills. Audio taping can be used to assess oral language development, but written cloze test and standardized achievement tests (C) are not. Repetition drills, choral reading, and chants (D) are generally used to assess pronunciation, which is only one of components of oral communication skills.

104. (B)

One of the main functions of portfolio assessment is to document and analyze the growth of students. For ELLs portfolio can be tailored to document the growth of language and content through a specific grading period. Teachers can show parents the kind of work done at the beginning of a grading period and at the end of it to provide evidence of the performance of children. Portfolio assessment can be used to document social development and interaction with native English speakers (A), but its main purpose goes beyond the social development of the child. Portfolio can be linked to the collection of assignments and daily activities (C), but its real meaning goes beyond the mere collection of daily work and artistic manifestations (D).

105. (C)

The threshold level is defined as an advanced level of literacy development in a given language. Students who arrive at this level possess a solid foundation in language and can easily transfer those skills to the second language. (A) is incorrect because there is no guarantee that student who have arrived at the threshold level will develop the positive self-esteem needed to acquire a second language; (B) is incorrect because there is no indication to suggesting that the mastery of L1 will lead to an understanding of culture and its implications for the acquisition of a second language. The Contrastive Analysis Theory alluded in (D) requires students to have a deep understanding of L1 and L2, which most ELLs obviously do not have.

106. (A)

The data from the Normal Curve Equivalent (NCE) is derived from actual scores of each students, which provides a more reliable indicators of individual performance; while the data, from the National Percentiles shows how a particular student compare with other students who took the test. (B) is incorrect because NCE does not use local or national norms to compare performance. (C) and (D) are incorrect based on the information presented.

107. (B)

Portfolio assessment allows teachers to track the performance of students through a systematic way of collecting data of the performance during a given period of time. (A) is incorrect because portfolio gathers data beyond the content areas. (C) is incorrect because portfolio assessment is an informal system to gather performance data, and results are shared with parents and teachers. (D) is incorrect because the main purpose of portfolio is not to guide students to understand the process; instead, it is designed to gather data to provide evidence of the student's performance.

108. (A)

When assessing the content knowledge of ELLs is very important to eliminate the role of language in the assessment process. To accomplish this goal, most state education agencies allows for linguistic accommodations. (B) is incorrect because summative evaluation describes the process of gathering data at the end of the give period. (C) is incorrect because the concept of content validity the process where the content of a given domain or standard reflects the content covered in a given assessment instrument. (D) is incorrect because there no connection between the concept of formative evaluation and linguistic accommodation.

109. (C)

The purpose of formative evaluation is to gather information about the performance of students and to make decision based on data. (A) is incorrect because gathering formative data is not generally used to compare it with a national norm. (B) is incorrect because formative data does not have to be restricted to the performance of special education students. (D) is incorrect because the data sent to comply with federal guidelines are summative in nature, not formative.

110. (A)

The purpose of criterion-referenced tests is to determine if students have mastered specific standards. Teacher-made test are generally designed to determine if students are mastering the local or state curriculum. (B) is incorrect because norm-referenced test compare students with a national norm. (C) is incorrect because teacher-made test are considered formal assessment. (D) is incorrect because teachers generally do not have the preparation to develop standardized achievement tests.

111. (C)

Morphology is the only appropriate choice because word formation is part of morphology. Understanding word formation helps speakers to understand new words. Choice (A), Syntax, is devoted to sentences, not word formation. Choice (B), Semantics, refers to the study of meaning at the level of the word or sentence. (D) Psycholinguistics refers to a host of issues.

112. (D)

Rubrics can be used to guide students in the development of an activity, and to guide teachers in grading of it. The use of concrete set of assessment components makes the process more concrete and objective. (A) and (B) are incorrect because a rubric is an assessment tool, not a classroom management or part of a lesson plan. (C) is incorrect because rubrics are ot design necessarily to promote higher order skills.

113. (A)

Under the NCLB, the implementation of services to ELLs becomes a state and district responsibility. The legislation requires states to insure that ELLs do not fall behind academically and learn English to be successful in the all-English classroom. The states are required to design an accountability plan to document progress toward goal completion. (B) is a strong distracter because the legislation attempts to empower students and to allow parents the option of accepting or rejecting participation of the children in the program. However, these two elements are not as important and encompassing as the program implementation presented in option A. (C) is incorrect because the role of the federal government is to regulate the process to deliver services, not to assume full control of the process. (D) is incorrect because the legislation does not endorse bilingualism as the goal. Actually, the words "bilingual" or "bilingualism" were purposely omitted from the legislation.

114. (A)

In the TBE model, students receive content are instruction in their native language to be sure that they do not fall behind academically. They receive English language development through ESL until they develop the proficiency needed to function in the all-English classroom. (B) is a strong distracter because content-area English has become the program of choice in situations where dual language instruction is not feasible—in classroom with students from multiple language backgrounds. (C) is also a plausible answer because some programs might use ESL pull-out to teach English, but this approach is an exception as opposed to the rule. Choice (C) is another strong distracter because school districts have often used ESL techniques to avoid providing the dual language approach required in Texas, for example. However, the true intention of TBE is not to replace dual language instruction with ESL.

115 (C)

In the pull-out system, children are removed from the classroom to receive English language development for a determined period of the day. While the child is getting ESL instruction, he/she misses instruction in the content areas and can fall behind academically. (A) and (B) describe elements that might be true but do not explain the key disadvantage of the pull-out program. (D) is not a true statement, since students in the pull-out program are generally able to develop some levels of English proficiency but at the expense of learning content.

116. (B)

Sheltered English provides content and language instruction in contextualize situations to be sure students are able to understand the content. Since English is the only language of instruction, a minimum command of the language is necessary to obtain the full benefit of the program. Having a strong foundation in L1 (A) and being literate in the language (D) are good predictors of second language acquisition, but there is no direct connection with specific ESL method like Sheltered English. (C) is incorrect because the native language of the students plays a very minimal role in the selection of ESL methods.

117. (B)

Newcomer programs were designed to support students from non-traditional backgrounds who can benefit from a special language program designed to facilitate adjustment to life in the United States. Traditionally, Newcomer programs provide linguistic and cultural activities to facilitate this adjustment. The socioeconomic status (A) or the language background (C) can be an important consideration for placement in the program, but the literacy status and the culture that the child brings to the process are more important considerations. (D) is incorrect because students at the intermediate or advanced level of English proficiency might not need the basic linguistic and cultural services of Newcomer centers.

118. (B)

As a result of the *Lau vs. Nichols* ruling, the OCR instituted the Lau Remedies to force school district to comply with the court ruling to offer meaningful education to ELLs. (A) is incorrect because the court just mandated the district to offer "meaningful education," but did not specify the type of remedy. Choice C is a true statement, at least two other cases *(ASPIRA vs. New York City Board of Education* and *Serna vs. Portales*) were decided based on the Lau ruling; however, these court cases impacted only two states (New York and New Mexico) and the Lau Remedies from the OCR impacted the whole nation. (D) is a false statement since there has never been a bilingual education

law mandating bilingual education. There is Title III of the NCLB legislation that provides funding to support bilingual education programs.

119. (B)

The AIR study compared the effectiveness of the bilingual and the English-only program and found no significant differences between the two. The research findings were questionable but as a result of this finding, Structure Immersion was conceptualized as an option to address the language needs of ELLs. The term Structured Immersion is a program designed to teach English and the term was coined to avoid confusion with the bilingual immersion programs in Canada. (A) is incorrect because Proposition 227 was the mandate that eliminated bilingual education in California. (C) is incorrect because the Bilingual Education Act has never identified dual language instruction as the program of choice. (D) is incorrect because the Bilingual Education Act of 1978 emphasized the transitional nature of bilingual education programs or TBE. The Act also prohibited the use of federal funding to implement developmental or maintenance bilingual education programs.

120. (B)

The bilingual education program is often perceived as a compensatory program for undocumented immigrant students. Since the program does not provide service to mainstream students, community leaders may opposed the program. However, when a program like the two-way dual language program allows English-speaking children the option of becoming bilingual; suddenly, it becomes a program for the gifted and the opposition to dual language instruction disappears. The 2-way program allows for the maintenance of L1 and L2 (A) but that is not the real reason why mainstream groups are supporting the program. (C) and (D) are not the best answer because while some 2-way programs are supported by federal funding and have a research foundation, but none of these features explains why the program is getting support from mainstream groups.

Index

Praxis English to Speakers of Other Languages

Index